17

A PROBE INTO THE HISTORY OF
ASHURA

By Dr IBRAHIM AYATI

Published by
Cultural and Guidance Section
AL-KHOEI FOUNDATION

A PROBE INTO THE HISTORY OF ASHURA

First Published in Pakistan in 1984 by
ISLAMIC SEMINARY PUBLICATIONS
A Publishing Division of
ISLAMIC SEMINARY PAKISTAN
P.O. Box 5425 KARACHI-74000

This impression 1991

ISBN : 0-941724-41-7

Mailing Address
The General Secretary,
Al-Khoei Foundation,
Chevening Road,
London NW 6, 6 TN
ENGLAND

Conditions for Sale

This book or any part thereof is sold subject to the condition that it shall not by way of any trade or otherwise circulated in any form of binding or cover other than what it is published in, without a similar condition including this condition being imposed on the subsequent purchaser or donee, except with prior written permission of the copyright owner.

بِسْمِ اللهِ الرَّحْمٰنِ الرَّحِيْمِ

اَلْحَمْدُ لِلّٰهِ الَّذِى عَلَّمَ بِالْقَلَمْ
عَلَّمَ الْإِنْسَانَ مَا لَمْ يَعْلَمْ
وَصَلَّى اللهُ عَلَى مُحَمَّدٍ وَّآلِهِ وَسَلَّمْ

CONTENTS

PREFACE ... 7
REGIME OF MU'ĀWIYA ... 41
REGIME OF YAZID ... 45
LETTERS OF THE KUFIANS TO THE IMAM ... 49
MUSLIM BIN AQIL PROCEEDS TO KUFA ... 50
MARTYRDOM OF MUSLIM BIN AQIL ... 56
MUHAMMAD BIN HANAFIYA ... 60
CAUSES OF THE RISE OF IMAM HUSAYN ... 63
PEACE TREATY OF IMAM HASAN ... 65
WHO WAS YAZID? ... 69
WHY THE IMAM REJECTS TO TAKE THE OATH? ... 70
MAIN CAUSES OF RISING OF IMAM HUSAYN ... 74
DEPARTURE OF IMAM FROM MADINA ... 75
MERITS OF IMAM HUSAYN ... 78
IMAM HUSAYN ENCOUNTERS HUR ... 88
ARRIVAL OF IMAM HUSAYN IN KARBALA ... 94
IMAM'S SERMON ON THE NIGHT OF ĀSHURA ... 99
IMAM HUSAYN CONSOLES LADY ZAYNAB ... 102
MORNING OF ĀSHURA ... 103
SUPPLICATION OF IMAM ON ĀSHURA ... 105
SERMON OF IMAM TO THE ARMY OF YAZID ... 105
NEGATIVE ATTITUDE TOWARDS THE TRAGEDY OF KARBALA ... 109
TRAGEDY OF KARBALA REMAINS UNFORGETTABLE ... 113
THE SERMON OF IMAM SAJJAD IN KUFA ... 121
IMAM SAJJAD IN THE COURT OF IBN ZIYĀD ... 127
SERMON OF IMAM SAJJAD IN THE MOSQUE OF DAMASCUS ... 130
JOURNEY OF AHLUL BAYT TO KUFA AND DAMASCUS ... 132
EVENTS OF KARBALA REMAINED SAFE FROM DISTORTION ... 135

ABU SUFYĀN ADMITS THE GREATNESS OF THE HOLY PROPHET	136
EXHORTATION OF IMAM ALI	139
TRAGEDY OF KARBALA REMAINS IMMORTAL	144
SELF-SACRIFICING LADIES	146
HISTORY IS VERY POWERFUL	153
SERMON OF LADY ZAYNAB IN THE COURT OF YAZID	156
BENEFITS OF HISTORY	159
DIVINE LAW IS UNALTERABLE	162
IMAM ALI'S SERMON ON DIVINE LAW	164
INVITATION OF THE PROPHET TO HIS KITH AND KIN	168
CONFIDANT COMPANIONS OF IMAM HUSAYN	171
MARTYRS OF ĀLE ABI TALIB IN KARBALA	172
ROLE OF ISLAMIC TRAINING	175
ALLEGIANCE OF THE MADINITES TO THE HOLY PROPHET	178
HISTORICAL DAYS OF MADINA	181
AHLUL BAYT RETURNS TO MADINA	186
NU'AMĀN BIN BASHIR	188
TRIBES OF AWS AND KHAZRAJ	191
AUTHORITIES ON THE EVENT OF KARBALA	195
EXPLANATION OF THE SERMON OF IMAM SAJJAD IN DAMASCUS	202
SERMON OF IMAM SAJJAD IN MADINA	207

APPENDIX I

ARRIVAL OF JĀBIR AND ATIYYA IN KARBALA	209
THE HOLY QUR'AN – THE KEY TO SUCCESS	211

APPENDIX II

DAY OF ARBA'IN (40th DAY OF IMAM HUSAYN'S MARTYRDOM)	217
MUSLIMS OUGHT TO UNDERSTAND ISLAM	217
POET-PHILOSOPHER DR. IQBAL ON IMAM HUSAYN	226

* * * * *

PREFACE

The tragedy of Karbala is an unparalleled event of the history of mankind. The great sacrifice made by Imam Husayn, the grandson of the Holy Prophet, on Āshura (the 10th of Muharram 61 A.H.) and the steadfastness shown by him is a beacon light for everyone, who has faith in his mission and is keen for its success.

When one studies the bewildering events of this incident, a number of questions arise in one's mind such as: What was the purpose of Imam Husayn's rising? Did he want to avoid taking oath of allegiance to Yazid or did he take this step in response to the invitation received from the people of Kufa? Did he wish, in the current terminology, to bring about a revolution?

Did he know that he would be killed or was he under the impression that his life would be spared? Did he act according to a predetermined plan or took decisions in the light of every new development?

When he received the news of the martyrdom of Muslim bin Aqil while he (Imam Husayn) was on his way to Kufa why did he suggest to his companions to go away and leave him alone, and thereafter why did he approach various persons to assist him?

Why did he ask all his companions during the night of Āshura to go away but also sent Habib bin Mazāhir to the tribe of Bani Asad to seek their help? Why did he seek help from Ubaydullah bin Hur Juafi in the palace of Bani Maqātil and why did he say to the sons of Aqil during the night of Āshura: "You should go away. It is sufficient that from amongst you Muslim bin Aqil has been killed?"

Why did he seek help from Zahhāk ibn Abdullah Mashriqi

and his friend and Zuhayr bin Qayn, in spite of their strong refusal, and insisted and even expressed willingness that Zahhāk ibn Abdullah should help him till the last moment and then go away? Does all this not show that Imam Husayn was not aware of the final result and had no definite plan in mind?

Does the step taken by him not amount to endangering his life? Does a person, who knows that he would be killed, proceed towards death along with his kith and kin including the suckling?

Many baseless answers and incorrect explanations have been given to these questions. Some have said that as the Imam was not prepared to take oath of allegiance to a person like Yazid and to recognize his unlawful government, he was obliged to leave Madina in a state of fear and reached Makkah. He considered Makkah to be a haven and intended to stay there, but the Kufians invited him and assured him of their assistance. The Imam himself, too, was afraid lest he should be assassinated in Makkah and thereby the sanctity of the Kāʻbah should suffer. He, therefore, accepted the invitation of the Kufians and went towards Karbala. Consequently he and his dear ones and companions were killed and the other members of his family were made captives.

Some have narrated that the Imam did not think that he would be killed, otherwise he would not have taken such a bold step.

Still others say that the Imam rose because he was under the impression that on account of his relationship with the Holy Prophet he would certainly not be killed, or he was fully convinced that even if he did not rise he would be killed disgracefully at the hands of Ibn Ziyad or someone else. He, therefore, preferred being killed while performing jihād (the Holy war) to dying a disgraceful death.

Some say that the step taken by the Imam amounted to endangering his life, but as the Almighty Lord had given orders in this behalf he was obliged to obey the same.

Some opponents, and those, who consider that everyone wishes to be a sovereign, also, say that love for rulership placed Imam Husayn in this perilous situation, but it was not proper to kill him in such a tragic manner. It would have been better to control and dissuade him by means of threats and allurements.

The correct answer to all these questions is that the factors for such a movement had commenced from the very beginning of the rule of Mu'awiya and were becoming stronger day after day. At last the matters had taken such a turn that if Imam Husayn bin Ali had not taken this step all the traces of Islam would have been obliterated and the pains taken by the Holy Prophet would have been wasted, neither the Qur'an nor Islam would have survived.

The root cause of all these events was the drama which was staged at Saqifa Bani Sāida immediately after the demise of the Holy Prophet. The most important development was the unprecedented method which was adopted for the selection of the Caliph. In violation of the Peace Treaty which Mu'awiya had concluded with Imam Hasan and according to which the Muslims were to choose the Caliph after him, he began obtaining the oath of allegiance for Yazid. Furthermore, he sent a circular letter to the governors and agents in the provinces saying: "Note carefully that in all the departments of the army and the State if it is proved that someone is a Shi'ah (supporter) of Ali or Ahlul Bayt (the progeny of the Prophet), you should withdraw his grant, cross out his name and violate his rights".*

Then Mu'awiya sent another circular letter saying: "If any person is suspected of being a supporter of Ahlul Bayt he should be subjected to torture and his house should be demolished". This order was implemented so strictly that as written by Ibn Abil Hadid, the Shi'ah took refuge in the houses of their relatives and friends. Even then they were afraid of their slaves and slave-girls lest they should divulge the secret, because if anyone was not on good terms with another he reported to the authorities that such and such person was a supporter of Ahlul Bayt. The people were, therefore, arrested on mere accusation and suspicion and were tormented and made homeless. This persecution was more severe in Iraq during the rule of Ziyad bin Sumayya as compared with other places. In spite of Imam Ali's brilliant past record and the honour enjoyed by him in Islam it was made necessary that, in all the Islamic countries and the areas which formed part of the territories of Islam, he should be

---

*Sharh-e-Nahjul Balaghah by Ibn Abil Hadid, vol. III, p. 15.

abused and cursed in the sermons of Friday prayers and also at other times, and Mu'awiya and Yazid should be honoured and praised. Mu'awiya wrote officially to Ziyad bin Sumayya, the Governor of Iraq, that the evidence given in any matter by a person, who was known to be a Shi'ah, should not be accepted, and those, who provided him shelter should also not be treated to be honourable.

Hujr bin Adi, Rashid Hujari and their eleven companions were subjected to the severest persecution and torture, so much so that Mu'awiya killed six of them who were at that time the best persons. There were many, whose hands and feet were amputated and pins reddened in fire were thrust into their eyes, and some others were buried alive.

The evil propaganda of Mu'awiya and his agents in Syria and other Islamic territories misled the people. Whosoever uttered a word against Mu'awiya was treated to be a murderer of Uthman and shedding his blood was considered lawful. Credulous persons, who are numerous in all ages, and are easily impressed by evil propaganda, came to believe that Uthman's blood was shed without any justification, and those, who were satisfied with this act deserved to be punished.

This was how Mu'awiya and his agents poisoned the public mind. The Khawārij, too, who were inimical towards both Mu'awiya and Imam Ali kept quiet with regard to Mu'awiya on account of fear, but abused the Commander of the Faithful openly and treated him to be an infidel. This thing in itself rendered great help to Mu'awiya and created a grudge in the hearts of the people against Imam Ali and his followers, so much so that when on the day of Āshura Imam Husayn mentioned the reason for his coming towards Kufa and then asked his opponents as to why they had gathered to kill him they replied: "It is due to the grudge, which we have against your father".

The only tragedy was not that the newly-converted ignorant Muslims, who constituted the majority of the society of that time, hated Ali owing to the evil propaganda of Mu'awiya. A tragedy many times greater than this was that they did not know Mu'awiya properly and considered him to be a distinguished companion of the Holy Prophet and scribe of the revelations! This belief about Mu'awiya was not new. During the time of the

Commander of the Faithful also (i.e. in the 37th and 38th year A.H.) most of the ignorant sanctimonious persons and those, who were more harmful to Islam than anything else, considered Mu'awiya to be honourable, a true Muslim, pious and a mujtahid or at least hesitated in believing him to be a hypocrite. Hence, they desisted from fighting against him in the Battle of Siffin and also obliged Imam Hasan to make peace with Mu'awiya.

In Kitāb-e Siffin, Nasr bin Muzāhim quotes on his own authority from Asmā bin Hakam Fazāri to have said: "In the Battle of Siffin we belonged to the battalion of Ammār Yāsir and were serving under his command. One day while it was noon we had taken shelter from the heat of the sun under a sheet of a red cloth, which we had fixed on our spears. Suddenly we saw a man, making his way through the ranks of the army, coming towards us. Approaching us he enquired about Ammār. Ammār introduced himself. The man said: "O Aba Yaqzān!* I wish to enquire about something. Should I mention it openly or in private?" Ammār said: "As you like". The man said: "It will be better to enquire about it openly". Then he said: "I left my house with perfect perspicacity and faith in my rightfulness and had no doubt about the fact that these people i.e. Mu'awiya and his followers were misled. I held this belief till I reached here and saw that our mu'azzin says: 'I testify that there is no deity but Allah and that Prophet Muhammad is His Prophet' and their mu'azzin also utters the same words. We believe in offering prayers and they also offer prayers like us. Similarly we xake supplications and they also make supplications like us. Our Book is the Qur'an and their Book, too, is the Qur'an. Their Prophet and our Prophet is the same.

Having seen this I fell into suspicion and Allah knows how uneasy I became. I approached Imam Ali, the Commander of the Faithful in the morning and placed the matter before him. He asked me: "Have you met Ammar Yasir?" I replied in the negative. Thereupon he said: "You must see him and accept whatever he says". Now I have come to you to find out what you have to say. Ammar Yasir said: "Do you know who is

---

*The patronymic appellation of Ammār Yāsir.

holding that black standard, which is before us? He is Amr bin Āsृ. I, who am Ammar Yasir, have fought against that very standard thrice in the company of the Holy Prophet of Allah at Badr, Uhud and Hunayn. It is now for the fourth time that I am fighting against it and as compared with the previous three occasions it has not become better but has become worse". Then he said: "Have you or your father witnessed those battles?" The man repleid: "No". Thereupon Ammar said: "You must know that the centres of our standard are the very centres of the standard of the Holy Prophet at the time of Badr, Uhud and Hunayn, and their standard, too, is at the place of the standard of the polytheists.*

Nasr also says that while Imam Ali was on his way to Siffin some companions of Abdullah bin Mas'ud including Ubayda Salmāni and others met him and said: "We are prepared to accompany you to Siffin, but we shall not join your army until we are satisfied as to which group is on the right, and which is on the wrong, so that we may fight against the wrong". Likewise he mentions some others, who were not willing to cooperate with Imam Ali, and said: "We have become suspicious about this fighting".

All these things go to prove that most of the Muslims had not yet realized the hypocrisy of Mu'awiya and considered him to be one of the distinguished companions of the Holy Prophet. They were not, therefore, prepared to fight against him in support of Imam Ali or Imam Hasan. Now that a period of twenty years and even more had passed since the event of Siffin, and Mu'awiya had propagated as much as he could in his own favour and against Bani Hashim and especially Imam Ali, and most of the companions, who had heard about the merits of Imam Ali from the Holy Prophet had departed from the world, and the belief that Mu'awiya was one of the companions of the Holy Prophet, a scribe of the revelations and the maternal uncle of the Muslims, definitely became more firm and gained currency. Thus if the matters had made their way in the same manner a day would have come when Muslims would not have recognized real Islam except that introduced by Mu'awiya and

---

*Kitāb Siffin, p. 320, second edition (Egypt).

all the troubles taken by the Holy Prophet during the period of twenty three years would have ended to the benefit of the descendants of Abu Sufyan, the sworn enemy of Islam.

Abu Sufyan and Mu'awiya, who fought against the Holy Prophet for twenty years and did all they could to exterminate Islam by all possible means, and professed Islam at the time of the conquest of Makkah, which took place in the seventh year of migration, were recognized by the people as the foremost persons of Islam and Imam Ali, who, according to the narrations of both the sects, was the first to embrace Islam, was now (God forbid!) treated by the people to be accursed, and cursing him was considered to be one of the greatest articles of Islamic worship. There were persons, who considered it obligatory for themselves to make amends for the lapse of this 'worship' if they forgot on any day to perform it. Although the Holy Prophet used to say: 'When heresies appear, and those, who have embraced Islam later, curse the early Muslims i.e. those, who expressed faith in the Prophet at the very outset, and one knows and does not manifest one's knowledge, is like one who conceals the Divine faith. A person who can distinguish between the Sunnah (The path of the Holy Prophet of Islam) and heresy should rise and save the people from deviation, otherwise he will become subjected to Divine wrath.*

According to this very authentic Hadith (tradition) Imam Husayn considered himself to be responsible, and did not deem it permissible for him to be negligent. He considered himself commissioned by Allah to defend Islam and the Muslim ummah from the danger of annihilation. During the ten years of his actual Imamate, therefore, he was not sitting at ease, and, as far as possible, did not remain silent. Letters were exchanged between him and Mu'awiya and he used to criticize Mu'awiya severely. The subject matter of the letters, which he wrote to Mu'awiya, was publicized in Madina or in Makkah at the time of Haj and almost prepared the ground for his rising, so much so that once when some wealth was being taken from Yemen to Syria via Madina for Mu'awiya, Imam Husayn confiscated it and distributed it amongst Bani Hashim. Later he sent its receipt to

---

*Jame'us Saghir Suyuti, vol. I, p. 31 narrated by Mu'az bin Jabal

Mu'awiya along with a letter of reproof.* These things themselves indicate that the Imam was thinking of revolution, for otherwise such an act would not have behoved the Imam.

All this was done by him to discharge his responsibility, and to prepare ground for his rising when it was necessary. He, therefore, performed this duty by means of letters, addresses and preaching. So much so that in reply to a letter of Mu'awiya, expressive of complaint, he wrote: "O Mu'awiya! I consider it a fault to give up campaign against you and deem myself responsible before Allah if I remain quiet and do not rise against you".

Until the time for formal movement and rising arrived, he acted according to the duty entrusted to him by Allah and the Holy Prophet in the form of ordering to do good and restraining from evil.

As regards his being commissioned by Allah it may be said that this claim is supported by a hadith (tradition), which has been quoted by Ya'qub Kulayni on a very reliable authority from Zurays Kanasi, who says: "Hamran bin A'yun Shaybani said to Imam Baqir: "Have you observed what events took place during the period of Imam Ali and Husayn? They performed jihad but were defeated and were eventually killed at the hands of the tyrants". The Imam replied: "Whatever happened had, of course, been ordained for them by Allah. He Himself ordered it, made it inevitable and then put it into force. The jihad performed by Imam Ali, Imam Hasan and Imam Husayn (Peace be upon them) was according to the previous knowledge and instructions, which they had received from the Holy Prophet, and every Imam who remained quiet also did so according to the same previous knowledge and instructions".

This tradition goes to show that the Holy Prophet had prescribed the duties of every Imam in advance, in accordance with the Divine Command, and each one of them carried out the Divine assignment during his own time.

It is possible that someone may doubt the correctness of such traditions or may be hesitant about their true meaning. Even then he cannot entertain any doubt about the rational fact that the leader of the Muslims must be loyal to Islam. It is also

---

*Sharh-e Nahjul Balaghah, Ibn Abil Hadid, vol. IV, p. 327.

obvious that if the Islamic Government falls in the hands of the enemies of Islam and they gain strength, they will uproot it. And Yazid, whose father Mu'awiya obtained oath of allegiance for him from all, during the period of his power and domination, was the very person, who made it a point to violate the Islamic commands. His corruption, deviation and blasphemies as contained in the verses composed by him before he attained to the caliphate are well-known and have been quoted by both the Sunni and the Shi'ah scholars.

Yaqubi and other historians have recorded that when Mu'awiya sent Yazid at the head of an army to conquer the Roman territories, the Muslim army camped at Ghazqazuna, where there was a convent named Murrān. In this convent Yazid had an illegal sexual alliance with a woman named Umme Kulsum. In the meantime fever and small-pox broke out in the Muslim army with such severity that the soldiers began dying and falling like autumn leaves. They insisted upon Yazid leaving the place as early as possible, but he did not pay any heed to their suggestion and composed the verses as translated below: "What do I care if the entire army of Islam dies of fever and small-pox. I am resting on a soft pillow and am embracing Umme Kulsum".

There are also some verses composed by him, wherein he has praised wine, and which show his mentality. In these verses he says inter alia: "If wine is unlawful in the religion of Ahmad (Islam), you should take it in accordance with the religion of Jesus son of Mary".

Yazid led an extremely voluptuous life and cared for nothing except revelry and merry-making. He spent most of his time in the convents of the Christians which constituted the fifth column at that time, and indulged in debauchery and amusements, so much so that even his father Mu'awiya wrote letters to him and admonished him. Qalqashandi has quoted* that when it was reported to Mu'awiya time and again that Yazid was leading a voluptuous life, he wrote a letter to him saying: "I am greatly concerned regarding the reports which I have received about you. They have pained me and destroyed

---

*Subhul A'shi, vol. VI, p. 387.

the hope of my affinity to you". He added: "O Yazid! You have thrown yourself into destruction and entrusted your soul to indecency and reproach, and have chosen for yourself destruction, disgrace and unlawful conduct instead of sublime deeds, virtues and noble acts. O Yazid! I wish that you had died at the very moment you were born. You made me happy and hopeful in your early youth. Having grown up, however, you have pained me and made me weep. Alas! Alas!"

These are the specimens of the personality of Yazid! Now Mu'awiya introduced to the Muslims as the successor of the Holy Prophet of Islam such an element, in whose person all the impurities were centred, and who was an embodiment of corruption and wickedness (as became very clear later) and completely ignorant of Islamic tenets. He made him dominate those on account of whose swords the father and grandfather of Yazid had adopted Islam, although not more than forty years had passed since the demise of the Holy Prophet, and his companions and even some of his wives were still alive.

It is, of course, evident that when rulership goes to a person, who does not believe in Allah and the Holy Prophet, does not offer prayers, drinks wine as if it were water, and insults all that is sacred according to religion, one should say goodbye to Islam and the Qur'an. In the circumstances was it possible that a godly person like Imam Husayn, the grand son of the Holy Prophet should be prepared to witness these crimes and see the religion of Allah a plaything in the hands of degraded persons, and endorse all this silently, or take the oath of allegiance to such a ruler? Certainly not. Furthermore, it was not only Imam Husayn who refused to take the oath of Yazid. No Muslim, who was acquainted with the Qur'an and recognized Allah, could agree to bear this insult, just as a number of the inhabitants of Kufa and Basra, and all those belonging to Madina, opposed Yazid from the very first day.

Imam Husayn knew well that the descendants of Abu Sufyān were basically hostile to Islam. They had endeavoured their best to exterminate Islam and were not at all prepared to tolerate that the name of the Holy Prophet should continue to exist. In case, therefore, the Caliphate remained with the descendants of Abu Sufyān no trace of Islam could remain.

Mas'udi, the renowned historian has quoted the following event: Mutarraf bin Mughira said, "My father and I were the guests of Mu'awiya in Syria. My father visited the court of Mu'awiya very often and praised him. One night when my father returned after meeting Mu'awiya, he was very sad and disturbed. I enquired from him the reason. He replied: 'This man i.e. Mu'awiya is a vicious person, rather the most abominable person of the age'. I said: 'But what has happened?' He replied, 'I suggested to Mu'awiya: 'Now that you have achieved your object, and attained to the Islamic Caliphate, it will be better that you should behave justly towards the people, and should not misbehave towards Bani Hashim so much, because, after all, they are your relatives and nothing is now left with them on account of which you may fear that they will rise against you'. Mu'awiya said: 'Alas! Alas! Abu Bakr became Caliph and administered justice, and nothing more than this happened that he died and his name, too, was eliminated. Umar and Uthman also died and although they behaved well towards the people, nothing except their names survived and they perished. As regards the Hashimi brother (i.e. the Holy Prophet), however, his name is pronounced in the world of Islam loudly five times a day and it is said: 'I testify that Muhammad is the Prophet of Allah'. What remains to be done when the names of the three Caliphs die and the name of Muhammad remains alive except that his name too should be buried and eliminated".*

Mas'udi has cited this event from the book Muwaffaqiyyāt by Zubayr bin Bakār which is one of the reliable documents. He says, "In the circumstances, could Husayn bin Ali sit and remain patient, and quietly observe those people fighting against Islam and the Qur'an, and endeavouring to eliminate them? Certainly not".

During those days the Islamic Caliphate had assumed the shape of the kingdoms of Kisra and Caesar. Mu'awiya, according to his corrupt thinking, decided to leave it as inheritance in his own family and there were two great impediments which hindered the achievement of this object. One of these impediments was the incapability of Yazid, who was known to the

---

*Murujuz Zahab, vol. II, p. 266, printed at Bolāq, Egypt, and Ibn Abil Hadid in Sharh-e Nahjul Balāghah has also alluded to it.

nobles of that time and the dignitaries of the Islamic territories, as a frivolous, incapable, shameless and wicked person, and the chiefs of the Islamic country had no regard for him. The other impediment was Imam Hasan with whom Mu'awiya had agreed in a peace treaty that after him, he (i.e. Mu'awiya) would not introduce anyone as the prospective Caliph.

As regards the first impediment, Mu'awiya found the remedy for it by suppressing the religious sentiments of the people with gifts, grants and big awards, and, if the object could not be achieved by these means, he would silence them with threats, cancellation of grants and dismissal from employment. He accomplished this task as quickly as possible.

In order to remove the second impediment he took steps to kill Imam Hasan and eventually poisoned him with a strange deceit through Ju'dah daughter of Ash'ath bin Qays. He then thought that the way was now clear and did not believe that any other impediment could exist after the death of Imam Hasan. Later he realized that in the presence of a person like Imam Husayn in Madina, which was more important than all other Islamic territories, its inhabitants would not at all take the oath of allegiance to Yazid. He was, therefore, obliged to resort to another deceit. The historians have written thus in this behalf: After the death of Imam Hasan, Mu'awiya resolved to obtain allegiance from the people for Yazid, whom he wanted to appoint as his successor. He, therefore, wrote letters to all the governors of Islamic provinces including Sa'id bin Ās Umavi, the Governor of Madina, whom he wrote: "Obtain oath of allegiance for Yazid from all the Muhajirs and Ansar and their descendants. Show harshness and severity in the matter, and do not be lax and negligent. However, do not exert pressure on a few persons, but leave them alone, like Abdur Rahmān bin Abi Bakr and Husayn bin Ali"

When Sa'id bin Ās received Mu'awiya's letter he invited the people of Madina to take oath of allegiance to Yazid. However, all of them declined to do so and said that they would take the oath when the above persons also had done it otherwise they would not. Sa'id wrote a letter to Mu'awiya telling him that all the people of Madina followed those few persons, and so long as they did not take the oath of allegiance, it would not be possible to obtain it from others even through harshness. Mu'awiya wrote in reply: "It does not matter. Do not disturb anyone till I have thought over the matter".

In the same year he decided to perform Haj and came to Madina and brought a large number of Syrians along with him. Then he met those few persons in Madina and expressed his displeasure. When they observed that they had been insulted, they left Madina for Makkah to perform Umra individually. However, Mu'awiya stayed on in Madina till the Haj season. During that period he bestowed abundant presents on the people of Madina in order to soften their hearts and win them over.

Later he proceeded to Makkah. When the people came to see him on his arrival, he met Abdullah bin Umar, Abdullah bin Zubayr, Abdur Rahmān and Imam Husayn. He showed them great respect, spoke affably to them, and ordered that an animal of riding might be brought for each one of them. He addressed each of them according to their status. He called Imam Husayn, the chief of the Muslim youth, Abdullah bin Zubayr, the cousin of the Holy Prophet, Abdur Rahman, the chief and master of Quraysh and so on.

After performing Haj he summoned them. Imam Husayn was asked by others to have a talk with Mu'awiya but he declined. They made the same suggestion to Abdullah bin Zubayr and he accepted it. They met Mu'awiya, who showed them due respect and said: "You have seen yourselves how kind I am to you. You are my kith and kin and I have great affection for you. As regards Yazid he is your brother and cousin. What I desire is that he should hold the title of Caliph whereas all the affairs of the State should be in your hands and you should exercise authority in all matters".

All of them kept silent. Mu'awiya asked them to give a reply but they said nothing. Mu'awiya repeated his words for the third time and turning to Ibn Zubayr he asked him to speak. Abdullah bin Zubayr said: "O Mu'awiya! You can do one of these three things; either, as it is said that the Holy Prophet departed from the world without nominating any successor, you should act in the same way and leave the selection of the caliph to the people, or you should nominate a person who is not related to you and is fit to hold that office, as was done by

Abu Bakr, or you should leave the matter to a consultative council, as was done by Umar". Mu'awiya asked: "Is there no way other than these three courses?" Abdullah replied in the negative.

Mu'awiya then turned to the others and said: "What is your view?" They replied: "Our view is the same as put forward by Abdullah bin Zubayr". Mu'awiya said: "All right. I shall be talking about it tomorrow and none shall have the right to object to what I say. If I speak the truth it shall be beneficial for myself, and if I tell a lie I myself shall suffer for it, but if anyone opposes me he shall lose his life".

On the following day a general meeting was called by Mu'awiya. It was attended by all those persons, who had come from different parts of the Islamic territories to perform Haj. Those few persons were also summoned and two armed men were stationed beside each one of them. Mu'awiya mounted the pulpit and the Syrians gathered round him. He delivered a speech in which he said: "I have seen that people say many baseless things. They say that Husayn bin Ali, Abdur Rahman bin Abi Bakr, Abdullah bin Zubayr and Abdullah bin Umar have not taken the oath of allegiance to Yazid. They are the best and the most distinguished persons among the Muslims. No task can be firm and permanent without them and nothing can be done without consulting them. I myself talked with them about the matter and found them submissive. All of them took the oath of allegiance to Yazid without raising any objection".

At this stage, as had already been settled, the Syrians shouted: "These few persons don't matter much. If they don't agree, you should permit us to chop off their heads".

Mu'awiya said: "How strange it is that people have become so hostile to Quraysh, and they don't want anything except shedding their blood. Keep quiet and don't repeat these words". Having said this he came down from the pulpit and his agents began taking the oath of allegiance from the people, whereas he himself mounted his animal and left Makkah.

After Mu'awiya's departure the people rushed towards Imam Husayn and others, and began criticizing them. They asked them: "How is it that you agreed to take the allegiance when you had been saying that you wouldn't do so?" Although they said that they had not taken the oath of allegiance and

Mu'awiya had told a lie, and had deceived them, the people did not accept their words. They said: "You are lying. If it was as you say, why did you not repudiate his allegation in the meeting?" When they replied that if they had done so they would have been killed, but their saying all this was of no use.*

Ya'qubi has quoted the words of Abdullah bin Umar and Abdullah bin Zubayr which they uttered when Sa'id bin Ās Umavi, the Governor of Madina, suggested to them to take the allegiance. He says: "When Sa'id bin Ās asked them to take the oath of allegiance to Yazid they declined and said: "What excuse shall we have before Allah if we take the oath of allegiance to one who plays with monkeys and dogs and drinks wine and is a confirmed licentious man. Can we cooperate with him and approve his actions?"

Ibn Jauzi says: "A group of persons went from Madina to Syria to observe the ways and conduct of Yazid. On their return they said: "We have come after seeing a man who doesn't at all have any religion. He drinks wine, plays on musical instruments and also plays with dogs. Abdullah bin Hanzala, Ghasilul Malāika used to say: "Yazid is a man, who doesn't spare even his mother, daughter and sister. He drinks wine and doesn't offer prayers".

Mas'udi says in Murujuz Zahab: "Yazid was notorious as a habitual drunkard. In the circumstances it was the duty of all Muslims not to agree to take the oath of allegiance to him, because such an oath meant approval of all his actions and an acknowledgement to assist him in whatever he did, and Islam does not permit the Muslims to remain quiet and observe patience, if Islam is being destroyed, the Qur'an is being trampled upon and the Divine religion becomes a plaything in the hands of idiots and bullies. Silence at such a stage is like the silence of the mean sufi, quoted by Syed Murtaza Dāi Rāzi in Tabsaratul Awām.**

---

*This incident has been mentioned by Ibn Abdu Rabih Undulusi in Iqdul Farid, vol. II, p. 248,; by Ibn Qutaybah in al-Imāmah Vas Siyāsah, vol. I, p. 138 and in the foot-note of Amāli Qāli, p. 177.

**Refer to Maqālāt-e Sufiya chapter sixteen. The story has not been reproduced here on account of its being obscene.

Imam Husayn considered silence in such circumstances to be unlawful and one of the points of the tradition of his grandfather, the Holy Prophet, which he quoted before the army of Hur while he was on his way to Kufa is this: "If a person observes such affairs and does not oppose them and keeps quiet, Allah will be entitled to include him with the oppressor and tyrant and subject them both to similar torture".*

During the last years of the life of Mu'awiya, therefore, Imam Husayn invited all those persons, who had seen the Holy Prophet and had the honour of being his companions, as well as their descendants, scattered in all Islamic regions, and wrote letters to all of them. About 1000 companions and Tābi'in gathered together in Mina and he addressed them in these words: "You can see how this bully treats us and our supporters. You should narrate to your fellow countrymen in your cities whatever is said in this meeting". Then he narrated one by one the virtues and merits of his father, Imam Ali, and exhorted them to enjoin others to do good and to restrain them from evil.

As is evident from the wording and sentences of the sermon** delivered before this gathering, it was there that the Imam commenced his mission of revolution.

We reproduce here, by way of specimen, a few sentences from that sermon so that the matter may become clear. After reciting the Qur'anic verses about the necessity of enjoining to do good and restraining from evil, he said: "O brave persons! You are well-known for your wisdom, virtue and benevolence and have created respect for you in the hearts of others through Allah. The noble persons honour you and the weak ones accord you respect. And those, who are your equals and are under no obligation to you, consider you to be superior to them".

Thereafter he said: "I am afraid lest you should get involved in difficulties, because you have attained a position of respectability which is not held by others, and you enjoy superiority over the people. Good persons aren't being respected and you are honourable among the people for the sake of Allah. You see

---

*The complete text of the tradition will be given later.

**Tuhaful Uqul.

with your own eyes that the convenants of Allah are being violated and His laws are being opposed, and you are not alarmed, although you are worried and alarmed when the convenants made with your ancestors are broken. The convenants made with the Holy Prophet have been broken and have become worthless, and are being held in contempt and you do not attach any importance to this fact. The blind, the dumb and the cripples in all the regions are without guardians and are not pitied. You don't discharge your responsibilities, and do not work according to your ability. You do not also pay attention to one, who performs his duty in this behalf, and do not show humility. You keep yourselves relieved by indulgence and collusion with the oppressors.

"All this is due to the fact that while Allah has ordered prevention of unlawful acts, and restraining the people from commiting them but you have neglected this duty, because you have been slack in protecting the honour and respect of your scholars and have not been able to preserve their status and have made others prevail over that rank. I wish you had realized this or had made an effort in that behalf".

He added: "The reins of administration should be in the hands of those, who are well-versed with the Commands of Allah i.e. lawful and unlawful things. It was you, who occupied this position, but you were deprived of it owing to your separation from truth and your differences about the Sunnah of the Holy Prophet in spite of clear proofs. If you had been patient and steadfast and had shown forbearance in the path of Allah, you would have assumed the reins of administration once again. However, you vacated your seat for the oppressors and handed over the Divine government to them, so that they might act in a dubious manner and pursue their carnal desires.

"It was your disregarding death and taking delight in this transient life which made the weak their subjects so that they might enslave and subdue some of them and deprive others of even a morsel of food. They ransack the Islamic territories for their personal benefit, and their cardinal desires bring disgrace to them. They follow the wicked person and have no fear of the Almighty Allah. In every city they make a preacher of their own mount the pulpit and all the Islamic territories are under their control. They do whatever they like and the people are their slaves. They cannot defend themselves against any maltreatment meted out to them. Tyrants and obstinate persons oppress the weak.

"There are some rulers, who do not believe in Allah and in the Day of Judgement. How astonishing this situation is! And why should I be not astonished when the land is possessed by either a deceitful person and a tyrant, or a wicked tax-collector, or a ruler, who is so cruel to the believers? Now it is Allah who can decide matters between us .... '*"

It is learnt from what has been stated that the Imam was thinking of bringing about a revolution before the question of taking oath of allegiance to Yazid arose, and he was waiting for an appropriate opportunity. Hence his movement should be treated to have commenced from the invitation which he extended to the companions and the Tābi'in in Mina.

Keeping in view the conditions of the Muslims in those days it was not an easy task to awaken the people and invite them to truth and this task could not be accomplished by means of correspondence and addresses and by sending messages. The Imam therefore, decided to bring about a revolution by means of which the inhabitants of all the Islamic regions might realize that if Yazid came into power Islam would be uprooted and no trace of it would be found anywhere.

The persons whose ancestors had considered Mu'awiya

―――――
*The Imam addressed those persons who were distinguished among the people. Their responsibility in the Muslim society was greater than that of others, but they were negligent of their duties, and were, therefore, reproached. They were evidently the very persons, who were invited by the Imam and addressed in Mina which is a part of the sanctuary and a place of peace, because it could not be that the Imam might have mounted the pulpit formally in Madina and gathered together and addressed the remaining Muhajir and Ansar, who were then reckoned to be the chiefs in the Islamic society and the ruler of the time might not have restrained him from doing so. This is confirmed by the contents of the later part of the tradition and there are other indications also in the light of which it cannot be said that the Imam addressed the people on these lines in Makkah after the death of Mu'awiya.

more than twenty years earlier to be a distinguished companion of the Holy Prophet, or at least doubted his falsehood and hypocrisy, could not be awakened with messages and addresses and could not be made to understand what a true Islamic Government should be. Moreover, Muʻawiya's agents were busy propagating in every town and region and making the people deviate from the right path. Persons like Hujr bin Adi and Rashid Hujari and his friends and Amr bin Humuq Khuzāi were being killed and none could pick up courage to protest, rather they were usually considered to be guilty. It was, therefore, necessary to start a sudden movement and bring about a revolution in the Islamic territories. It should thus influence all the regions, and its effects should continue for a very long period and should not cease till the matters were reformed, and the intentions of Bani Umayya in general and of the descendants of Abu Sufyan (who always wished that the people should cease to utter the name of the Holy Prophet and should no longer understand Islam) were known to the people. The people should consequently recognize them (Bani Umayyah) and join their opponents, and the campaign should start. In this their rulership should come to an end. Hence the Imam started his movement with the purpose of enjoining to do good and restraining from evil.

In the testament which Imam Husayn wrote and handed over to Muhammad bin Hanafiya, while leaving Madina, he said after expressing his belief in Allah, in the Prophethood of his grandfather Muhammad bin Abdullah, in the Day of Judgement, and in Paradise and Hell:

"I have not come out with the intention of violence and rebellion or in obedience to my passions, and it is not my object to create mischief on the earth or to oppress anyone. My only object is to reform the affairs of the Muslim nation and to act according to the conduct of my father and grandfather".

When he decided to depart from Madina he went to his grandfather's grave many times at night and said: "O Allah! I love good deeds and hate bad deeds".

Imam Husayn commenced jihad knowing fully well that he would be martyred and his men and women would be made captives, but Islam and its commands would survive and the opposing powers would be annihilated; Yazid, whom his father had nominated his successor during his own lifetime, contrary to the practice followed by the previous Caliphs, and made him dominate the Muslims, would not be able to repeat this act; Mu'awiya bin Yazid would not be at the helm of the State; Mu'awiya's scheme would come to nought; all the people would wake up from slumber with the assistance of the organization itself and distinguish between real and artificial Islam. Consequently Bani Umayya would be disgraced and their dead bodies would always serve as an eye opener denouncing cruelty and oppression.

It is possible that an objection may be raised at this stage as Allah says: *Do not subject your lives to destruction with your own hands* (Surah al-Baqarah, 2:195) and discharging the responsibility of enjoining to do good and restraining from evil is itself subject to certain conditions. It may be said in reply that Imam knows better than all others the conditions pertaining to enjoining to do good and restraining from evil and his action is in itself the best authority.

It is, of course, true that it is not permissible to subject oneself to destruction, but the jihad performed by Imam Husayn did not amount to this. If a person considers being killed for the sake of Allah to be subjecting oneself to destruction, he must also place most of the battles fought by the Holy Prophet under the same category. He must also consider whether confronting of twenty Muslim warriors with two hundred enemies in the early battles of Islam, when the Muslims were not numerically strong enough, amounted to subjecting themselves to destruction! But the Muslims unanimously agree that this viewpoint is not correct.

Furthermore, the Qur'anic verse does not mean that the Muslims should not perform jihad, because in the event of their being killed they have subjected themselves to destruction with their own hands. In fact this verse was revealed when the Muslims had been ordered that in the event of war every one of them should provide equipment, arms, foodstuffs and animals of riding according to his capacity. Apparently some persons were making excuses in the matter and were not prepared to make necessary contributions. It was then that this verse was revealed saying: *Spend your wealth for the cause of*

Allah and do not subject yourselves to destruction with your own hands (on account of negligence or stinginess). (Surah al-Baqarah, 2:195) This meaning is confirmed by the narration of Huzayfa bin Yamān, a distinguished companion of the Holy Prophet, who has been reported to have said that this verse was revealed in connection with expenditure. This narration has been quoted by Ibn Ali Hâtim and Bukhâri from Huzayfa and A'mash, and by Suyuti from Ibn Abbas, Mujāhid, Ikrima, Sa'id bin Jābir, Atā, Zahhāk, Hasan Basri, Qatada, Saddi and Maqâtil bin Hayyān. All of them were companions or Tābi'in.

In another narration Aslam bin Yazid Abu Imran says: "During the siege of Constantinople one of our soldiers attacked the enemy and split their rows. Some of our men said: "This man has subjected himself to destruction". Abu Ayyub Ansāri was with us. He said: "We know the meaning of this verse better and you only guess. This verse was revealed about us, the Ansar, who had the honour of receiving the Prophet and becoming his companions. When Islam flourished, we became negligent in assisting the Holy Prophet and said to ourselves: "Now that Islam has gained popularity and become powerful, we should take care of our families. We, therefore, paid no attention towards helping the Holy Prophet. Thereupon this verse was revealed: *Spend your wealth for the cause of Allah and do not subject yourselves to destruction with your own hands.* Destruction was involved in spending on one's wife and children and in abandoning jihad. Hence, one subjects oneself to destruction by abandoning jihad and not by performing it.

This narration has been quoted by Abu Dāud Sijistāni, Tirmizy, Nisāi, Abd bin Hamid, Ibn Abi Hātim, Ibn Jurayr Tabari, Ibn Marduya, Abu Yāla and Ibn Habbān in Sahih and Hākim Nishapuri in 'Mustadrak'. All of them have quoted it from the tradition of Yazid bin Abi Habib through Aslam. Tirmizy declares that this tradition is authentic.

In another narration Abi Ishaq Sabi'i has been quoted as saying: A man said to Barā bin Āzib. "If, during a battle, I attack the enemy alone and am killed, will it amount to my subjecting myself to destruction with my own hands?" Barā replied: "No, because Allah says to His Prophet: *So fight in the way of Allah. You are not responsible except for yourself."* (Surah al-Nisa,

4:84) Then Barā added: "This verse relates to spending money at the time of war. This narration has been quoted by Ibn Marduwayh and by Hākim in Mustadrak. Hākim says that this tradition fulfils the conditions laid down by the two shaykhs (Bukhāri and Muslim).

A similar remark of Huzayfa bin al-Yamān has also been quoted in Tafsir-e 'Ayyāshi and reproduced in Tafsir-e Burhān. In Luhuf Sayyid bin Tāwus has also given the same meaning to this verse on the authority of these very narrations.

Furthermore, the verse relating to destruction occurs in the context of defensive jihad and a reference to the context makes the position clear.

The basic thing is that, in the terminology of Islam, being killed for the cause of Allah is not taken to mean destruction. The Holy Qur'an says about the martyrs of Islam thus: *Think not of those who are slain in the way of Allah, as dead. They are alive with their Lord and receive sustenance from Him.* (Surah Ale Imran, 3:169)

In one of his sermons* Imam Ali said to his companions at the time of the Battle of Siffīn: "Your death and destruction lies in your being subdued and your life consists of death when you are predominant. The life which makes one submit to every worthless person is worse than dying and being destroyed a thousand times".

However, at this stage, Imam Husayn was not prepared to be martyred like his father and brother, because such a martyrdom could not produce the desired results. It was possible that none might have paid any heed to such martyrdom and the Imam's blood might have been shed in vain.

Those who think that the Imam was not aware of the consequences of the step taken by him are gravely mistaken, because apart from the traditions saying that the Imam, who does not know what he is going to face is not the vicegerent of Allah, and the Imams were also aware when they would die, and they had an option in the matter.

The question of the martyrdom of Imam Husayn was basically well-known in the family of Bani Hashim and especially

---

*Nahjul Balaghah.

in the household of Imam Ali. Umme Salama, Umme Ayman and others had all heard from the Holy Prophet that Husayn would be martyred in Karbala.

Besides this in the sermon, which he delivered in the sanctuary of the Holy Kā'bah before his departure, the Imam said: "Man is destined to die". It is quite clear that the Imam knew that he would be martyred, or else he would not have said: "I can see as if the desert wolves are piercing my body between Nawāwis and Karbala". Similarly it becomes clear from what he said on other occasion that he was fully aware of the consequences and to deny this is nothing except baseless contention.

Muhammad bin Hasan bin Farrukh Saffār says in the beginning of Basāirud Darajāt and similarly Kulayni says in Kāfi, that a man belonging to Kufah met the Imam in Thālabiya (and apparently dissuaded him from going to Kufah and warned him that he would be killed). Imam Husayn replied to him: "If I had met you in Madina I would have shown you in my house the signs of Jibril bringing revelations to my grandfather. O brother Kufi! How can it be that the source of knowledge of the people should be with us, and they may know whereas we may be ignorant".

Furthermore, at the time of his departure from Madina he said: "Whoever accompanies me will be martyred and whoever lags behind will not share the victory".

If anyone says that Sayyid Murtaza has been quoted as having said that Imam Husayn did not know that he would be killed, we say in reply that Imam Bāqir and Imam Sādiq have been quoted as saying that he was aware that he would be killed. And if an objection is raised that when he knew that he would be killed why did he take his women and children along with him, which resulted in their being made captives, our reply is the same as given earlier. It was not his intention merely to be killed along with his companions. What he aimed at was to draw the attention of the people to the malpractices of Bani Umayya and to the fact that their rule was not an Islamic rule, and their aim was to efface and destroy Islam and especially the name of the Holy Prophet Muhammad.

Hence, he acted according to a correct plan and proved to

the world that they were not prepared to let any member of the family of Bani Hashim live, and would make even a suckling the target of their arrows. He also proved that they treated the members of the Holy Prophet's family more harshly than they treated the polytheist captives of Turkey and Dailam, and they had no intention except that of effacing Islam and the traditions of the Holy Prophet and ruling unjustly over the people.

We have said earlier that the people had not recognized Bani Umayya correctly. They were mostly mistaken and they honoured them. Mu'awiya, who had been an infidel and a polytheist during the larger part of his life and was obliged to embrace Islam at the time of the conquest of Makkah, was considered by them to be a peer of Ammār Yāsir and Zush-Shahādatain and Ibn Tayyahān and even Imam Ali ibn Abi Talib.

Rabi bin Khuthaym who was one of the distinguished Tābi'in and was considered to be a great ascetic, came to Imam Ali at the time of the Battle of Siffin and said: "O Commander of the Faithful! Though we are aware of your rank and position, we are doubtful as to whether this battle is justified or not."

There were many other persons also upon whom the people depended for guidance. Public opinion had been completely perverted and this was especially the case with the Syrians and those, who had been under Mu'awiya's influence from the very beginning.

Nasr bin Muzāhim says: "Hashim Marqāl, along with a group of the reciters of the Holy Qur'an of Kufa, was busy fighting against the enemy. In the mean time a Ghassānian came in the field and began reciting epic verses and abusing Ali and insisted on cursing and vilifying him. Hāshim Marqāl said to him: "Young man! There is a time when one has to account for whatever he says. You should fear Allah to whom you have to return, because he will question you about your stand and your aim". The man turned and said: "I am fighting against you, because I have been told that your chief does not offer prayers and the same is the case with you people". Hashim then admonished him and removed the misunderstanding which had been created in his mind and he went back.*

_____
*Kitāb Siffin, P. 354, Second edition (Egypt).

What we mean to say is that more than twenty years before the rising of Imam Husayn the people of Syria did not know Imam Ali in spite of all his virtues quoted from the Holy Prophet and the matters had turned much worse during Mu'awiya's twenty years rule. During this period he carried out intensive and extensive propaganda to distort the Islamic realities. His agents were putting his orders into practice in all Islamic regions and the foundation of Islam had terribly shaken. Lawful things had become unlawful and vice versa. And during the rule of Yazid bin Mu'awiya the Islamic traditions would have been eliminated further and the position would have been what was assessed by Imam Husayn himself who said: "If the Muslim ummah becomes subjected to the rulership of a person like Yazid one should say goodbye to Islam and abandon it".

There are some, who say that the Imam was invited by the Kufians and as he was afraid lest his blood should be shed in Makkah and the sanctity of the sanctuary violated, he accepted the invitation of the Kufians and started his movement from that time, and in case they had not invited him he might not have possibly taken this step. They mean to say that in fact there was no movement at all, and the Imam took the decision, because he was compelled by the circumstances to do so.

In reply we ask: "When he came to know that Muslim bin Aqil had been martyred and became sure that the Kufians were not faithful and no assistance could be expected from them, why did he not return from that very place and did he not hide himself in the desert especially when Hur's army had not yet arrived?" And he could return even after encountering Hur's army i.e. he could fight against them. Furthermore, why did he deliver the wonderful fiery sermon which has been quoted by Tabari etc. and in which he said: "Whoever sees the cruel ruler making the unlawful things lawful and breaking Allah's pledge...".

If the question was of accepting the invitation of the Kufians why did he write letters from Makkah to the five chiefs of Basra namely Yazid bin Mas'ud Nahshali, Malik bin Musma, Ahnaf bin Qays, Munzir bin Jārud and Mas'ud bin Amr and sought assistance from them?

Certainly Imam Husayn wanted to bring about a revolution, and its voice should be heard in all Islamic territories and the

31

victorious enemy, intoxicated with his power, should himself drag the family of the Holy Prophet to various cities and regions so that the people should see them from close view and learn that Bani Umayya did not believe in Allah and in the Holy Prophet and the fact of his being oppressed should become known universally, so that Bani Umayya might be uprooted. Otherwise, how could the people who heard Imam Ali being cursed from the pulpits for more than twenty years, distinguish between truth and falsehood? How could the Syrians, who had never perhaps heard the names of Hasan and Husayn being uttered with honour (and did not possibly know about one out of thousands of the merits of Bani Hashim) be made aware of truth and awakened from slumber? This could be done only by Imam Ali ibn Husayn (Imam Sajjād) mounting, in the centre of Yazid's regime, the same pulpit from which propaganda had been carried on against Imam Ali and telling the Syrians about his virtues disgracing Yazid and Muʻawiya and causing the Syrians to revolt against Yazid, so that the tragedy of the martyrdom of his father and brothers in Karbala should be discussed by the Syrians for a long time in their assemblies, and the inauspicious effects of Muʻawiya's propaganda should be totally eliminated so that notwithstanding all his despotism, he should not be able to distort the facts.

Imam Ali was martyred while he was praying in the arch of the Kufa Mosque. The Syrians wondered at this event and said: "Did Ali also offer prayers that he came to the mosque and was killed in the arch?"

It is possible that someone may raise an objection and say: If Imam Husayn intended to rise, why did he say on the day of Āshura: "Let me go. I shall proceed to a safe place". We say in reply: It is true that such a statement of the Holy Imam has been quoted by Tabari in different words but this does not prove that the Imam said: 'I am prepared to return and abandon my mission and shall no longer enjoin others to do good or restrain them from evil'. No, not at all. Of course, the Kufians had invited him and then went back on their words whereupon he said: "Now that you are regretful for what you said and wrote, it doesn't matter, and I am prepared to return". He did not say that he wanted to abandon his mission.

As regards his seeking assistance from various persons it was because they were usually those Iraqis, who wielded influence in their regions. Now whether they responded to his call (like Zuhayr bin Qayn, Zahhāk etc.) or not, all of them played their part sincerely in supporting the revolution.

Let us take the case of Zahhāk Mashriqi.* He observed all the happenings of Āshura with his own eyes and later mentioned the same to everyone in Kufa. Most of the events of Āshura have been quoted from him. He thus proved to be a true recorder of the events and proclaimer appointed by the Imam. Or else what benefit can one derive from the company of such a person for a few hours when he is sure that he is going to be killed?

Another person was Ubaydullah bin Hur Juafi, who served under Mu'awiya in the Battle of Siffin, and was one of those, who claimed to be the avengers of the murder of Uthman. Although he did not come to the Imam's help and excused himself, but when the Ahlul Bayt (the family of the Holy Prophet) proceeded from Kufa to Syria, Ibn Ziyad summoned the nobles of the city one by one and made enquiries about them, but could not see Ubaydullah bin Hur amongst them. After a few days Ubaydullah bin Hur arrived in Kufa and went to see Ibn Ziyad, who asked him: "Where have you been and why did you not assist us?" He replied: "I have been sick". Ibn Ziyad said: "Was it your heart that was sick or your body?" Ubaydullah bin Hur replied: "My heart was not at all sick. I was not feeling well for a few days and Allah has cured me". Ibn Ziyad said: "You are lying. You were with our enemy". He replied: "If I had been with your enemy this would have been evident and could not remain hidden from you".

The narrator says: Ibn Ziyad being inattentive, Ubaydullah bin Hur suddenly went away from there and mounted his horse. In the mean time Ibn Ziyad became conscious of this and said: "Where is Ubaydullah? Bring him". The guards ran out and said to him: "The emir has summoned you and you must respond". He spurred his horse and said: "Tell him that I swear by Allah that I shall never come to him voluntarily". He then left and dismounted at the house of Ahmar bin Ziyad Tāi. His friends

---

*A detailed account of this man will be given later.

and companions gathered round him there, and all of them went to Karbala. He was very much grieved on seeing the graves of the martyrs and composed some verses lamenting the death of the Imam. Possibly he was the first person who visited the grave of the Imam and composed an elegy for him.

Later Hur rose in company with Mukhtār to avenge the murder of Imam and opposed the government of the time and continued harassing it till the end of his life. In his well-known book, Najjāshi, the biographer of *muhaddithin* (traditionalists) has included him among the pious predecessors and says that he compiled a book consisting of the sermons of Imam Ali.

Another person from whom the Imam sought help was Zuhayr bin Qayn. He was one of the notables of Kufa and wielded great influence over his tribe named Bujayla. At the time of the Battle of Siffin he was one of those, who claimed to avenge the murder of Uthman and later on supported the government of Kufa. Now that he joined the Imam this had a very good effect on others. Furthermore, his being killed grieved the tribes of Kufa, and, consequently, they refrained from cooperating with the government and were always awaiting an opportunity to take vengeance. And it was not Zuhayr alone whose martyrdom became the source of indignation and rancour among the tribe of Bujayla but other tribes also associated with them against the government. The martyrdom of all those belonging to Basra and Kufa, who lost their lives along with the Imam, wounded the hearts of most of the tribes, because all of them were the nobles and dignitaries of these two cities, and most of the tribes residing there mourned their death. The government had to pay dearly for their bloodshed.

From the very early days the Shi'ah of Kufa became active and formed a secret party. Every night they used to gather in the house of one of them, mourned the martyrs, and secretly put the people on their oath that they would oppose the government and avenge the blood of Imam Husayn. Their number increased gradually and the political conditions of Iraq became more dangerous day after day. After three years and a few months when Yazid died they formally made their call public and arrested Amr bin Hurayth, the Governor of Kufa and expelled him from the city. They gathered in the Masjid of Kufa and all the chiefs of the tribes also attended the meeting. Names of a few persons were recommended for the interim government; one of them was Amr bin Sa'id* according to Tabari, and Umar bin Sā'd as stated by Hāj Farhād Mirza in his book entitled Qumqām. On hearing this the women of Hamdān tribe poured out of their houses and began lamenting. Later the women of Nakha Rabia and Kehlān tribes also joined them. Their men, armed with swords, guarded them on all sides, and the women gathered round the pulpit, lamented and cried and said: "Is it not sufficient for Umar bin Sā'd that he has killed the son of Fatima? Now he wants to govern us and to become the ruler of Kufa!" They reminded themselves of the tragedy of Imam Husayn. Till that day formal mourning for the martyrs of Karbala had not taken place in the central Masjid of Kufa.

Disturbance also took place in Basra as in Kufa. Ibn Ziyad began to be opposed from all sides and he had to flee Basra to Syria in disguise. In Makkah Abdullah bin Zubayr took the oath of allegiance from the people for himself, and in Syria also a strange revolution took place which culminated, after Yazid's three or four years hideous rule, in the extinction of the caliphate for which Mu'awiya had been strenuously trying for four years. Thereafter none of the descendants of Abu Sufyan attained to the caliphate.

As regards the Imam's permitting his companions to leave and insisting upon it, it was evident because he did not wish to keep in the dark anyone, who might have joined him for worldly gains. It was necessary that his steps as well as those of others, who were going to be martyred along with him should have been indentical. They should not have acted blindly but with perfect cognition, and no coercion should have been involved. This in itself is one of the distinctions of Islam that all its soldiers are vigilant and intelligent and know what they are doing and this shows the difference between truth and falsehood.

*Tabari's account is absolutely incorrect and we are not aware of any person named Amr bin Sa'id who might have participated in the murder of Imam Husayn. Exactly the same error has appeared in Ibn Qutaybah's al-Imamāh Vas Siyāsah wherein he has throughout written Amr bin Sa'id instead of Umar bin Sā'd.

The pretenders who recruit soldiers for themselves are not at all prepared to lose even one of their devotees easily. However, the godly persons are not like this. They leave the people free to choose their path with their own will and only point out to them the right path.

Imam Husayn had not undertaken this journey with the object of acquiring a kingdom so that he should have kept with him by all possible means those, who had accompanied him, and should not have allowed them to go away. On the contrary he said in very clear terms: "I think that a battle will take place with these people. I release you from the oath of allegiance taken by you. Now that it is night time and it has enveloped you in its darkness, you should avail of the opportunity and go away". However, his companions and Bani Hashim gave a pertinent reply. They said unanimously: "Praised be Allah, who has honoured us with martyrdom in your company. Even if it be supposed that this world had been eternal and we had to live in it for ever, we would certainly have preferred to be killed along with you to living in this world".

Furthermore, the Imam wanted to put them to test and granted them full freedom, so that those, who were cooperating with him willingly, might be distinguished from those, who were reluctant, and none of them should regret his action later, and say that he had become involved in difficulty and had no way out, or show weakness before the spiteful enemy, so that it might be said that Husayn bin Ali duped the people for the sake of rulership and worldly gains. He, therefore, said in very clear words: "You should disperse and go to your homes, because these people are after me only and if they succeed in subduing me they will have nothing to do with anyone else". He said this so that they should select the right or wrong path after careful consideration.

In short Imam Husayn did such a job that his martyred body became the symbol of Islam till eternity, and his memorial continues to be a permanent threat to the oppressive regime and will always be combating against the enemies of Islam.

Bani Umayya and Bani Abbas always restrained the people from visiting the grave of Imam Husayn. To achieve this end they constructed watch towers and forts around his grave and posted a large number of soldiers there for the purpose of observation. The supervision was so strict that a pilgrim could hardly escape. Usually they had to face torture and death. As persecution by the caliphs increased insistence by the people on visiting the grave of the Imam grew more intense and as the resistance gained strength the administration became more worried and took serious measures in the matter. Consequently many hands were amputated, many heads were chopped off, and many limbs were cut into pieces. However, all these actions were absolutely ineffective.

During the days of Bani Abbas the grave of Imam Husayn was repeatedly demolished. However, as soon as the people felt that the government was inattentive they prepared it immediately. Hence, when one studies the history of the grave of the Imam, it becomes obvious as to when and by whom it was demolished, and who ordered its demolition, but it is not usually clear as to who repaired it, and who bore the expenses of its construction and repairs. This in itself shows the devotion and sincerity of the people in the matter.

What could be the reason for restraining the people from visiting the grave of Imam Husayn except that the oppressive regimes of the time considered the enthusiasm of the pilgrims and their assembling there to be a threat to their very existence.

The pilgrims of Imam Husyan knew well that he was martyred, because of his upholding justice. He laid down his life to check oppression and to maintain the principle of enjoining virtue and restraining the people from vice. He made the supreme sacrifice, but did not submit to the tyrannical, despotic and oppressive regime and opposed it valiantly. Hence, none of the rulers could bear the devotees of Imam Husayn and their being ready to lay down their lives for the sake of pilgrimage of his grave and mourning for him.

Although the sentry posts and guards of the regime were constantly vigilant, the people reached the grave of Imam Husayn, taking advantage of the darkness of night, and took refuge before sunrise to places like Ghāziriya and Naynava which are situated near Karbala. This statement is confirmed by the following incident:

Abul Faraj Isfahani has quoted in Maqātilul Tālibiyin

Muhammad bin Husayn Ashnāni as saying: "On account of fear I had not visited the grave of Imam Husayn for a very long time. At last I said to myself: "Come, whatever may be the consequences, I must go and pay homage to the sacred grave of the Imam". Accompanied by a perfumer I left for Karbala. We used to hide ourselves during daytime and travelled at night till we reached Ghazariya. We left Ghazariya at mid-night and, passing through the watchmen, who were asleep, slowly approached the sacred grave of Imam Husayn. However as the grave had been demolished, its exact location could not be easily found. We found it after great difficulty. A box which covered the grave had been thrown aside and was half-burnt. The grave had been watered and consequently the earth had caved in and assumed the shape of a ditch. We paid homage to the sacred grave. The place was giving a pleasant smell. I asked my companion who was himself a perfumer as to what smell it was. He replied: "I swear by Allah that I have never smelt such a sweet smell so far." We then departed from the grave and left certain signs at some places. After Mutawakkil was killed we visited the grave with some of the descendants of Abu Talib and restored it to its original shape with mutual assistance".

This incident shows the interest which the people took in the matter. Imam Husayn was recognized to be the criterion of truth. Whoever opposed Husayn in any manner, even though the opposition consisted of restraining from mourning his martyrdom or visiting his grave, was considered to be false and was opposed.

Of course, it should not be forgotten that the Holy Imams who succeeded Imam Husayn encouraged the people to perform the pilgrimage to his grave. It is learnt from the narrations that the Holy Imams considered the pilgrimage of the grave of the Chief of the martyrs to be a vital matter for Islam. In the case of the pilgrimage of the grave of Imam Husayn, however, the Holy Imams have said that as the danger from and prevention by the enemy increases, the spiritual reward for the pilgrimage also increases. Now how can it be that the performance of the ceremony of Haj, in spite of all its importance, should not be permissible if there is danger for life, whereas pilgrimage to Karbala should be recommended emphatically although there was ninety per cent possibility of one's being killed.* Its only reason can be that in those days the Holy Imams considered the continuance of the ceremony of Haj and the pilgrimage of the House of Allah to be dependent upon the pilgrimage of the grave of Imam Husayn. Otherwise there can be no occasion for such narrations.

There is a well-known tradition of the Holy Prophet in which he has been reported to have said: "Husayn is from me and I am from Husayn". By this sentence the Holy Prophet did not mean to say only that Husayn was a part of his body, because every child is a part of the body of his father and grandfather and there is nothing particular about it. Supposing that we take this meaning of the first part of the sentence what will be meaning of its second part i.e. "I am from Husayn?" The correct meaning of the tradition, therefore, is that the Holy Prophet said: "Husayn has acquired his existence through me and is the means of the survival of my religion".

During most of the risings of the Alavis against Bani Umayya and Bani Abbas after the martyrdom of Imam Husayn their slogan was vengeance for the blood of Husayn and they usually took the oath of allegiance from one another by the side of his sacred grave. Hence the rulers were afraid of the grave of the Holy Imam as their very rulership was in a state of instability. Otherwise what reason could there be for their preventing the people from the pilgrimage to his grave? Bani Umayya remained at the helm of affairs after his martyrdom for seventy years, and their agents regularly obstructed the people from reaching there.

It may also be said that they were justified in doing so, because Husayn had been killed by the Umayyad administration and it was a matter of shame for them that the people should go to perform pilgrimage to his grave. But the question arises as to why Bani Abbas, who were not the culprits themselves, opposed the pilgrimage to his grave so much? In fact it was Bani Abbas, who were more harsh and who cut off the hands and heads of the people, who wanted to go to perform the pilgrimage of the sacred grave of Imam Husayn.

However, Bani Umayya did not destroy the grave of the

---

*Kāmiluz Ziyārāt by Ibn Quluyah, p. 261.

Imam for seventy years, but Bani Abbas demolished, watered and ploughed it. Why did they do all this? Evidently it was because they were afraid of even the martyred body of Imam Husayn, because they knew very well that the dust of the Martyrs of Āshura always tells the intelligent pilgrims expressly: O passerby! Tell our supporters that our bodies were cut to pieces because we opposed the oppressive government. It made us welter in our blood. We endeavoured to restrain the rulers of the time from their wicked deeds and they butchered us. Our bodies were torn to pieces and crushed under the hooves of the horses of the tyrants, because we supported Islam. However, we did not give up struggle and endeavoured to disgrace the spiteful enemy in the eyes of mankind. With our devotion and self-sacrifice for the protection of Islam we opened an institution for the maintenance of Islamic law for the inhabitants of the world.

Now O you, the future comers! Recognize the worth of your religion and do not sell it for petty gains, because the blood of millions like us has been shed to support and protect it. Honour the blood of the martyrs, believe in the worth of your religion, and do not be negligent in the matter of piety. The meaning of pilgrimage coupled with sincerity is that the pilgrim should know whose pilgrimage he is undertaking, what his real message is, what his position is, and why he has attained to this position?

Ali Akbar Ghifari

REGIME OF MU'AWIYA

The topic of this book is an account of the sacred rising of Imam Husayn, which is a glorious chapter in the history of Islam. We propose to state briefly the important events of this period of less than a year which is quite short from the viewpoint of duration but extremely effective and eternal so far as its role is concerned.

Distortions have taken place and continue to take place in every chapter of Islamic and non-Islamic history. They change the very shape of events and make the task of the future researches more difficult. Usually these distortions are made either by the extravagant supporters or by spiteful opponents. There is not a page of history which has escaped distortion. We find that treacherous hands have changed the real features of historical facts. It can, however, be said in connection with the event of the rising of Imam Husayn that the spiteful enemies have not been able to temper with this chapter of history and this movement has been so explicit, clear, sacred and unblemished that even the enemies of his father Imam Ali and his brother Imam Hasan have bowed their heads respectfully before him and admired his movement whole-heartedly. Of course the circumstances in which this movement was started and the condition of the Islamic government of that time have helped understand the need for this movement, and whoever has undertaken to write about it has admitted the greatness, bravery, frankness, courage, and love for freedom, of its leaders.

It is a matter of great regret, however, that many baseless matters, vulgar stories, and misleading falsehoods by ignorant supporters and extravagant friends have become a part of the writings and speeches about this movement. One of the greatest

41

services, which can be rendered to the Doyen of the martyrs, is to keep the event of Karbala free from every sort of falsehood, myth and baseless matter. However, this is a task, which the common and illiterate people cannot be expected to perform, because it is they, who have been instrumental in bringing about this calamity. They act against the sacred object of the leader of this revolution and think that it is possible to promote truth by means of falsehood, honesty by means of treachery and piety by means of impiety and carelessness.

To segregate the event of the movement of Imam Husayn from all sorts of unreliable, irrational and baseless matters and to content themselves with the writings of the writers of third and fourth centuries A.H. is the task of pious research scholars, and it is their duty to tell the truth with their tongues and pens and promote it, and refrain from telling false and baseless things in their writings and speeches. It is possible that one day this very sacred, clear, and explicit chapter of the history of Islam as befits the magnanimous and infallible leader may be based on truth and honesty in writing and speech. It is in this way only that the value of this great movement, and the greatness of its leader, will become evident all the more, and even in the mourning groups signs of his greatness, devotion, sincerity, jihad, steadfastness and manliness will be clearly apparent.

About fifty years after the death of the Holy Prophet, twenty years after the martyrdom of Imam Ali, and ten years after the martyrdom of Imam Hasan Mu'awiya bin Abi Sufyan breathed his last in the middle of the month of Rajab of the year 60 A.H. He was the governor and caliph in Damascus for about 42 years. He held the office of the governor of Syria for five years under the Second Caliph and for twelve years under the Third Caliph. He also ruled over Syria for a little less than five years during the Caliphate of Imam Ali and for about six months during the Caliphate of Imam Hasan and campaigned against both of them. He also held the Islamic Caliphate for a little less than twenty years, and towards the end of his life he obtained oath of allegiance from the people for his son Yazid for the office of Caliph.

Mu'awiya was the progenitor of the fourteen Umayyad caliphs, who were the descendants of Abu Sufyan and Marwan and held the Islamic Government in their hands for one thousand months from 41 A.H. to 132 A.H.

During the time of his caliphate Mu'awiya had complete control over the situation and could violate openly the agreement which he had concluded with Imam Hasan; for example, one of the conditions of the peace treaty was that the supporters of Imam Ali would not be persecuted and killed and all of them would enjoy security.

The name of Hujr bin Adi Kindi, who was one of the companions of the Holy Prophet and a supporter of Ali was specially mentioned in the Peace Pact. However, as the Islamic historians have written unanimously, Mu'awiya killed Hujr bin Adi and six of his companions, and one of them named Abdur Rahman bin Hannān Ghazzi was buried alive by Ziyad bin Abihi in Iraq. Mu'awiya's power and domination had assumed such proportions that he did what he liked and none could raise any objection.

Ali bin Husayn Mas'udi, one of the greatest Muslim historians and geographers of the 4th century writes thus in his book entitled Murujuz Zahab: At the time of return from the Battle of Siffin a Kufian, mounted on a camel, came to Damascus. One of the Syrians disputed with him and said: "This she-camel which you have mounted is mine. It was looted in the Battle of Siffin and has fallen in your hands". Their dispute got prolonged and both of them went to Mu'awiya. The man belonging to Damascus produced fifty witnesses, who deposed that the she-camel belonged to him. On the authority of the evidence given by fifty persons Mu'awiya also decided that the she-camel belonged to the Syrian and compelled the Iraqi to surrender it to him. The Iraqi said: "May Allah bless you. It is a he-camel and not a she-camel". Mu'awiya, however, said: "I have already given a decision and it cannot be altered". When the people dispersed Mu'awiya called the Iraqi and asked him as to what his he-camel was worth. Then he gave him something more than the price of the he-camel and said to him: "Tell Ali that to fight against him I have 100,000 men, who do not distinguish between a he-camel and a she-camel" (i.e. if I say that a he-camel is a she-camel or vice versa, they will not dispute).

After narrating this story Mas'udi writes that Mu'awiya

acquired such a grasp over the people that at the time of proceeding for the Battle of Siffin he called them to Friday prayers on Wednesday and offered Friday prayers with them, but none asked him as to why Friday prayers was being offered on that day when it was Wednesday.

Thereafter he has narrated another incident which we reproduce below in detail from the book entitled An-Nasāyah al-Kāfiya Li Mun Yatawalla Mu'awiya: Ammar Yasir was killed in the Battle of Siffin at the hands of Mu'awiya's men. As narrated by Bukhāri in his Sahih, as well as by others, Ammar was striving more than others at the time of the construction of the Masjid of Madina and when the Holy Prophet saw him he said: "Alas! Ammar! An oppressive group will kill him at a time when he will be calling them to Paradise and they will be calling him to Hell". Ammar's being killed made truth manifest, and it was established that the oppressive group was Mu'awiya and his supporters. In order to extricate himself from this difficulty he said: "We have not killed Ammar. He has been killed by him, who brought him in the battlefield" (i.e. by Ali). When Imam Ali was informed about the stand taken by Mu'awiya he said: "If that be so Hamza, the Doyen of the Martyrs was killed by the Holy Prophet, because he brought him along with him to fight against the polytheists".

However, as Mu'awiya was confident that his friends would accept whatever he said, he remarked: "It is true that we have killed Ammar, but the word Bāghiya used by the Holy Prophet does not mean unjust and oppressive. On the contrary it means one, who seeks or demands, and it is we, who have risen to seek vengeance for the murder of Uthman. Hence the meaning of the Holy Prophet's remark is that Ammar would be killed by those who rose to seek vengeance for the murder of Uthman and there is nothing wrong about it".

This argument of Mu'awiya was also absurd and the later part of the tradition provides a reply to it, because the Holy Prophet said: "Ammar will be killed by those, who will invite him to Hell, and whom he will invite to Paradise". However, Mu'awiya had become so powerful and dominant that none could convince his followers by argument. We do not intend to study the period of Mu'awiya's rule and the short account given above appears to be sufficient to invite the attention of the readers to the social and religious conditions of those days. In case, however, someone desires to become fully conversant with the period of Mu'awiya's rule he should refer to An-Nasâyah al-Kâfiya Li Mun Yatawalla Mu'awiya and then judge fairly.

REGIME OF YAZID

When Yazid attained to the caliphate, the Governors of Madina, Makkah, Kufa and Basra were Walid bin Utba bin Abu Sufyan, Amr bin Sa'id, Nu'amān bin Bashir and Ubaydullah ibn Ziyad respectively. In the first instance Yazid decided to obtain oath of allegiance from Husayn bin Ali, Abdullah bin Zubayr and Abdullah bin Umar, who had not acknowledged him heir-apparent during the time of Mu'awiya. He, therefore, wrote a letter to Walid bin Utba, the Governor of Madina, desiring him to obtain allegiance from these three persons as early as possible and not to accept any excuse from them. To accomplish this task Walid called Marwan bin Hakam for consultation, ignoring their previous strained relations. Marwan said: "Summon them immediately, and ask them to take the oath of allegiance to Yazid. If they agree to take the oath well and good otherwise execute them before they come to know about the death of Mu'awiya, because, if they learn about his death, everyone of them will become a claimant for caliphate and refuse to obey, excepting Abdullah bin Umar, who need not be feared, because he is not the type of man, who may rise or oppose".

Walid sent Abdullah bin Amr bin Uthman to Imam Husayn and Abdullah bin Zubayr. He found both of them in the mosque and conveyed to them the message of Walid. They said to him: "You may go back and we too shall meet Walid soon" Then the Imam said to Abdullah: "I think Mu'awiya is dead and the object of this untimely call is that we should take the oath of allegiance to Yazid".

Imam Husayn summoned a group of his men and told them to arm themselves. He said to them: "Walid has called me just now, and I think that he will propose something which I may not accept. In that event I cannot trust him. You should, therefore, come with me and when I enter his house you should stay at the door and as soon as you hear me speaking aloud

45

enter the house to prevent him from doing me any harm".

The Imam went to meet Walid and saw that Marwan was also there. Walid informed him about the death of Mu'awiya and also conveyed to him the orders of Yazid. The Imam said: "You will not certainly be contented with my taking the oath secretly and would like that I should take it in the presence of the people". Walid said: "Yes". Thereupon the Imam said: "Then you should wait till tomorrow so that I may arrive at a decision in the matter". Walid said: "All right. You may go now and come tomorrow along with the people to take the oath of allegiance". Marwan said: "I swear by Allah that if Husayn bin Ali leaves this place without taking the oath of allegiance it will no longer be possible for you to lay hands on him without bloodshed. You should, therefore, detain him till he takes the oath and in the event of his refusing to do so, you should chop off his head. On hearing the words of Marwan the Imam got up from his place and said: "O bastard! Is it you, who will kill me or Walid? By Allah you have told a lie and become a sinner". Then he departed and reached his house along with his men.

Marwan said to Walid: "Now that you have not accepted my advice I swear by Allah that you will not be able to lay your hands on him again". Walid said: "Marwan! What are you saying? You have suggested to me something which must spoil my faith. By Allah, even if the entire wealth of the world is placed at my disposal I will never kill Husayn bin Ali. Should I kill him if he declines to take the oath of allegiance to Yazid? By Allah I believe that whoever sheds the blood of Husayn, the grandson of the Holy Prophet, shall be very unlucky and helpless before Allah on the Day of Judgement". Marwan who did not like Walid's words said to him: "It is all right if you think so".

On the following day which was saturday the 28th of Rajab 60 A.H. Walid sent for the Imam again so that he might take the oath of allegiance from him. The Imam, however, told his messenger to tell him to wait for that night, so that he might take a decision by the following day. During the same night he left Madina along with his wives, brothers and nephews and most of the members of his family, and proceeded on his journey to Makkah, remembermg the words of Prophet Musa, son of Imran: *So he left the city afraid and cautious saying:*

Lord! Protect me against the unjust people. (Surah al-Qasas, 28:21)

When it was said to Imam Husayn that it would have been better if he had adopted a deviated path so that the enemies might not have been able to lay hands on him he replied: "By Allah I shall not go by a deviated path. Let that which Allah wills happen". Eventually he arrived in Makkah on Friday night after the 3rd of Shāban. Remembering the story of Prophet Musa, he said: *When he started his journey to Midian he said, "Perhaps my Lord will show me the right path".* (Surah al-Naml, 28:22)

The pilgrims used to visit the Imam in Makkah. Even Abdullah bin Zubayr, who knew very well that none would take the oath of allegiance to anybody in the presence of the son of the Holy Prophet and the Imam enjoyed a position higher than everyone in all respects, came to see the Imam every day.

The news of the death of Mu'awiya spread throughout Iraq and the people also came to know that Imam Husayn and Abdullah bin Zubayr had declined to take the oath of allegiance to Yazid and had gone to Makkah.

The distinguished supporters of Imam Ali gathered in the house of Sulayman bin Surd Khuzāi and thanked Allah for the death of Mu'awiya. Sulayman bin Surd then said addressing those present: "Mu'awiya has departed from the world and Husayn bin Ali has declined to take the oath of allegiance to Yazid and has gone to Makkah. You are the supporters of Husayn as well as of his father Ali. If you think that you are ready to assist him and to fight against his enemy and can lay down your lives for his sake, you should inform him of your readiness through a letter. In case, however, you are scared that you will show slackness and will abstain from rendering him assistance, you should not deceive him by claiming unduly to be his supporters and devotees".

When Sulayman bin Surd said these words he had in mind the fact that so long as there is no question of making sacrifices the people can distinguish very well between truth and falsehood and make no mistake about it. They understand clearly as to who is truthful and who is a liar; where lies the truth, and where lay the falsehood; who is wise and who is ignorant and who is a guide and who is a bandit. However, they can make such a correct assessment only so long as the question of profit and loss does not arise and they do not suffer any loss by supporting the truth and fighting against falsehood. But when the preliminaries for test become available and truth and falsehood stand facing each other most of the people side with falsehood, and as truth cannot be supported without sacrifice the views of the people alter and they abandon truth and support falsehood.

Sulayman bin Surd knew well that the sentiments of the people at that time could not be relied upon, because it might so happen that if Husayn bin Ali rose against Bani Umayya later and they employed their full strength to kill him and rendering him help became something dangerous, the same people might turn away their faces from him, ignore the letters written by them, close their doors in his face and even join his enemies. They might consider it a religious duty to kill him and might put him and his friends to sword to gain the pleasure of Allah and His Prophet. And after killing those godly persons they might stand and cry: "Allah is the Greatest. I testify that there is no God but Allah and I testify that Muhammad is His Prophet"; as if they had committed no sin at all! It was for this reason that he explained the position to the distinguished supporters and said: "Even now you should judge the result in your minds and visualize the situation which is bound to arise and then decide whether you can make him hopeful of your assistance and invite him to Iraq with perfect confidence and final determination. It should not be that today, when your sentiments are roused, you should be writing letters, making covenants and taking oaths and pull the son of the Prophet of Allah from Allah's sanctuary to Iraq, but tomorrow when the enemy surrounds him and compels him either to take the oath of allegiance or lose his head you should desert him and forget the promises made by you". The distinguished supporters replied with one voice: "We are prepared to perform jihad and make sacrifices and shall lay down our lives for the sake of our Imam". Thereupon Sulayman said: "In that case you should write a letter to the Imam". They, therefore, wrote a letter as follows:

In the name of Allah, the Beneficent, the Merciful.

This letter is being written by Sulayman bin Surd, Musayyab bin Najbah, Rafā bin Shaddad Bajali, Habib bin Mazahir and other Muslim and faithful supporters of Husayn bin Ali residing in Kufa. They write to Husayn bin Ali: Peace be upon you. We join you in praising the Almighty Allah except whom there is no god. Praised be Allah Who has destroyed your oppressive and spiteful enemy, the man who prevailed over this nation, assumed unlawfully the reins of government, usurped the public treasury and became the ruler of the Muslims without their consent. He then killed the pious persons and spared the bad ones and placed the property of Allah at the disposal of the oppressors and the rich. May Allah deprive him of His blessings as He deprived the people of Thamud. At present we, the Iraqis, do not have any leader and Imam. Hence, we request you to proceed to us. Maybe the Almighty Allah may draw us together on truth through you. We have nothing to do with Nuaman bin Bashir in the matter of Friday and Eid prayers. He is alone in the governor's House. If we come to know that you have left to join us we shall turn him out and shall, God willing, pursue him up to Syria".

They sent this letter through Abdullah bin Suba Hamdāni and Abdullah bin Wāl and instructed them to leave for Makkah immediately. They reached the Imam in Makkah on the 10th of Ramazan, 60 A.H. and delivered the letter to him.

LETTERS OF THE KUFIANS TO THE IMAM

After two days the people of Kufa sent about 150 letters, each of which was from one, two or four men. Most of these letters were brought from Kufa to Makkah by Qays bin Mashar Saidāwi, Abdur Rahman bin Abdullah bin Shaddād Arhabi and Ammāra bin Abdullah Saluli. Two more days passed and then the supporters of Kufa sent a letter to the Imam through Hāni bin Hāni Sabi'i and Sa'id bin Abdullah Hanafi. The following are the contents of the letter:

In the name of Allah, the Beneficent, the Merciful.

This is a letter to Husayn bin Ali from his Muslim and faithful supporters. Be quick and hurry up, for the people are waiting for you, and they do not look towards anyone other than you. Hurry up. Hurry up. We repeat: Make haste. Make haste. And peace be upon you."

Thereafter Shabath bin Rabie, Hajjār bin Abjar, Yazid bin Hārith bin Ruwaym, Urwah bin Qays, Amr bin Hajjāj Zubaydi and Muhammad bin Amr Taymi wrote the following letter:

"The gardens and the deserts are green and fresh and the fruits have ripened. Proceed whenever you like. Your Iraqi soldiers are ready to receive you. And peace by upon you".

Letters from the Kufians piled up with the Imam and the messengers from Iraq gathered in Makkah. The Imam sent the following reply to the Kufians:

"In the name of Allah, the Beneficent, the Merciful.

From Husayn bin Ali to the believers and Muslims of Iraq. Hāni and Sa'id, your last messengers, have brought your letters. I have read what you have written and pondered over it. You have written that you do not have an Imam and asked me to come to you so that Allah may perhaps draw you together on truth and guidance through me. Now I am sending to you my cousin Muslim bin Aqil in whom I have full confidence. If he writes to me that your elders and wise men confirm what your messengers say and what you have written in your letters I may proceed towards you soon. I swear by my life that a true Imam and leader is only he who takes decisions according to the Qur'an, establishes justice, promotes the Divine religion and dedicates himself to the path of Allah. And peace be upon you".

The Imam sent this letter through Hāni and Sa'id. Then he ordered Muslim bin Aqil to proceed to Iraq along with Qays bin Mash'ar Saidāwi, Ammāra bin Abdullah Saluli and Abdul Rahmān bin Abdullah Araji. He instructed him to tread the path of piety, to keep his mission secret, to be lenient and moderate, and to inform the Imam immediately if he found that the people supported the rising and revolution.

MUSLIM BIN AQIL PROCEEDS TO KUFA

Muslim went to Kufa via Madina and stayed in the house of Mukhtār bin Abi Ubayda Thaqafi. The supporters perhaps thought that the task would be accomplished quite easily. Husayn bin Ali would gain victory over Yazid without facing any trouble. Justice and piety would replace injustice and sin, and the people would easily forget what Mu'awiya had taught them for forty two years. They used to visit Muslim frequently and when the Imam's letter was read for them, they shed tears of delight with perfect sincerity, and took the oath of allegiance at the hand of the special representative of the Imam. According to Shaykh Mufid seventeen thousand persons took the oath of allegiance to Muslim bin Aqil, but the number mentioned by Tabari is twelve thousand.

Now Yazid came to know that Muslim had arrived in Kufa and the supporters of Imam Ali had taken the oath of allegiance to him, and Nua'man bin Bashir had shown weakness in taking action against him. He, therefore, appointed Ubaydullah bin Ziyad, the Governor of Basra as the Governor of Kufa as well, and also entrusted him with the task of carrying out his oppressive orders. He wrote to him: "You should go to Kufa, pursue Muslim and captivate, kill, or banish him." Ubaydullah proceeded to Kufa immediately and on the very first day of his arrival in the city he addressed the people and spoke about the kindness as well as harshness of Yazid. He summoned the chiefs of the tribes and various classes of the society and behaved very harshly towards them. Now the people of Kufa reached the stage at which the number of the supporters of truth diminishes, and that of the followers of falsehood increases. The Almighty Allah says: *Do people think that they will not be tested because they say, "We have faith?" We tested those who were before them. Thus Allah knows those, who are truthful, and knows those, who are liars.* (Surah al-Ankabut, 29:2 — 3)

The truthful are those persons who stick firmly, even at the time of test and trial, to what they have said and assessed. Fear and desire do not dissuade them from the truth, which they have recognized. Nothing can place them amongst the supporters of falsehood. As regards the liars they are those, who really speak the truth and correctly distinguish between truth and falsehood before they are involved in the difficulties of Divine test, and think themselves to be the supporters of truth and enemies of falsehood, and say that they would defend truth even if they have to lay down their lives for it. The promises of falsehood and the allurements of the world would not make them deviate from the right path, but as soon as the circumstances change and the time for making sacrifices for truth arrives their mental attitude changes. Fear and poor spirit take the place of courage; doubt and hesitation that of faith; and polytheism and treachery that of sincerity. The liars are not only those, who have no intention of siding with truth and opposing falsehood even before the time for test arrives, but liars are also those, whose condition changes at the time of Divine test, and what they consider falsehood today was considered truth by them till yesterday.

The people of Kufa i.e. those who, after receiving the news of the death of Mu'awiya, gathered in the house of Sulayman bin Surd Khuzāi, delivered speeches, took into consideration the position of the Muslims at that time and wrote a letter to the Imam from that very place and similarly those who visited Muslim after his arrival in Kufa and took oath of allegiance to him in his capacity of the special representative of the Imam of the time, did not in fact intend to tell lies and deceive their Imam and to provide means for his martyrdom and the captivity of the members of his family. Truly speaking their intentions were quite good. They deemed the caliphate of a person like Yazid, and that too after fifty years of the death of the Holy Prophet, to be shameful and inadmissible for the world of Islam, and did not consider anyone amongst all the Muslims to be more competent and more deserving than Husayn bin Ali the son of the Holy Prophet. They thought that they had always rendered him assistance and would continue to do so in all circumstances and would bear all hardships to achieve their Divine object. They turned out to be liars and forgot what they had been thinking about themselves earlier. So long as Nu'aman bin Basir Ansari had been running the administration of the city moderately and leniently the supporters were very enthusiastic. They claimed at every place and in every meeting to be the supporters of Husayn bin Ali and wrote that they would pursue Nuaman bin Bashir up to the gates of Damascus. However, as they had previous experience of the harshness of Ubaydullah bin Bashir Ansari had been running the administration of the changed as soon as Ubaydullah assumed the Governorship of Kufa. Previously they talked about Jihad (the Holy war), but now they began to recite the Qur'anic verse: *Do not subject your lives to destruction with your own hands.* (Surah al-Baqarah, 2:195)

The greater was the hold of Ibn Ziyad over the affairs of Kufa, the greater was the danger for Muslim and his companions and now there was no possibility of their success. The mental and religious disposition of the people proceeded towards a direction contrary to that which they had assessed earlier, so much so that the entire atmosphere of the city was completely changed. The attitude of the people, who really wished that Imam Husayn should come at the helm of affairs and Bani Umayya should be deprived of the Islamic Government, underwent such a change that although Muslim bin Aqil was keeping himself aloof and seldom met the people, he was obliged to shift from the house of Mukhtar bin Abi Ubayda Thaqafi to that of a well-known and powerful person named Hāni bin Urwa Murādi. His supporters used to visit him there secretly.

The conditions in Kufa at that time indicated that all the letters which had been sent to Imam Husayn and the promises made with him were mere lies and could no longer be relied upon. Ibn Ziyad succeeded in locating the place where Muslim was then residing. He gave three thousand dirhams to his slave named Ma'qal and said to him: "Associate with the friends and supporters of Muslim for a few days and pretend to be one of them. Give them this money also and say that you are interested in their success and the money is meant for being spent on the procurement of implements of war. After gaining their confidence you may find out the place where Muslim is residing and meet him". Ma'qal acted as ordered by Ibn Ziyad. In the first instance he contacted, in the Masjid of Kufa, Muslim bin Awsaja (who was one of the distinguished supporters of the Imam and was martyred on the day of Āshura) because he had heard that Muslim bin Awsaja was obtaining the allegiance from the people on behalf of Imam Husayn. Ma'qal, who was prepared to tell any lie, and commit any treachery to achieve his end, said to Muslim bin Awsaja: "I am a man from Syria and Allah has blessed me with love for the Holy Prophet's family and their supporters". Saying this he also shed some crocodile tears and then said: "I have got three thousand dirhams. I wish to present this money to the man who, I understand, has come from the Hijaz to Kufa to take the oath of allegiance for the son of the Holy Prophet. However, I have to say with much regret that it has not been possible for me to see him and have not yet met anyone, who may guide me to him, and thus enable me to achieve this blessing. I have enquired from various persons and have since come to know that you are acquainted with this Holy household. I have, therefore, to request you to take this petty amount from me and take me to Muslim bin Aqil. I am your Muslim brother and you should trust me. If you so wish I am prepared to take the oath of allegiance to the Imam before I go and see Muslim".

Muslim bin Awsaja said: "I am glad to meet you, for you may possibly render some assistance to Ahlul Bayt. However, I am worried on account of the fact that the people have come to know before the accomplishment of the task and achievement of the goal that I am associated with this movement. I am apprehensive of the tyrannical Ibn Ziyad in this regard". Ma'qal said: "God willing, all will be well. You may please take the allegiance from me". Muslim took the oath from him and obtained a promise that he would remain loyal and would not divulge the secret. Ma'qal made all the promises and took all the oaths demanded by Muslim bin Awsaja without any hesitation. He even added something to it and satisfied him.

Then he visited the house of Muslim bin Awsaja for a few days and eventually had access to Muslim bin Aqil and took the oath of allegiance once again. As directed by Muslim bin Aqil he also presented three thousand dirhams to Abu Thamama Sāidi Hamdāni, a staunch supporter and one of the martyrs of Karbala, who was then responsible for the procurement of arms, food and other provisions.

Ma'qal used to come to see Muslim bin Aqil earlier than all others and was the last to leave. He thus acquired information about all their activities and submitted reports to Ibn Ziyad regularly. Ibn Ziyad thought that he should first arrest Hāni and then take steps to arrest Muslim. Consequently Hāni also confined himself to his house on the pretext of illness and did not go to the Governor's House till Muhammad bin Ash'ath, Asmā bin Khārija and Amr bin Hajjāj Zubaydi approached him in compliance with the orders of Ibn Ziyad. As a measure of expediency they made him mount an animal, and took him to Ibn Ziyad.

With the arrest of Hâni the situation in Kufa became absolutely favourable for Ibn Ziyad. Although Hani expressed ignorance about the presence of Muslim bin Aqil in his house the secret was divulged by the arrival of Ma'qal there. Hâni was, therefore, obliged to confess before Ibn Ziyad and said: "I did not take Muslim to my house. He himself came and asked me to admit him. I felt ashamed to refuse his request and, therefore entertained him. As regards his activities whatever has been reported is correct. Now I can promise you that no harm will come to you from me and I will have nothing to do with him. As an alternative I can go and apologize to him, and ask him to go wherever he likes". Ibn Ziyad did not, however, accept either of the two offers made by him and said: "By Allah you must surrender him to me". Hâni replied: "By Allah I will not surrender him to you". When he declined to surrender his guest Ibn Ziyad broke his face, nose and head with a stick, which he had in his hand, and put him under arrest. Then he went to the Masjid, mounted the pulpit and severely threatened the people in a brief speech. He had not yet come down from the pulpit when the spectators rushed into the Masjid and said that Muslim bin Aqil was coming. Ubaydullah then entered his palace hurriedly and shut the gates.

It is very surprising that twelve or seventeen thousand persons had taken the oath of allegiance to Muslim, but, when he came to know about what had happened to Hâni and called his supporters to rise, not more than four thousand persons turned up. And still more surprising is that at the time when Muslim came out with four thousand armed men and Ibn Ziyad closed the doors of his palace, not more than fifty persons were with him, and out of them thirty were policemen and the remaining twenty were some dignitaries and the members of his family. The people had encircled his palace and were abusing him and his father. This apparently favourable state of affairs became so unfavourable in the early part of night that Muslim bin Aqil offered evening prayers in the night of 9th Zil-Haj in the Masjid of Kufa with only thirty persons and when he left the Masjid only ten persons were with him, and when he came out of the Masjid there was not even one person, who might accompany him.

Allah knows those who are truthful, and knows those who are liars. (Surah al-Ankabut, 29:3)

It is a sufficient proof of the falsity of the claims, correspondence and pretences of the Kufians that four thousand armed men could not subdue Ibn Ziyad, who had not more than fifty persons with him, and gain control over the city, and only one false rumour spread by the supporters of Ibn Ziyad that the Syrian army was arriving, scattered all of them.

MARTYRDOM OF MUSLIM BIN AQIL

The situation in Kufa became so dangerous that even good and distinguished supporters like Sulayman bin Surd, Musayyab bin Najba and Rafā bin Shaddād were not seen anywhere and the person, who was the chief of twelve thousand men a day earlier, was wandering in the streets of Kufa in a state of distress and perplexity and could not find his way. Tabari's account of this event which is almost identical with that quoted by Shaykh Mufid in "al-Irshād" is as follows: "Muslim bin Aqil came out of the gate of the Masjid and suddenly found himself alone. There could be seen not even one person, who might show him the way or guide him to a place or defend him if he faced an enemy. He, therefore, wandered in the streets of Kufa without knowing where to go".

There is a point which it will not be inappropriate to mention here. It has been for centuries now that the people have reproached the Kufians for their perfidies and breach of promise. Just as they have praised and greeted the faithful companions and friends of the Imam, they have cursed these persons who promised support to him on one day but drew their swords against him on the other day and continued their opposition till he was martyred. To be fair, however, it may be said that the people of Kufa did not do anything which might be unusual or surprising and on both the occasions they acted according to rule i.e. when they wrote the letters to the Imam and also when they drew their swords against him. So long as they were leading peaceful lives and the swords had not been unsheathed and a lenient man namely Nu'amān bin Bashir was the ruler of Kufa they could distinguish between truth and falsehood by means of the light which Almighty Allah has bestowed upon man to enable him to differentiate between right and wrong, and between truth and falsehood, and correctly assessed as to who was fit for the Imamate and leadership of the people. They did not consider any other Muslim of that time to be equal to him. This correct discernment of truth and falsehood by them was as usual and according to rule, because so long as a person has not deviated from the path of nature and sound mind by means of factors of deviation, and fear, hope, avarice, profit or loss have not confused and misled him, he knows which is the right path and which is the wrong one and makes no mistake in distinguishing between them.

Allah says: *Have We not given him two eyes, a tongue and two lips. Have We not shown him the ways of good and evil?* (Surah al-Balad, 90:8 — 10)

However, when these very persons, who could distinguish between truth and falsehood were put to test, the question of fear and avarice and profit and loss arose; hence the paths of religion and expediency got separated from each other. They acted as most of the people usually do i.e. they kept aloof from truth and the truthful, and began to talk about prudence, wisdom, precaution and foresight instead of jihad, sacrifice, resistance, reform and valour. Truly speaking it is not strange that the Kufians did not sacrifice their lives to carry out their responsibility. Those who wonder at their conduct should in the first instance imagine themselves to be placed in the same situation and then decide fairly whether in these conditions and circumstances, would they have acted in a different way?

In fact one should wonder at those persons, who remained steadfast in all circumstances, and in spite of all hardships, supported truth and laid down their lives for it. So much so that even when their bodies were torn to pieces and they fell down on the ground, they were worried whether they had performed their duty of self-sacrifice and combating against injustice and oppression properly, and consequently would feel ashamed before Allah and His Prophet on the Day of Judgement!

Qarza bin Ka'b Khazraji was one of the companions of the Holy Prophet. He participated in the Battle of Uhud and later battles. During the Caliphate of Umar he came to Kufa and imparted instruction in jurisprudence to the people. His son

Amr bin Qarzi Ansari was one of the devoted companions of Imam Husayn. As stated by Ibn Tawus in Luhuf so long as Amr did not collapse on the day of Āshura owing to excessive wounds, the Holy Imam did not sustain any injury. Amr received the arrows on his hands and the blows of the swords on his body, and when eventually he fell on the ground and rolled in dust he looked at the Holy Imam's face and said: "O son of the Prophet of Allah! Have I acquitted myself of my duty? Then Imam said in reply: "Yes, you have, and you will enter Paradise earlier than me. Convey my greetings to the Holy Prophet and tell him that his Husayn is also arriving soon".

The steadfastness and constancy of these noble souls is really astonishing. One must wonder at their resolution and firmness and praise and greet them, because the different aspects of life and severe pain did not change their attitude and did not make them deviate from their Divine course. Many persons who have read or heard Zahhāk bin Abdullah Mashriqi Hamdāni have regretted his weakness, bad luck, and lack of foresight and wondered that while his Imam was surrounded by the enemies this man took leave of the Imam and went away. However, very few have judged fairly and realized that in the particular circumstances it might not have been possible to show even that firmness and steadfastness which was shown by him. One should wonder at his staying with the Imam and participating in the battle rather than upon his eventual departure.

Tabari quotes the story from Zahhāk himself in these words: "Mālik bin Nazr Arji and I went to see Imam Husyan and sat down before him after paying due respect to him. He welcomed us and said: "For what purpose have you come to see me?" We said: "We have come to greet you and to seek your blessings, so that we may renew our pledge, and also inform you that the people of Kufa are ready to fight against you. The Imam said: "Allah is sufficient for me and He is the best Helper".

When we bade farewell to him Imam Husayn said: "Is there anything against your rendering me assistance? My companion Mālik bin Nazr said: "I am indebted and have also to support my wife and children". I said: "I, too, am faced with the same problems. Notwithstanding this, however, if you give me an option that I may go away in case you become alone and my support is no longer of any use to you, I am prepared to stay on and assist you till that time". The Imam accepted my services on this condition and I stayed on with him. When on the day of Āshura all his supporters were martyred and the enemy reached up to the Imam and the men belonging to his family, and none remained with him except two persons namely Sawayd bin Amr bin Abi Muta Khasami and Bashir bin Amr Hazrami I said to him: "O son of the Prophet of Allah! As you are aware, we had agreed that so long as you have supporters I I shall also remain with you and assist you and when they are killed I shall be free to go away. The Imam said: "You are right, but how can you escape this army? If you can find a way out I have no objection to your going away".

Zahhāk adds: "When the soldiers of Amr bin Sā'd were pursuing our horses I had tied my horse in one of the tents and was fighting on foot, so that I succeeded in killing two enemies of the Imam and amputated the hand of another. On that day the Imam praised my performance repeatedly and said: "When he permitted me to leave I brought out my horse, mounted it, and struck it till it stood up on its hind hooves. Then I let it go. The enemies were, therefore, forced to let me pass and I came out of their rows. Eleven persons pursued me and were about to capture me, but Kathir bin Abdullah Shābi, Ayyub bin Musrah Khaivāni and Qays bin Abdullah Sāidi identified me and I was saved on account of their intercession".

It is true that one must feel sorry for this man, because he missed such a blessing, left such an Imam alone, and lost such an opportunity in vain, although he could also become one like Habib ibn Mazahir Asadi and Burayr bin Khuzayr Hamdāni. However, his case is quite different from that of the people of Kufa. This man had not written any letter to the Imam and had not promised any sacrifice. He had also not taken an oath of allegiance to Muslim bin Aqil. And when he reached the Imam he did what he had undertaken to do, and did not boast that he would go to any length in making sacrifices. On the other hand he himself stated to what extent he was prepared to go. However, the people, who took the oath of allegiance to Muslim bin Aqil left him alone during the night of 9th of Zilhaj in the streets of Kufa, and if a woman had not admitted him into her house and quenched his thirst, there was no one who might have rendered him even that much service. Muslim spent the last night of his life in that woman's house and when on the following day Ibn Ziyad took steps to arrest him and his men besieged the house, he was obliged to come out of the house to meet martyrdom.

When Muslim was taken prisoner he made a request to Muhammad bin Asha'th that he might send someone to inform Imam Husayn about his (Muslim's) martyrdom and also to convey the following message to him: "May my parents be your ransom! Return from this journey along with the members of your family lest the Kufians should deceive you. They are the companions of your father, who wished to get rid of them by means of death or martyrdom. The people of Kufa lied to you as well as to me, and nothing can be achieved by means of falsehood". In the court of Ibn Ziyad also he made two requests to Umar bin Sā'd; firstly that he should sell his coat of mail and sword and repay his debt amounting to seven hundred dirhams; secondly that he should obtain his dead body from Ibn Ziyad and bury it".

Muslim and Hani were martyred on the same day and their heads were cut off and sent to Yazid in Damascus.

MUHAMMAD BIN HANAFIYA

When Imam Husayn left Madina for Makkah along with the members of his family, his brother Muhammad bin Hanafiya remained in Madina. The mother of Muhammad, the son of Ali, belonged to a tribe named Bani Hanafiya and on this account he was called Muhammad bin Hanafiya. He was a magnanimous, brave and pious person. Although Kaisāniya sect considered him to be an Imam he himself believed in the imamate of his brother Imam Hasan after his father Imam Ali, and thereafter in the imamate of his second brother Imam Husayn and then in the imamate of his nephew Ali bin Husayn. He was a distinguished person among the Ahlul Bayt and showed great valour in the battles fought by Imam Ali the Commander of the Faithful.*

---

*It is said that the Roman Emperor sent two herculean athletes to Muawiya to measure their strength with the Muslim athletes. One of them was tall and corpulent and the other was powerful with a strong grip. Muawiya said

Continued...

When Imam Husayn left Madina for Makkah he wrote a testament for his brother Muhammad bin Hanafiya. It has been narrated by Ibn Tawus. In this testament the Imam mentioned the motive for his rising and clarified the policy which he intended to pursue in all circumstances. He also referred to the false motives which instigate a man and make him fight to satisfy his carnal desires and stated that the godly persons are free from such motives. The testament reads as follows:

to Amr bin As: "We have got a match for the tall man in the person of Qays bin Sād bin Ubada, but as regards the other man you should think over it as to who can measure his strength with him and defeat him". Amr said: "I have two persons in view but you are inimical towards both of them. One of them is Muhammad bin Hanafiya and the other is Abdullah bin Zubayr". Muawiya said: "You should summon him who is nearer to us at present. Amr asked Muhammad bin Hanafiya to meet the challenge. Muawiya took his place in the general assembly and the dignitaries of the State also attended.

The powerful person was the first to enter the field and came face to face with Muhammad. Muhammad said to him: "Either you should sit down and let me hold your hand so that I may pull you off from your seat, or I may sit down and you may lift me from my place. Now let me know whether you are going to sit down or I should do so?" The Roman said: "You may sit down. Muhammad sat down and let the Roman hold his hand. In spite of his best efforts, however, the Roman could not move Muhammad from his place, and acknowledged his weakness. Then Muhammad stood up and the Roman sat down and let Muhammad hold his hand. Muhammad immediately lifted him from his place with one jerk, held him in the air, and then threw him on the ground. Those present applauded him for his strength and Muawiya too was very happy.

Now the second Roman champion who was tall statured entered the field to compete. Qays bin Sād who was present went in a corner, took off his underwear and gave it to the Roman to wear. When the Roman put it on it reached his breast and also trailed along behind his feet. Thereupon, he felt ashamed and sat down.

The elder amongst the Ansar were very much annoyed on Qays having taken off his underwear in such a formal meeting and rebuked him. He, however, composed some verses in which he apologized for his conduct.

In the name of Allah, the Beneficent, the Merciful.

"This is the testament of Husayn bin Ali bin Abi Talib written by him for his brother Muhammad, known as Ibn Hanafiya. Indeed Husayn testifies that there is no god except Allah and no being other than Him is fit to be worshipped and He has no partner. He also testifies that Muhammad is Allah's servant and messenger, who has brought truth from Him, and that Paradise and Hell do exist and the Day of Judgement is bound to come and there is no doubt about it, and on that day Allah will bring the dead to life".

What the Imam said consists of the very doctrines which it is necessary for every Muslim to hold, and one who does not hold them cannot be a Muslim. Apparently the Imam meant to say that these very principles were in danger and, if the matters were allowed to continue in that manner, it was possible that the regime of the time might not refrain even from attacking these Principles of Faith. In fact the real motive for the Imam's rising was the protection of these very principles on which other religious and social tenets of Islam are based.

The Imam continued: "This movement of mine is not on account of stubbornness, rebellion, worldly passions or instigation by Satan. It is also not my object to create trouble or to oppress anyone. The only thing which invites me to this great movement is that I should reform the affairs of the followers of my grandfather, eradicate corruption, undertake enjoining to do good and restraining from evil and follow the tradition of my grandfather, the Prophet of Allah and my father, Ali".

This testament does not mention the formalities which usually form part of the last will made now a days. On the other hand the Imam wished to clarify his motive. He wanted to tell the people that his movement was not an ordinary one based on human passions and worldly desires. He, therefore, says: "I am not going out for merry-making and amusement or to create mischief. I am also not persuing the path of oppression". He adds: "I have come out to reform the followers of my grandfather". These words show that in the year 60 A.H. the Muslim ummah was faced with a dreadful social and religious crisis, which could not be overcome with a severe and bloody revolution. It was a danger which could be faced only by a leader like Husayn bin Ali, whose infallibility has been testified by the Holy Qur'an in the verse of Purification of Surah al-Ahzab (33:33). It was a peril which could not be dealt with by means of speeches and religious sermons.

He added: "If the people respond to my call, and accept truth from me, well and good; and if they do not accept it, I shall observe patience and am not afraid of unpleasant events, hardships, and sufferings". By saying that he would observe patience, the Imam did not mean to say that he would sit with folded hands so that Yazid might do whatever he liked. On the contrary he used this word in its correct sense, which is suited to the position of an Imam, and is the basis of faith and godliness. In other words he said: "Even if I am alone I shall pursue this path till Allah decides justly between me and these people, and He is the most Wise and the most Powerful of the judges".

Thereafter he wrote: "O my brother! This is my testament for you. I do not seek assistance from anyone except Allah. I depend on Him alone and have to return to him".

CAUSES OF THE RISE OF IMAM HUSAYN

Truly speaking if we wish to find out the causes of the rising of the Imam we shall have to make a search for its preliminaries during a period of at least thirty years preceding that time, because about thirty years after the migration of the Holy Prophet, there had taken place such developments as had made necessary a movement like this in the Islamic society.

Uthman bin Affan Umavi ruled over the Muslims for about twelve years as the Caliph of Islam. It is clearly recorded in the history of Islam that the shape of the Islamic Government underwent a change during the six years covering the second half of the Caliphate of Uthman. In fact the Islamic rule should strictly enforce law otherwise the people should be free in all matters and no limits should be laid down for them except those prescribed by law. This Islamic method underwent a change and it assumed another posture which made the Muslim free in all matters, except that it was necessary for them to have regard for the interests of the ruler.

Taking advantage of this state of afairs the people began to amass wealth and property from the *Baytul Māl* (public treasury) of the Muslims. It was the same *Baytul Māl* which was guarded so carefully by Imam Ali during the period of his caliphate. The same policy was adopted by the caliphs preceding Uthman and even Uthman exercised necessary care in spending from it during the earlier part of his caliphate. However, later this wealth, instead of being spent on the general welfare of the Muslims, fell into the hands of a few persons. These were the malpractices, started thirty years earlier, which Imam Husayn decided to restrain in 60 A.H. by means of a sweeping and bloody revolution, which resulted in his own martyrdom and his everlasting honour.

Mas'udi writes in Murujuz Zahab that at the time of his death the Third Caliph left behind in cash 150,000 gold dinars and one million dirhams. However, according to the same Mas'udi, when Imam Ali was martyred Imam Hasan mounted the pulpit and announced: "My father has not left behind any gold or silver except 700 dirhams. This money, too, had been saved by him from his salary to procure a servant for his house".

Thereafter Mas'udi writes: "The value of the property owned by the Third Caliph in Wādiul Qura and at other places reached 100,000 gold dinars. Besides it he also left behind a large number of horses and camels".

About Zubayr he writes: "Besides the well-known palace at Basra he built a large number of houses in Basra, Kufa and Alexandria and at the time of his death he owned 50,000 gold dinars, one thousand horses, one thousand slaves and slave-girls and numerous estates in different cities.

Talha bin Ubaydullah was a well-known companion of the Holy Prophet. His daily income from the property owned by him in Iraq alone reached 1000 gold dinars and according to another version it exceeded this amount. In Syria he owned even larger property.

Abdur Rahman bin Awf Zuhari was one of the distinguished companions. He had 100 horses, 1000 camels and 10,000 sheep. At the time of his death he had four wives and as he had children also his wives inherited, according to the Islamic law of inheritance, 1/8 of the property left by him. This was decided between the four wives and every wife got 1/32 of the property. This 1/32 amounted to 84,000 gold dinars.

When Zayd bin Thābit died he left behind such a large amount of gold and silver that it was broken with a hatchet and distributed among the heirs and the value of his other property was 100,000 gold dinars.

Yāla bin Umayya, whose mother's name was Munayya, is also called Yāla bin Munayya. The Battle of the Camel was started against Ali with his financial assistance and most of its expenses were borne by him. At the time of his death he left behind 500,000 gold dinars and the people also owed him large sums of money. Besides this the value of property etc. left by him was 300,000 dinars".

Thereafter Mas'udi himself writes: "During the Caliphate of Umar there was no such financial disorder and he did not permit these persons to grab all this wealth from the property of the Muslims. On the other hand everything was done in a straightforward manner and according to a clear-cut policy. In the light of the system of government and collection of wealth and its distribution among the Muslims none of the Muslims could acquire so much wealth.

After Caliph Uthman Imam Ali attained to the caliphate. The difficult task for Ali, on account of which battles were also fought, was to control these influential persons and not to permit any person any longer to take even one dinar from the *Baytul Māl* of the Muslims without proper accounting. He wanted to restrain the people from all sorts of covetousness, greed, and bad habits. For about four and a half years covering the period of his caliphate he had to struggle against these very persons who had been prevented by him from amassing wealth. He used to say: "It is no longer possible that I should be at the helm of affairs and this plundering should be renewed. On the contrary I shall recover whatever has been given or taken unlawfully and shall deposit it in the *Baytul Māl*". On this very account Ali was eventually martyred.

PEACE TREATY OF IMAM HASAN

After Imam Ali, Imam Hasan attained to the caliphate. At this time the Muslim society had assumed a peculiar form. Their strength had been divided almost evenly, and if Imam Hasan had continued fighting against Mu'awiya neither of the two parties could expect victory without severe bloodshed. The result of such a fighting would have been disastrous for the Muslims. Hence, Imam Hasan was faced with a situation in which he had no alternative but to come to terms with Mu'awiya and prevent senseless bloodshed. If he had persisted in fighting it would have resulted in gain to the Eastern Roman Empire on the external front and to the Khawārij within the Islamic territories. If those 400,000 or 500,000 Muslims had attacked one another on that day and fighting with Mu'awiya had been continued only Allah knows what calamity would have fallen on the Muslims from the side of the Eastern Roman Empire and what dimensions the danger from Khawārij would have assumed, and what the history of Islam would have been!

Hence, Imam Hasan retired from the caliphate and thus safeguarded the blood of the Muslims and the strength of Islam, and prevented the external and internal enemies from taking undue advantage of the situation. This does not, however, mean that he surrendered to Mu'awiya and recognized him as the caliph and the Commander of the Faithful.

One of the conditions of the Peace Treaty between Imam Hasan and Mu'awiya reads thus: "Hasan bin Ali makes Peace on the condition that he will not be under an obligation to call Mu'awiya, the Commander of the Faithful". It meant that he did not recognize Mu'awiya to be the caliph and the Commander of the Faithful. Those, who think that by retiring, Imam Hasan bin Ali surrendered to Mu'awiya and Mu'awiya became the caliph of the Muslims and Hasan bin Ali also became one of his obedient subjects, should keep in mind this valuable narration by Ibn Athir which refutes this false belief:

"After Hasan bin Ali retired and Mu'awiya became the caliph, Farwa bin Nawfal Ashjaie Khāriji, who had deserted the Khawārij earlier along with five hundred men and gone to the city of Zur said: "Now there is no doubt about the fact that we should fight against Mu'awiya's adminstration. As Mu'awiya has come at the helm of affairs and become the caliph we must wage war against him". They, therefore, marched towards Iraq and reached the palm-grove of Kufa. In the meantime Imam Hasan had left Kufa and was on his way to Madina. When Mu'awiya came to know that the said Khāriji had revolted along with his five hundred men, he wrote a letter to Imam Hasan, possibly with a view to strengthening the Peace Treaty with the Imam. He wrote thus: "I understand that Farwa bin Nawfal Khāriji is proceeding to Kufa along with five hundred men. I, therefore, direct you to go and fight against him and ward him off, and after you have vanquished him there will be no objection to your proceeding to Madina".

Imam Hasan received Mu'awiya's letter when he had arrived at Qādisiya. He sent him the following reply: "O Mu'awiya! You have appointed Hasan bin Ali to go like one of your officers and to ward off a rebellious Khariji. I, Hasan bin Ali, have retired, in the interest of the Muslims, from the caliphate, which is my right. If I had wished to fight against one of the people of the Qibla i.e. with a Muslim, whoever he might be, and to which ever sect he might belong, I would have fought against you in the first instance".

The Imam meant to say that he desisted from fighting against Mu'awiya in spite of the latter's being deviated from Islam as compared with all others. It will be observed that the Imam did not say: "I have recognized you as the caliph". On the other hand he wrote: "I let you go and did not fight against you". And possibly a better interpretation of the words "I let you go" may be this: 'I have set you at liberty in the field of politics and have myself retired only in the interest of Islam and to avoid the bloodshed of the Muslim i.e. I considered it futile that these two forces of Islam which are evenly balanced should fight and kill and weaken each other and be annihilated, and the external and internal enemies should take undue advantage of this situation'.

After the martyrdom of Imam Hasan Imam Husayn did not also rise up in arms against Mu'awiya during the last ten years of his rule (49 — 60 A.H.) and did not undertake that campaign against him — the campaign, which he considered necessary during the regime of Yazid. However, he continuously criticized and reprimanded Mu'awiya and denied his rightfulness to the caliphate in the same manner in which his brother Imam Hasan had done.

After the martyrdom of his brother Imam Hasan, Imam Husayn wrote the following letter to Mu'awiya which has been reproduced by Ibn Qutayba Denuri:

"O Mu'awiya! Are you not the same person who killed Hujr bin Ady and his pious friends unlawfully? They were the persons, who condemned heresy and ordered the people to do good and restrained them from evil. You killed them cruelly after granting them security and making firm promises and covenants with them. By doing so you defied Allah and considered the Divine covenants to be frivolous. Did you not kill Amr bin Humuq Khuzāie, who was one of the distinguished companions of the Holy Prophet? He was the man whose face had worn out and whose body had grown thin on account of excessive worship. You killed him after granting him security and holding out promises of safety to him. If such promises had been held out to the desert deer, they would have come down to you from the hills with perfect confidence.

"Are you not the man who associated Ziyad, the son of an unknown father, with your father Abu Sufyan and called him your brother, as Ziyad bin Abu Sufyan, and supposed that he is the son of Abu Sufyan although the Holy Prophet has said: "The child belongs to the man on whose bed (i.e. in whose house) he is born and the woman giving birth to the child is married to him and the adulterer is to be stoned to death as commanded by Allah. And then you have appointed Ziyad to rule over the Muslims so that he may kill them and amputate their hands and feet and hang them on date-palm trees. Allah be praised!

"O Mu'awiya! It appears that you are not a member of the Muslim community and the Muslims have no connections with you. Fear Allah and beware of the Day of Judgement, because Allah has a document from which nothing, whether small or big or good or bad, is omitted and everything is taken into account. You must remember that Allah does not forget these acts of yours, that is, you kill people on mere suspicions and false accusations and have made a boy, the ruler of the Muslims, who drinks wine and plays with dogs.

"O Mu'awiya! I see that you have destroyed yourself, spoiled your faith and made the Muslim ummah helpless".

This was the manner in which Imam Hasan and Imam Husayn, the two sons of the Holy Prophet addressed and wrote letters to Mu'awiya bin Abu Sufyan and called him to account.

WHO WAS YAZID?

In order to learn more clearly as to how far the views expressed by Imam Husayn about Yazid are indisputable according to the history of Islam, one should refer to the following remarks of Mas'udi in respect of Yazid.

"Yazid was a pleasure-seeking person. He was a man, who kept beasts of prey. He had dogs, monkeys and panthers. He always arranged wine-drinking parties. One day after the martyrdom of Imam Husayn while he was sitting in such a party, Ibn Ziyad was seated on his right side, Yazid turned to the cup-bearer and recited two couplets which are translated below:

"Give me a cup of wine which should satiate my bones. Then give another such cup to Ibn Ziyad, the man who is my confidant and who has strengthened my position and the foundation of my caliphate".

Yazid meant to say that Ibn Ziyad by killing Imam Husayn had strengthened the foundation of his caliphate.

Thereafter Mas'udi writes about the injustice and oppressions committed by Yazid and then says: "In the Muslim ummah Yazid was like Pharaoh amongst his subjects" and then writes: "It is not so, because Pharaoh was more just to his subjects". He adds: "The injustice, intrepidity and impiety of Yazid also penetrated into the Muslim ummah". The sins committed by Yazid were also committed by his favourites and they adopted his ways and manners. During the period of his caliphate music became current in Makkah and Madina, and all sorts of amusements and funs began to be used. The people began to drink wine openly. It is also the more surprising that the man, who claimed to be the successor to the Holy Prophet and occupied the seat of the caliphate, had a pet monkey, which was named Abu Qays. Yazid used to bring it in his drinking parties and he spread a mattress for it. He also mounted it on the back of a she-ass, and made it participate in the horse-race. One day Abu Qays won the race. The monkey was then dressed in red and yellow silken clothes and cloak, and an embroidered cap was placed on its head".

This was the import of the sentence which Imam Husayn

wrote to Mu'awiya about Yazid. However, this person attained to the Islamic Caliphate and pressed Imam Husayn to take the oath of allegiance i.e. to acknowledge him to be the lawful successor of his (i.e. Imam Husayn's) grandfather, the Prophet of Allah.

WHY THE IMAM REJECTS TO TAKE THE OATH?

Now let us see as to why Imam Husayn did not take the oath of allegiance to Yazid and preferred, instead, to lay down his life and be martyred.

Some writers have given a very flabby and incorrect answer to this question. They say that the Imam came to the conclusion that he would be killed whether he took the oath of allegiance or not. In no case would Bani Umayya spare him. He considered it perferable to be killed honourably and to lay down his life for the sake of Allah.

This answer appears to be very superficial and insufficient. The martyrdom of Imam Husayn is much above that it may be said that when he realized that he would inevitably be killed he sacrificed his life saying to himself: 'Now that I am going to be killed let me be killed honourably and achieve martyrdom in the path of Islam'.

However, this is not the case, and it is necessary that the conditions prevailing in the Muslim society at that time should be studied more carefully and the sermons and addresses of the Imam himself should also be understood more accurately so that the facts may become clear.

Taking into account all the developments which had been taking place for thirty years Imam Husayn concluded correctly that at that time i.e. in the year 60 A.H. the Muslim ummah had deviated to such an extent that its deviation could not be remedied merely by means of speeches, preaching and writings and by delivering religious sermons and discourses. Of course, if the deviation of the caliphate and the people of that time had been only superficial it would have been possible to reform it easily and the deviated ones might have been brought to the right path. However, the deviation existed in 60 A.H. was so acute and critical that it was affecting the very basic and political foundations of the Muslim society.

Furthermore, it was a general and collective deviation and

not of some individuals so that it could be reformed by preaching and exhortation. Corruption had penetrated into the entire society and could not be eradicated by these means. Imam Husayn, therefore, concluded that a severe and quick rising was necessary to obtain a final and decisive result from the elementary work done by the Commander of the Faithful and Imam Hasan, and the effects of the conditions created by Bani Umayya before the conquest of Makkah as polytheists and thereafter in the garb of Muslims could not also be eliminated without taking an earnest and energetic stand.

Of course, Imam Husayn can explain for us better than anyone else the causes of his rising, and he has actually done so. We therefore, propose to study the sermons of the Holy Imam and find out as to what he says about the causes of his rising and how he commences the event and where he ends it.

If the sermons and writings of the Imam are taken into account, especially in their chronological order, it appears that in the beginning he did not make an open announcement of his movement but when he began to advance towards his goal gradually he made the spirit of his movement and the causes of his rising known to the people. Commencing with the testament which he wrote in Madina for his brother Muhammad bin Hanafiya till the last speech which he delivered before Hur bin Yazid Riyahi and his companions at the halting place named Bayzah, he gradually told the Muslims as to why he took that step and also that he had no other alternative. He made it clear that the grave corruption which had taken place in the Islamic Caliphate in the first instance and had then affected all social aspects of the Muslim society could not be remedied without earnest rising, self-sacrifice and martyrdom.

When the Governor of Madina pressed the Imam to take the oath of allegiance, Imam Husayn visited the grave of the Holy Prophet for two consecutive nights and offered prayers there. During the second night after he had paid homage to the sacred grave, he performed a few rakats of prayers and then said: "O Almighty Allah! This is the grave of Your Prophet and I, too, am the son of the daughter of Your Prophet. O Lord! you know with what predicament I am faced".

It is possible that some persons may imagine that the

Imam meant to say that the enemies wanted to kill him and it was immaterial whether he surrendered to them or not.

However, we are sure that no Muslim will conceive from Imam's invocation that he was in danger of being martyred in the path of Allah and could not ward off this danger and live in peace along with his wives and children and, therefore, lamented and showed weakness and lack of self-possession, and also introduced himself to Allah saying that he was the son of His Prophet's daughter. This is a very strange interpretation. Was not the Holy Prophet poisoned and killed? Were not Imam Ali and Imam Hasan martyred? Then why should Imam Husayn have moaned for fear of being martyred and complained against being killed? The Muslims who had received training at the hands of the Holy Prophet for a few years or at times for a few months and even for a few days did not complain against martyrdom in spite of the fact that previously they were idolaters and polytheists. On the contrary, while leaving their houses they prayed that they might not return alive and might attain to the Divine blessing of martyrdom. Now how could it be that the son of the Holy Prophet, the spirit of Islam, and the off-spring of towering personalities like Imam Ali and Lady Fatima the daughter of the Holy Prophet should be afraid of martyrdom and beseech Allah and His Prophet to protect him from this calamity and let him remain alive?

Amr bin Jumuh who was a Muslim and resident of Madina was previously an idolater and the custodian of an idol-temple in Madina. He remained steadfast in idol-worship and notwithstanding the fact that Islam had spread in Madina he continued to bow down with perfect devotion before an idol, which he had in his house. For many consecutive nights it so happened that the young men of the family of Bani Salma stole his idol and threw it in some well or dirty pit of Madina. In the morning this old man went in search of his god, retrieved it from dirt, washed and perfumed it and then stood before it with great meekness and apologized to it, said: "If I had known as to who treats you like this I would have seen him, but you should believe me that I don't know that person and should, therefore, be excused".

The young men of Bani Salma did not give up the practice

and persisted in the matter till one day the dormant nature of Ibn Jumuh became enlightened. On that day he found his deity in a well, tied in a rope with the dead body of a dog, and said to it: "Had you been a god you would not have been lying in a well along with a dog". He returned to his house very much dejected and disappointed and gave up idol-worship. Possibly he embraced Islam on that very day.

This man was an idolater previously. However, when he became a Muslim, Islam elevated his spirit so much that, with the Islamic training of about a year or two, the level of his thinking became so high that in the month of Shawwal 3 A.H. he got ready to participate in the Battle of Uhud. His four sons were already ready accompanying the Holy Prophet. They and his other relatives dissuaded him from participating in the jihad saying: "You are an old and disabled man and also limp. Furthermore, your four sons are already accompanying the Holy Prophet. You should, therefore, remain at home and should not expose yourself to trouble". Amr got agitated on their suggestions. Then he approached the Holy Prophet and said: "O Prophet of Allah! Don't withhold Paradise from me. I shall walk into it with this limping foot". When he got ready to leave his house he raised his hands in prayer and said: "O Lord! Let me be destined to be killed in this journey and to attain martyrdom. Let it not be that I may return home from this journey being despaired of martyrdom".

Now the point for consideration is that if a Muslim, who had spent his past life in worshipping idols, and embraced Islam under the pressure of the youths of his tribe, could be elevated so much spiritually by Islam that he considered returning alive from the battlefield to his wife and children to be privation and bad luck, and sincerely prayed to Allah that he might not return to his home alive, how could it be that Imam Husayn who was an embodiment of nobleness and virtue and the offspring of the Holy Prophet and the Commander of the Faithful, should complain of the danger of death and say to his grandfather: "O Prophet of Allah! Come to my help as the enemies are going to kill me!" No. This is not the position, and the sentence: "You know with what predicament I am faced" should not be interpreted to mean this, because this meaning will degrade his eternal movement and make it seem superficial. In his supplication to Allah the Imam says: "O Lord! You know with what predicament I am faced". Predicament means the condition which the Holy Imam mentioned clearly in his sermons, letters and discourses. It is the very assessment made by Imam Husayn. It is the same deplorable state of affairs and the serious deviation which had developed in the Muslim society at that time. Predicament means that after careful study of the conditions prevailing in the Islamic territories and the activities of the Umayyad Caliphate and the ways and manners adopted by the people, Imam Husayn came to the conclusion that the Muslim society could not be saved from the danger of serious deviation without rising, self-sacrifice and martyrdom.

Then the Imam said: "O Lord! You know that I like good deeds and hate indecent deeds". With these words the Imam mentioned his object to some extent, but not so clearly that the common people might understand as to what he meant to say.

Then he said: "O Almighty Lord! I beseech You in the name of this grave and the master of this grave to show me the path by means of which You as well as Your Prophet may be pleased with me".

MAIN CAUSE OF RISING OF IMAM HUSAYN

In these words as well as in his testament the Imam made his mission known to the people. He said: "I am going to enjoin the people to do good and to restrain them from evil". What did he mean by this? Possibly most of the people who heard these words of the Imam imagined that he wanted to go to Kufa and tell the grocers and bakers of that city: "Do not weigh less. Do not sell bad curd and cheese and improperly baked bread to the people". Or that he might tell the merchants of Kufa not to charge interest. This would be restraining from evil! Or that he might tell the residents of Kufa: "Do not be careless about obligatory prayers. If you can afford you must go to Makkah and perform Haj". This would be enjoining to do good. But the Imam's object was much higher than this. Of course this kind of enjoining to do good and restraining from evil is something good and essential, but this task could be performed by the ulema of Kufa and did not necessitate the Holy Imam's going there. In fact Imam Husayn wanted to do something which none else could do. In the conditions then prevailing it was only he, who could perform a memorable deed whose freshness cannot fade with the passage of time, and which cannot be effaced from the pages of the history of Islam.

DEPARTURE OF IMAM FROM MADINA

After his departure from Madina Imam Husayn reached Makkah on 3rd of Shābān and sent his cousin Muslim bin Aqil to Kufa in the middle of Ramazān. From that time till the 8th of Zil Haj he continued to stay on in Makkah. None could imagine that on the 8th of Zil Haj when the people were putting on Ehrām (pilgrim's garb) to perform Haj the son of the Holy Prophet of Allah and child of Makkah and Mina would leave Makkah without performing the ceremonies of Haj and would abandon *Ehrām* after performing Umra. However, the Imam decided to depart from Makkah. He went round the Kāba, performed Sai between Safa and Marwa and then abandoned *Ehrām*, because there was the danger of his being arrested or killed within the precincts of the sanctuary, and in case he was killed in that way his object could not be achieved. The Imam did not leave Makkah to escape from being killed. He left Makkah so that if he was killed it should be in such a way that Islam should always benefit from his martyrdom.

According to Luhuf the Imam addressed a gathering before his departure. After praising the Almighty Allah he said: "Death has marked the human beings in the same manner in which a necklace leaves its mark on the neck of a young woman" (i.e. every human being is destined to die). In these words he hinted at the fact that during those days the social and religious corruption could not be remedied except by the martyrdom of one like him, who was the son of the daughter of the Holy Prophet of Allah.

In the discourse delivered before his departure from Makkah he speaks about martyrdom, death, going before his grandfather, the Holy Prophet of Allah, and before his parents and falling into the clutches of the hungry wolves of Karbala. He told the people that his journey would end in this manner. We know that Imam Husayn delivered this discourse earlier than the 8th of Zil Haj and possibly on the seventh of that month before a gathering of the pilgrims of the House of Allah. At that time the political conditions were apparently favourable for Imam Husayn, and the people thought generally that Yazid bin Mu'awiya would soon step aside and his caliphate would topple down and the Imam who was entitled to the caliphate would attain to it. This was because Muslim bin Aqil, his special representative, had sent a report from Kufa saying: "All the people are with you and do not recognize the caliphate of anyone else. They are also not prepared to acknowledge anyone as their ruler except you. Hence you should come as early as possible". Apparently the conditions were very favourable and reassuring, but in spite of this Imam Husayn was talking about death and martyrdom and the fierceness of the Iraqi wolves.

The fact is as already stated by us i.e. Imam Husayn wanted to tell the people that he had already assessed that no result could be achieved and nothing useful and positive could be done without his own martyrdom as well as that of his friends. That is why he said that man cannot avoid death. He said: "I am keen to see the Prophet of Allah, Ali, Hamza, Ja'far and my mother Fatima in the same way in which Ya'qub was keen to see Yusuf. A site of martyrdom has been selected for me by Allah and I am going there". It transpires from this sentence that this was a Divine plan and not one drawn by Husayn bin Ali. The Almighty Allah had destined since eternity that such deviation and corruption, could take place in the Muslim society, and Husayn bin Ali would make an unprecedented self-sacrifice and meet martyrdom to remedy the situation.

The Imam said: "I can see as if the desert wolves of Iraq are attacking me between Nawāwis and Karbala and tearing me into pieces. They are filling their hungry flanks and empty pockets. It is for them to fill their pockets and to feed themselves to satiety, and for me to fight against this social and religious corruption. This is the plan devised by Allah and it is He who has considered my martyrdom to be the remedy and the means of reforming the present state of affairs. It is impossible to escape from whatever has been destined by Him. We the family of the Holy Prophet are happy with what Allah is pleased with, and like whatever He likes. We bear with patience all the difficulties which He makes us face and He also gives us full reward which is admissible to the patient people. I am a part of the body of the Prophet of Allah and a part of his body cannot remain separate from him. I shall join him in Paradise so that he may be pleased to see me and fulfil the promises made with me. Only he, who is prepared to sacrifice his life for my sake and to meet Allah, should accompany me. God willing I intend to depart tomorrow morning".

The Divine religion, the rights of the people and the interests of the Islamic society can be defended at different times in different ways. It may be by spending money in the path of Allah. It may be by speaking for the sake of Allah and bringing the people to the right path by means of useful and instructive words. It may be by writing a book for the sake of Allah and bringing the people nearer to truth and reality with useful publications and increasing their religious and moral insight. However, Imam Husayn declared that at that juncture the problem with which Islam was faced could not be solved with financial assistance or through writing or verbal benevolence. On the contrary the matters had taken such a turn that it was not possible to restrain corruption and eradicate its foundation except by means of self-sacrifice and martyrdom.

It would not have been right for anyone to think that as Imam Husayn was going to take a step forward in the path of Allah he too would contribute some money or present five swords, seven coats of mail and four spears to him or say like Ubaydullah bin Hur Juafi in response to the Imam's call that he would give him a strong horse. Husayn bin Ali did not, however, require swords, lances, horses or money, but was prepared to accept only that person who was sincerely prepared to lay down his life for his sake. He said: "Only that person, who is prepared to sacrifice his life for the sake of Allah and to meet the Almighty, can join me in this journey. God willing I shall be departing tomorrow morning".

It is surprising that in spite of all these emphatic pronouncements of the Imam many unfortunate opportunists also joined him under the impression that the circumstances were favourable and perhaps most of them remained with him till the news of the martyrdom of Muslim bin Aqil was received. The fact is that from the very beginning these people sided with him, who became caliph and assumed authority.

They were not prepared to support the Imam who was going to die and meet martyrdom, who was to be deprived of water, and whose companions were one day going to die the honourable death of martyrs.

MERITS OF IMAM HUSAYN

We should now like to quote some traditions relating to Imam Husayn from Ibn Athir's book entitled Usudul Ghabah:

A man asked Abdullah bin Umar: "What will be the position if the blood of a mosquito touches the dress of a man?" Abdullah bin Umar said: "Look here! This Iraqi enquires about the blood of a mosquito, although these very Iraqis killed the son of the Prophet of Allah and I myself have heard the Holy Prophet saying: "Hasan and Husayn are my two fragrant flowers in the world".

The Holy Prophet said: "Husayn is from me and I am from Husayn. Allah loves him who loves Husayn. Husayn is the son of the Prophet and father of the Imams".

Anas bin Harth Kāhili, and his father who were the companions of the Holy Prophet, says that he heard the Holy Prophet saying: "This very son of mine (i.e. Husayn) will be killed at a place in the region of Iraq. Whoever is present at that time and is in a position to assist him should assist him".

The prelude to what had been said by the Holy Prophet became apparent in 60 A.H. and Imam Husayn also got ready to meet martyrdom. However, it was not, as some persons have imagined, that, as there was no chance of his escaping death, and he knew that even if he surrendered he would be killed, he became helpless and exposed himself to martyrdom. In fact this was not the position, and whoever says or writes this says something flabby and baseless. If that had been the case what value would there have been of the Imam's action and how could the world attach all this importance to this sacred rising? This movement is the central point of all the sacred movements of the history of Islam and is in fact the centre of all sacred religious movements, whether they were initiated before Imam

Husayn or were led after him by Zayd bin Ali, Husayn bin Zayd, Sāhib Nafs Zakiyya and his brother Ibrahim, Husayn Shahid Fakh and others. How is it possible that such a movement should be analyzed with such baseless explanations?

The correct position is the same to which we have referred earlier and said that towards the end of 60 A.H. and in the beginning of 61 A.H. Imam Husayn felt that the Islamic society had reached a stage of spiritual and moral degradation which could not be reformed except by means of rising and martyrdom. It does not, however, mean that it was not possible for him to continue to live and he, therefore, chose to be martyred. What is meant is that he could not find any prospect for the existence of religion and the Islamic ummah except by means of sacred revolution. He concluded that if he wanted the Muslim ummah to live, and there should be a Muslim ummah in the world, he himself must be sacrificed and his dear ones like Zaynab, Umme Kulthum, Fatima bintul Husayn and Ali bin Husayn (Peace be upon them) who were the greatest and the most eloquent orators of the world of Islam should continue Imam Husayn's mission by inviting the attention of the Muslim ummah to its shameful condition, in the bazaars of Iraq and Syria, deliver the Muslim ummah permanently from the danger of death and annihilation, keep alive the sacred movements which were started before Husayn bin Ali and open a smooth path for the future religious movements of the Muslims.

After Walid bin Utbah, the Governor of Madina, tried to coerce the Imam under the orders of the caliph of the time to submit and take oath of allegiance, and the incident of the night of 28th Rajab took place, the Imam did not take the oath of allegiance and deferred his final decision to the following day. Thereafter Abdullah bin Zubayr got alarmed and ran away from Madina on the following day, but the Imam stayed on in Madina. On that day he came out of his house to find out whether there was any fresh news. Marwan bin Hakām met him on the street and said to him during the course of their conversation: "Sir, I am your well-wisher. You should hear me and listen to what I say". The Imam replied: "Let me know what you have to say. If it is something good for me I shall surely accept it". Marwan said: "I suggest that you should take the oath of allegiance to Yazid. This will be beneficial to your world as well as to your faith (i.e. if you recognize Yazid as the caliph, Imam and leader of the Muslim nation, and endorse his leadership of the Muslims of the world, you will preserve your faith as well as your worldly interests, but in case you do not take the oath to him, and oppose him, you will destroy your faith and the world will also slip away from your hands)."

The Imam said in reply to these presumptuous words of Marwan: *"We are from Allah and to Him we shall all return."* (Surah al-Baqarah, 2:156). This verse is usually recited to console ourselves or others when a calamity befalls us. The calamity in connection with which the Imam recited this verse to console himself and others was the intellectual degradation of the Muslims i.e. they had deviated from the true path of religion to such an extent that Marwan had the audacity to say that if Husyan bin Ali took the oath of allegiance to Yazid his faith as well as his worldly interests would be secure, but otherwise both of them would be jeopardized. Then the Imam said: "If the affairs of the Muslim ummah have really taken such a turn that a person like Yazid is going to be the protector of Islam and the Muslims and the ruler of the Muslim world and successor of the Holy Prophet, one should say: "May Allah save Islam", because I have myself heard the Prophet of Allah saying that caliphate is unlawful for the family of Abu Sufyan". Thereupon the discussion between the Imam and Marwan got protracted and eventually Marwan parted with the Imam in a state of anger.

Imam Husayn went from Madina to Makkah and on the 8th day of Zil Haj, which is called tarwih day and which coincided with the day on which Hāni bin Urwah was arrested by Ibn Ziyad, and Muslim bin Aqil staged a rising in Kufa, he (Imam Husayn) proceeded to Iraq. The Muslims wondered much at the Imam's sudden departure from Makkah at a time when the ceremonies of Haj were to be performed.

Farazdaq, a poet whose name is well-known in the history of Islam says: "In 60 A.H. I took my mother to Makkah to perform Haj. When I arrived in the precincts of the sanctuary and was driving my mother's camel I saw Husayn bin Ali. He was armed and was going out of Makkah. I asked the people: "To whom do these camels belong?" They replied that they belonged to Husayn bin Ali. Thereupon I went to the Imam, saluted him, and said: "O son of the Prophet of Allah! May Allah grant your wishes and may my parents be your ransom, why are you leaving Makkah without performing the ceremonies of Haj?" He replied: "If I had not made haste and not come out of the city I would have been arrested". Then he asked me: "Who are you?" I replied: "I am an Arab." I swear by Allah that he did not make any further investigation or inquiry about me. Then he said: "Do you know anything about the people you have left behind (i.e. the Iraqis)?" I replied: "You have enquired about it from the right person. I know those people very well. Their hearts are with you and their swords are against you. The Divine decree descends from heaven and Allah does what He likes". The Imam said in reply: "You have spoken the truth. Only that thing which Allah wills happens. If the Divine decree is according to our wishes we shall thank Allah for His blessings, and it is also He who can make one succeed in the matter of thanksgiving. And if the Divine decree does not accord with our wishes, and blocks the path of hope, even then one, who has good intentions and a pure heart, does not perish". Farzdaq said: "May Allah grant your wishes and protect you from all calamities".

Then Farazdaq enquired from the Imam about Haj ceremonies and took leave of him after obtaining the requisite answers.

What the Holy Imam said to Farazdaq needs very careful consideration. The Imam meant to say: 'I am not one of those persons who have an object in view and strive to achieve it, but may or may not meet success. I have a set objective before me and, whatever the circumstances may be and whoever gains victory or sustains defeat, I shall attain to that objective. A person may work hard to acquire wealth. Another may strive to attain to a high position. Another may go to a doctor for his own treatment or that of his patient. Another may step into the battlefield to defeat his rival. Some may perform good deeds or apparently good deeds to acquire renown and honour. It is possible that such persons may achieve their object, and it is also possible that in spite of their best efforts they may not meet success. It is not necessary that man should achieve what he desires. More often than not our earnest desires suddenly turn into failures. That is what happens to most of the people. They make efforts to achieve their object. At times they are successful, but at other times they not only fail to achieve success but also lose their wealth, and occasionally their life, without getting anything in return.

The Imam says: 'I am not one of those people and whatever the future circumstances and the political conditions of Iraq may be, I shall achieve my object. I have risen only to perform the duty which devolves upon me from Allah in the present circumstances. It is not my object to become a caliph or to rule over the Muslims. If I am successful I shall have performed my duty and it will be quite right, and if my enemy is the winner, even then I shall have performed my duty. There is no other object of my movement'. Truly speaking it makes no difference for the godly persons, and those, who have no material motive and perform jihad for Allah, with a view to perform their duty, whether they are victorious or defeated. This interpretation is also on account of the inadequacy of words, otherwise the word defeat does not exist in the dictionary of the godly persons. This was what Imam Husayn said while going to Iraq when he told Farazdaq: "If we succeed we shall thank Allah, but even if destiny does not favour us we shall not perish, because our intention is good. It is possible that we may be killed but we shall not die, because there is a great difference between being martyred in the path of Allah and for the sake of enjoining to do good and restraining from evil on the one hand and dying and perishing on the other".

The Imam said exactly the same thing on the day of Āshura in one of his addresses to the people of Kufa. By reciting some poetical verses of the companion of the Holy Prophet named Farwa bin Murādi, he hinted that if some of his friends or enemies thought that that was a day of his death, defeat and destruction, they were sadly mistaken, for the fact was that it was the day of his martyrdom — a martyrdom which would be the first step towards his eternal life.

Ibn Tawus writes that when Burayr bin Khuzayr Hamdāni counselled the people but they did not pay any heed to him, the Imam himself mounted a camel and asked them to become silent. When they became silent and attentive he praised Allah in a befitting manner and invoked blessings for Muhammad, the angels and other Prophets. Then he said: "O People! Woe be to you! You have deceived us. You cried for help, and we got up quickly to come to your rescue. However, you wielded against us the same sword, which we had given in your hands and kindled for us the same fire, which we had lit to destroy our common enemy. You joined your enemies to fight against your friends and well-wishers, although you have not received justice from them (i.e. from the enemies) in the past and cannot also entertain any hope in the future. Woe be to you! Why did you not take a final decision and forsook us when the swords were still sheathed and the people were tranquil and calm? Why did you begin to fly hurriedly like newly-winged locusts, and why did you fall in the fire of mischief like moths? May you never be blessed, O mean people! who have thrown the Qur'an away and tampered with its words.

"O You supporters of sins and friends of Satan and those who have wiped out and destroyed the traditions of the Prophets! Have you withdrawn your hands from our assistance and are you going to support the oppressors? I swear by Allah that you have always been unfaithful. You are inherently faithless people. You are the most filthy fruit, which is of no use to your friends and well-wishers, and chokes their throats, but is easily swallowed by the enemies. By choking the throats of the friends it is meant that you promise assistance and support and boast of your devotion and manliness, but when you are put to test and when it is time to defend Islam and offer sacrifice, you are not only useless, but your oppression and injustice does not spare even your friend, and threatens his life like a choking morsel!"

Then the Imam said: "O people of Kufa! You should know that this bastard (i.e. Ubaydullah) son of that bastard (i.e. Ziyad) has obliged me to choose one of the two things; either the swords be unsheathed i.e. there occurs a fierce battle, which culminates in my martyrdom and self-sacrifice or I should fall into disgrace and humiliation and submit to his will so that he may do with me whatever he likes. However, disgrace and humiliation are not acquainted with us. Allah does not like that we should be put to shame and humiliation. The Prophet and the godly persons do not yield to abjectness and humiliation.

We have been brought up in the laps of pure mothers. The young men with the sense of honour and the gentlemen with undaunted courage will not go the way of ignoble and weak persons so long as the path of death and martyrdom is open before them, and will not also agree to our humiliation and abjectness. Although at present my faithful friends are few, and many others have ceased to support me, I shall not choose any path other than fighting, and shall not go except the way of martyrdom".

It was here that the Holy Imam recited the following poetic verses of Farwa ibn Musayk Murādi which represent a world of spiritual greatness, peace and vigour:

"If we have been victorious today it is not something new, because we have always gained victory; and even if we are defeated, predominance and victory is ours; and truth is victorious in all circumstances, whether it wins or loses.

We are treading this path with courage and manliness and are not accustomed to fear and cowardice. However, what can be done if it be so destined that we should meet martyrdom and others should attain to rulership.

It is customary in the world that after attacking the people and trampling upon them death goes back and then renews its attack and crushes another group.

Fate is drawing the gentlemen of Bani Hashim towards death in the same manner in which it did in the past ages.

If the kings of the world had been immortal, we, who are the rulers of the Kingdom of heaven, would have lived for ever. And if the virtuous and magnanimous persons had continued to live in the world, we, who are the basis of magnanimity and the essence of virtue, would have continued to live.

Tell those who rejoice at our misfortune and affliction today: "The time of your affliction is also drawing near, and time will bring down a terrible disaster on you".

With this spirit, showing his greatness, determination, devotion and faith, the Imam proceeded from Makkah to Iraq. He knew very well what he was doing, where he was going and what the result of his action would be. However, others and even the relatives and devotees of the Holy Imam were worried lest the favourable circumstances should become unfavourable and eventually the Imam should be martyred. The Imam was going to meet martyrdom but his friends and relatives were requesting him not to go lest he should be killed.

One of those persons was Abdullah bin Ja'far, the nephew and son-in-law of Imam Ali. After the departure of Imam Husayn from Makkah Abdullah sent him a letter through his sons Awn and Muhammad. In that letter he entreated the Imam in the name of Allah to return. He also wrote: "I am afraid that you and your men will be martyred, and if you are killed today light will disappear from the world, because people are guided by you and all faithful persons count on you. You should not, therefore, be in a hurry, because I am coming after this letter". Then Abdullah left along with the brother of Amr bin Sa'id, the Governor of Makkah. He was carrying a letter from his brother (the Governor of Makkah) to the Imam wherein he assured him of security and asked him to return to Makkah with full confidence. Both of them came to the Imam, presented the letter of the Governor of Makkah to him and insisted on his returning. The Imam told them in reply: "I have seen my grandfather, the Prophet of Allah, in a dream and he has directed me to continue my mission". They asked him as to what else he had dreamt, but he told them that he had not informed anyone about his dream and would not do so throughout his life. Abdullah bin Ja'far lost hope of the Imam's return. However, he ordered his two sons, Awn and Muhammad to join the Imam. Later they were martyred on the day of Āshura.

The Imam continued his journey towards Iraq till he reached near Kufa. From there he wrote a letter to the people of Kufa and sent it to them through Qays bin Mashar Saidāwi. He had not yet received the news of the martyrdom of Muslim bin Aqil. In this letter he wrote to the Kufians: "I have received Muslim's letter and have come to know about your allegiance, sincerity, and firm determination to assist me in the path of Allah. I pray to Allah that He may not withhold His kindness from us and grant you handsome reward for your sincerity and firm determination. I left Makkah on Tuesday the 8th of Zil Haj i.e. on **Tarwih Day** and have proceeded towards you. When my messenger reaches Kufa you should reinvigorate your resolve and quicken your efforts. If Allah wills I, too, shall join you soon".

Qays took the Imam's letter and proceeded to Kufa, but when he reached near the city he was arrested and taken before Ibn Ziyad. Ibn Ziyad asked him to mount the pulpit and abuse Husayn bin Ali. Qays mounted the pulpit, praised Allah and then said: "O people! Husayn is the best of all creatures living at present, and is the son of Fatima, the daughter of your Prophet. I have been sent by him. All of you should rise to assist him". Thereafter he cursed Ubaydullah and his father and invoked blessings for Imam Ali ibn Abi Talib. As ordered by Ubaydullah he was hurled down from the roof and consequently all his bones were cracked.

The Imam continued his journey towards Kufa till he reached a place called Zurud. There he learnt about the martyrdom of Muslim and Hāni and said: "We are from Allah and to Him we all will return." He also said repeatedly: "May Allah's blessings be upon both of them".

At the halting place called Uzaybul Hajānāt he received the news of the martyrdom of Qays bin Mashar. He invoked blessings for him and prayed that Allah might grant him a place in Paradise. At the halting place called Zabala he informed his companions about the martyrdom of Muslim and Hāni and the state of affairs in Kufa, and said: "Our supporters have withdrawn their support from us. Whoever wishes to leave us and go his way should do so". It was here that most of his companions went away, and only a few of them remained with him.

Muhammad bin Jarir Tabari, the famous Islamic traditionalist, exegetic, historian and jurist, in his famous history book entitled **Tarikh-e Umam Wal Muluk**, has stated that "Imam Husayn addressed the people at the halting place called Zi Hasam and delivered a brief speech. In this speech he stated more clearly the motive of his rising and announced his readiness to be martyred. He said: "You can see what turn the matters have taken. The people are becoming disloyal and unkind. Their goodness is disappearing. The world is passing quickly and nothing except something insignificant and a mean and worthless life remains out of it. The world today is just like a pasturage in which nothing grows except harmful grass".

Why did the Imam speak ill of the state of affairs at that time and why did he complain and express regret? He himself explains this in his concluding sentences. There he does not speak about the anxieties of life, or drought or lack of security and peace. The thing which had made life unpleasant and unbearable for the Imam was other than those things which usually make life unpleasant and unwholesome for the people.

Just think what the situation at that time was. It was the time when the vanguard of the needy had arrived and there was a danger of the Iraqi soldiers crowding round the Imam. Some persons, therefore, wished that the Imam had not taken this step. Possibly some short-sighted persons imagined that the Imam himself also thought in the same way and regretted his action and its consequences. It was, therefore, necessary that the Imam should reveal the motive of his rising to some extent and mention more clearly what had made his life unpleasant, difficult and unwholesome. It was for this reason that in the above-mentioned brief address he also said: "The present condition of the Muslims is such that truth is not being followed and falsehood is not being abandoned".

Imam Husyan meant to say: 'In these circumstances it is necessary for an able and self-sacrificing personality like me, the son of the Prophet of Allah, to rise. Don't you see and in other words why don't you ask me as to why I don't surrender and take the oath of allegiance, and why I don't recognize the present Islamic Government formally and acknowledge Yazid, the grandson of Abu Sufyan as the leader and Imam of the Muslims of the world? Don't you know that there is now no occasion for asking these questions? Don't you see the present condition of the Muslims and don't you realize that the people do not act upon Truth?' Apparently the Imam might mean that, for example, the people told lies or indulged in back-biting in their meetings or kept asleep in the morning and allowed their prayers to lapse. However, it is not so, because such sins have always existed among the people to a more or lesser extent. It seems that the Imam wanted to say: 'Don't you see that the present leadership of the Muslims does not conform to the real Caliphate and Succession of the Prophet of Allah. It does not follow the Prophet and has deviated from its natural course which ought to be adherence to truth and justice. The present caliphate is committing oppression, leaving the tyrants free and even encouraging them.'

Then Imam Husayn said: "In such circumstances a pious person should crave for death and this regrettable condition makes a believer fond of martyrdom and meeting Allah".

In the sermon delivered by Imam Husayn in Masjidul Harām he spoke about death, martyrdom and self-sacrifice. Here also he spoke about martyrdom and lack of interest in life. He said: "Living with oppressors does not bear any fruit except weariness, annoyance and vexation". What the Imam said here briefly was stated by him in detail and he explained more clearly the conditions prevailing in those days when he came face to face with Hur bin Yazid Riyahi who had come from Kufa along with one thousand horsemen to arrest him.

IMAM HUSAYN ENCOUNTERS HUR

Imam Husayn encountered Hur and his companions on the 1st of Muharram, 61 A.H. and provided them water to satiate their thirst. It was now the time for noon prayers and Hajjaj bin Masruq Juafi, one of the honourable martyrs of Karbala, pronounced *azān* (call to prayers) under the orders of the Imam.

The Imam then came out of his tent and conversed with them after the call to prayers. Then after praising the Almighty Allah he said, "O people! My excuse before Allah and you Muslims of Kufa is that I did not proceed to Iraq without reason. Your representatives came to me and you wrote in your letters that you had no Imam and asked me to come to you so that Allah might guide you through me. I have come now. If you are prepared to assure me by renewing your promises and covenants I shall come to your city, but if you don't do so or are worried and disturbed on account of my arrival I am prepared to return to the place from which I have come". Hur and his companions did not, however, give any reply to the Imam.

As directed by the Imam, Hajjāj pronounced *iqāmah* and both the armies offered congregational prayers led by the Imam, and after taking rest they also offered the afternoon prayers in a similar way. After the prayers the Imam spoke to the companions of Hur once again and said: "O people! If you fear Allah and are pious and recognize the right of the rightful persons Allah will be pleased with you (here also by the word 'right' the Imam did not mean to tell the people that, for example, they should not pare the wall of their neighbour while they are constructing a building, or should not try to board a vehicle earlier than another passenger who enjoys priority. The Imam meant the right, which is the basis of all the rights i.e. the right of Imamate and leadership of the Muslims of the world, for if that right is secure all other rights are also secure, but if that right is eliminated all other rights are also violated). Then he said: "We the members of the family of the Holy Prophet are the fittest persons to govern you and to exercise authority over you in material and religious matters as compared with the persons, who are at the helm of affairs these days. They are unreasonable persons and claim to hold a very sacred and delicate office which they do not deserve. They oppress you. Such persons cannot be recognized to be the successors of the Holy Prophet, Imams of the Muslims, defenders of the sacred religion of Islam and the protectors of the Holy Qur'an".

Hur bin Yazid Riyahi said in reply to the remarks of the Imam: "I swear by Allah that I am not aware of the letters and the messengers. "The Imam asked Uqbah bin Samān (who was made captive on the day of Āshura but was set free later) to place the letters of the Kufians before Hur and his men." However, Hur said again: "We have not written any letter and we shall not leave you until we take you before Ibn Ziyad". The Imam said: "This is not possible before death". The Imam and Hur mounted along with their respective companions and adopted a route which led neither to Madina nor to Kufa. In the meantime Hur said to the Imam by way of sympathy and advice: "I entreat you in the name of Allah not to fight, because if you fight you will be killed". The Imam got excited and said: "Do you threaten me with death? Will you be comforted by killing me? My reply is the same which the man from Aws tribe gave when he wanted to support the Holy Prophet, but his cousin warned him of being killed and said: "Where are you going? You will be killed". That Awsi man replied: "I have selected my path and for a brave man, whose intentions are good, who does not lose the spirit of Islam in the path of jihad and does not care for his life in assisting the good people, keeps aloof from the ignoble persons, and does not accompany the wicked, it is not a matter of shame to die honourably. If

I live I will not have to regret and in case I lay down my life in this path I shall not be reproached. The baseness of man lies in the fact that he should live an ignominious and shameful life".

Imam Husayn and Hur accompanied by their respective companions, reached a halting place called Bayza. Here also the Imam spoke to those people and made it more clear than before that at that time he was under an obligation to perform a duty. The contents of this speech of his are as follows:

"Yazid is a tyrannical and oppressive caliph, who considers lawful the things declared by Allah to be unlawful. He breaks Divine covenants, opposes the path of the Prophet and oppresses the people. The Holy Prophet has said that in such circumstances if someone does not restrain such a caliph with his words and conduct from committing evil deeds it is necessary for Allah to send him to the same place to which He sends that oppressive caliph".

It is the same thing to which the Holy Qur'an has alluded in these words: *We have made some of the Imams (leaders) lead their followers to the Fire.* (Surah al-Qasas, 28:41) i.e. all the leaders do not take their followers to Paradise. Some of the Imams and leaders of the nation guide the people towards Paradise and good fortune, and that Paradise means in the general sense of progress, prosperity and greatness in this world as well as in the Hereafter. However, according to the Holy Qur'an and historical experience some Imams, like Yazid, drag their followers towards fire, torture and certain downfall.

The Imam then explained more explicitly the conditions prevailing during those days i.e. in 60 A.H. and said: "You should know that these people namely the agents of the Caliphate of Bani Umayya follow Satan, carry out his orders and do not forsake his obedience. In the same proportion they have disobeyed Allah and started committing crimes openly and have suspended the Divine punishments. They have appropriated the property of the Muslims to themselves i.e. they have allocated to themselves the money which should have been credited to the public treasury of the Muslims; spent for their own selfish desires. They have treated the things made lawful by Allah to be unlawful and those made unlawful by Him to be lawful. Now that they have created these conditions, who can be more responsible to change them and eliminate the causes of the decline of the Muslims in accordance with the orders of the Holy Prophet than myself. I am Husayn bin Ali, the son of Fatima, and one of those for whose sake the verse of Purification (33:33) and the verse of *Mubāhila* (3:61) were revealed, and I am the disciple of Imam Ali, the Commander of the Faithful".

Indeed, who could perform the task performed by Husayn bin Ali? Who could obtain friends like his friends and who could take his place in this movement?

Ibn Abbas was a great scholar and commentator of the Holy Qur'an, a distinguished companion of the Holy Prophet and his cousin. However, he could not perform the task performed by Husayn bin Ali. Muhammad bin Hanafiya was the brother of the Imam and son of Ali ibn Abi Talib but he was not equal to this occasion.

Habib ibn Mazāhir Asadi was a companion of the Holy Prophet, but was not capable of doing what Imam Husayn did. Same was the case with Muslim bin Awsaja and Hāni bin Urwa Murādi. Imam Husayn's cousin Muslim bin Aqil, his worthy and honourable brother Abbas, and his dear, brave and pious son Ali bin Husayn were all very great and magnanimous persons, who displayed astonishing valour and self-sacrifice in this great Islamic movement and cooperated with him fully. However, notwithstanding all their magnanimity and great personality none of them could become the central point of this sacred movement. The nucleus and the spiritual power of this Divine movement was hidden in the personality of Imam Husayn. It was this very spiritual power which guided this movement till its last stage and even prepared his survivors for its guidance till they were subjected to extreme torture and captivity.

Then the Imam said: "I am in receipt of your letters through messengers telling me about your allegiance and steadfastness in the path of truth. You have written that whatever the circumstances might be you would not forsake me and would not surrender me to the enemy. Now if you stick to your oath of allegiance and your decision and, as was written by you, do not desist from assisting me you will enjoy good luck, for I am the son of Ali and Fatima and shall remain with you in this sacred jihad. My wives and children will share the fate of your wives and children. It does not also behove you to hold the lives of your wives and children more dear than the lives of my family. When I am ready to sacrifice my own life as well as the lives of the members of my family, you, too, should not spare your own lives as well as the lives of the members of your family".

In other words he said: "Now that I am prepared for being martyred along with my companions and for my women and children being made captives in the path of enjoining to do good and restraining from evil and have brought my dear ones along with me so that you may have no excuse left, it is also your duty that you should follow your Imam and should not falter in the path of Allah. You should not be distressed on account of being killed or made captives, and should not lag behind in assisting the Imam of the time and son of your Prophet. However, if, in spite of all this, you break your promise and abandon allegiance to me I swear by my life that such an action by people like you will not surprise me, because you have behaved in this very manner towards my father Ali, my brother Hasan and my cousin Muslim bin Aqil. A person who trusts you and becomes proud of your promise is deluded. Nevertheless you should know that if you do so the loss will be yours. You will be deprived of good luck. Whoever breaks his promise is a loser himself and it is possible that Allah may soon make me independent of your assistance".

The Imam delivered this address before one thousand persons who were the companions of Hur and all of them heard it, but there was only one person who was impressed by it and showed after a few days that he had properly comprehended the lesson taught by the Imam. That person was Hur bin Yazid Riyahi. In the morning of the day of Āshura he went to Umar bin Sād and said to him: "Are you really going to fight with Husayn bin Ali? Umar replied: "I swear by Allah that I shall fight with him and it will be a tough fight too". Hur said: "Is there any harm if you accept one of the offers made by the Imam?" Umar replied: "If I had possessed authority there would have been no harm and I would have accepted it, but Ibn Ziyad is not prepared to accept anyone of them."

It was at this time that a dangerous conflict commenced between the intellect and passions of this lucky man. It was necessary that he should submit either to the spiritual power or the Satanic temptation. At last, however, the celestial spark which the Imam's words had kindled in his heart prevailed over the devil of his passions and he chose the Divine path and said: "By Allah; I have reached a place where the ways to Paradise and Hell part. By Allah, even if I am cut to pieces and burnt a number of times I shall not prefer anything to Paradise".

Then Hur proceeded to the camp of the Imam. There he confessed his sin, adopted the right path and said: "Almighty Allah knows that I was not aware that the matters would take such a turn. I have now come to repent, but I do not know whether my repentance can be accepted". The Imam replied: "Of course, Allah will accept your repentance and shall forgive you". Then the Imam asked his name. He replied: "I am Hur bin Yazid". The Imam said: "You are a free person as your mother named you Hur (free). You are free in this world as well as in the Hereafter. You should dismount now." He said: "Will it not be better that I should combat with these horsemen for some time and dismount after attaining the honour of martyrdom?" The Imam replied: "May Allah bless you. You may do as you like".

Hur returned to the people of Kufa and began talking to those persons who were his colleagues and fellow-soldiers an hour earlier. He reproached them for their betrayal and faithlessness and spoke thus to the army of which he himself had been a commander: "O people of Kufa! May you die and may Allah make your mothers mourn. You invited this servant of Allah, and when he accepted your invitation and came to you, you withheld your assistance from him. You who promised earlier that you would sacrifice your lives for his sake, have encircled him today and have drawn your swords to kill him. You have besieged him and made it impossible for him to breathe. You are troubling him from every side and do not wish that he should be free, and he and the members of his family should find refuge somewhere. You have made him helpless like a captive. You have deprived him and his women, children and companions of the water of the river Euphrates which is drunk by all Muslims and non-Muslims, and in which the desert birds of Iraq bathe. They are almost exhausted on account of thirst.

How badly you have treated the descendants of the Holy Prophet after him! If you do not repent even now, and do not abandon the idea of killing him Allah will not quench your thirst on the Day of Judgement".

These were the words of the fortunate man who had one day blocked the way of the Imam of his time, alarmed his women and children, made him camp under the orders of Ibn Ziyad in a desert away from human habitation and had collaborated with his enemies from the 2nd of Muharram till the morning of the 10th Muharram. However, within less than an hour his spirit underwent a change and he suddenly began to crave for martyrdom. He became so self-sacrificing in the path of truth that he could no longer content himself with worldly thoughts and hope for life; he did not forsake eternal happiness.

Allah says: *Allah is the Guardian of the believers. He takes them out of darkness into light.* (Surah al-Baqarah, 2:257)

The same invisible Hand, which pulls out the undeserving persons from martyrdom and eternal good name, aids the people of noble spirit from different places into the domain of martyrdom and self-sacrifice and places Hur bin Yazid Riyahi, the commander of the enemy's army into the row of Habib ibn Mazahir Asadi and Burayr bin Khuzayr Hamdāni and even in the row of Ali bin Husayn, Qasim bin Hasan and other Hashimi young men.

ARRIVAL OF IMAM HUSAYN IN KARBALA

On Thursday, the 2nd of Muharram 61 A.H. Imam Husayn camped at a place in the region of Naynava called Karbala. On the following day Umar bin Sād bin Abi Waqqas Zohari reached there from Kufa with 4000 soldiers and encamped opposite the camp of Imam.

Sād belonged to the family of Bani Zohra bin Kilāb of the tribe of Quraysh and was a near relative of Lady Āmina, mother of the Holy Prophet. Umar's father Sād bin Abi Waqqas was one of the five persons who embraced Islam, in the beginning of the Holy Prophet's mission, owing to their acquaintance with Abu Bakr. He is well-known in the history of Islam and in connecttion with the Islamic conquests.

Umar bin Sād sent someone to the Imam enquiring of him

as to why he had come to Iraq. The Imam said in reply: "The Iraqis themselves sent letters to me inviting me to come. Now if you do not like my coming I am prepared to return to the Hijaz".

Ibn Sâd wrote a letter to Ibn Ziyad and informed him of what the Imam had said. Ibn Ziyad said: "Now that he has been caught in our clutches he hopes to escape and return to the Hijaz. There is now no question of showing indulgence and no way is open for him". Further he wrote to Ibn Sâd: "I have carefully read your letter and understood what you have written. Tell Husayn bin Ali that he and all his companions should take oath of allegiance to Yazid. When this has been done we shall take some decision about them".

Soon after Ibn Sâd received another letter from Ibn Ziyad asking him to prevent Husyan and his companions from utilizing water and not to allow them to drink even a drop of it. Umar immediately despatched 4000 men under the command of Amr bin Hajjaj to stand between Imam Husayn and the river Euphrates and to check the use of water by the Imam and his companions. This event took place three days before the martyrdom of the Imam. The Imam asked Ibn Sâd to see him. They met at night at a place situated between the camps of the two armies and had protracted discussions. When Umar bin Sâd returned to his camp he wrote a letter to Ibn Ziyad saying: "Allah has extinguished the flames of war. We have reached an agreement and the matter has been settled according to the national interests. Husayn bin Ali is now prepared to return to the Hijaz or to proceed to some Islamic frontier". In order to make Ibn Ziyad agree to his suggestion he also added a lie justified by its motive.

Ibn Ziyad cooled down and was impressed by the suggestions made by Ibn Sâd. However, Shimr bin Zil Jawshan, who was present there said: "You are making a mistake. You should make the most of this opportunity and now that you have gained control over Husayn bin Ali, you should not let him go, because you will not get such an opportunity again". Ibn Ziyad said: "You are right. You should, therefore, go to Karbala personally and deliver this letter to Ibn Sâd telling him that Husayn and his companions should surrender unconditionally, and then he (Ibn Sâd) should send them to Kufa, and failing that he should fight with them. If Ibn Sâd is not agreeable to this and is not prepared to fight with Husayn bin Ali, you yourself should assume the command of the army and cut off his (Ibn Sād's) head and send it to me".

Then he wrote a letter to bin Sād saying: "I have not sent you to behave leniently toward Husyan Ibn Ali and to intercede with me for him and to make his life secure. Now you should note that if he himself (i.e. Husayn) and his friends surrender, you should send them to me, and if they decline to do so, you should attack and kill them and mutilate their bodies i.e. cut off their ears and noses, for they deserve this treatment. And if Husayn bin Ali is killed you should make the horses trample upon his chest and back because he is a cruel, quarrelsome and ungrateful man. This does not mean that I wish to hurt him after his death. However, I have pledged my word that if I kill him I shall get him trampled upon by the horses. Now if you act according to my directions I shall reward you, but if you do not act as you have been advised, you should hand over charge of the army to Shimr bin Zil Jawshan, who has been given necessary instructions by me".

When Ibn Ziyad wrote this dangerous letter and gave it to Shimr, Ummul Banin's nephew (brother's son) Abdullah bin Abil Mihāl bin Hizām was also present. He stood up and said: "O Emir! My cousins Abbas, Abdullah, Ja'far and Uthman, sons of Ali bin Abi Talib have come with their brother. If possible you may please write a letter of security for them". Ibn Ziyad replied: "All right".

What a great difference there is between the thinking and assessment of the two parties! The cousin of Abi Fazal renders, in his own opinion, a great service to his cousins (aunt's sons) and obtains a letter of security for them from Ibn Ziyad. But the question is: Will they make use of this letter and go away deserting their brother, master and Imam?

When the slave of Abdullah brought the said letter of security to Karbala and called the sons of Ummul Banin and said to them: "Your cousin Abdullah has sent a letter of security for you". He was perhaps thinking that on hearing this the sons of Ummul Banin would become extremely happy. However, the sons of Imam Ali ibn Abi Talib replied to him with one voice: "Convey our greetings to our cousin and tell him that we do not stand in need of security from Ibn Ziyad. Divine Security is better than the security granted by the son of Sumayya".

When Shimr reached Karbala he delivered Ibn Ziyad's letter to Umar Sād and they exchanged views. Eventually Umar Sād agreed to carry out the Emir's orders himself. Shimr was related to the mother of these young men (Abbas and his three brothers) and, therefore, announced that they had been granted security. However, he received the same reply.

Then Umar Sād mounted his horse, occupied a place in front of his army and said: "O riders of Allah! Mount, and be it known to you that your place is in Paradise". Strangely enough this is the same expression which was uttered by the Holy Prophet in a battle when he invited his companions to defend Islam, and Ibn Sād uttered the same words on the 9th of Muharram against the son and the right successor of the Holy Prophet and his sons and dear ones. At this moment the Imam was sitting in front of his tent with a sword in his hand and had gone to sleep with his head resting on his knees. Suddenly the uproar of the army approached nearer and nearer. Lady Zaynab ran to her brother in a state of perplexity and said: "Brother! Don't you hear the uproar of the enemy army which has reached near? The Imam raised his head from his knees and said: "Just now I saw the Holy Prophet in a dream and he told me that I was going to him. On hearing this Zaynab slapped her own face and said: "How sad it is for me!" The Imam said: "Sister! Don't be sad. Be tranquil. Allah will bless you".

In the meantime Abbas bin Ali arrived, submitted a military report and said: "My master! The enemy has reached. What is to be done?" The Imam stood up and said: "My brother Abbas! May my life be sacrificed for you. Mount your horse, go and ask them as to why they have launched an attack at this time and what new development has taken place".

Abbas approached the enemy army accompanied by twenty horse-men including Zuhayr bin Qayn and Habib ibn Mazahir Asadi and enquired from them about the reason for their sudden attack. They replied: "We have received orders from our Emir that either you should surrender immediately or we should fight against you". Abbas said: "Don't be in a hurry. Let me go to the Imam and inform him of the position".

While Abbas went and informed Imam Husayn of the matter, his companions remained in front of the enemy forces and counselled them. Imam Husayn said to his brother: "Go back to them and, if possible, obtain extension of time from them till tomorrow morning, so that tonight we may offer prayers to Allah and make supplications and seek His forgiveness. Allah knows that I love to offer prayers, to recite the Qur'an, to make supplications and to ask His forgiveness".

Somehow they granted respite to the Imam and his friends till the following morning. The Imam also availed of this short opportunity and prepared himself for martyrdom. He tested his companions once again so that if anyone had been ignorant of the result of the rising, he should come to know that the Imam had no way before him except martyrdom and sacrifice, and whoever had not stayed on with a view to meeting martyrdom should go away and vacate the field of sacrifice for those noble persons who did not care for their lives.

Imam Zaynul Abidin Ali bin Husayn, the fourth Imam, who had accompanied his father during this journey says: "My father called his companions after sunset and addressed them. Although I was ill I went there to hear his speech". It should be kept in mind that this speech was delivered by a person, who had less than a hundred supporters with him and was encircled by more than 20,000 men of the enemy and had been given extension of time till the following morning only. The Holy Imam knew very well that he could not agree to surrender and take the oath of allegiance and tolerate the ignoble persons. He also knew that the enemy would not leave him alone and the matter would not be settled without fighting and in the circumstances his own martyrdom as well as that of his companions at the hands of the Iraqis, who had gathered to kill him, was certain. In spite of all this he spoke to his companions with perfect composure and confidence. He pointed out to them that the following day was the day of martyrdom, and insisted upon them that each one of them should hold the hand of one of the members of his family and get out of trouble, and then they could go to their respective cities, so that Allah might grant them relief, because the enemies were after him only, and, after having overpowered him, they would have nothing to do with anyone else.

IMAM'S SERMON ON THE NIGHT OF ĀSHURA

The Imam commenced his speech thus: "I thank Allah to the best of my ability and praise Him during the time of weal and woe. O Lord! I thank You, because You have honoured us by means of Prophethood, taught us the Qur'an, made us comprehend the religion and its commandments, granted us eyes, ears and hearts; kept us free from the pollution of polytheism and then enabled us to thank You for Your blessings. It is a fact that I am not aware of any companions more faithful and honest than my companions, and any relatives more righteous and kind than my relatives. May Allah grant all of you a good reward. I think that the day of our fighting with this army has arrived. I permit all of you to go away. You are free to depart without any restriction and should take advantage of the darkness of night".

This speech has been quoted by Shaykh Mufid, Tabari, Abul Faraj and Ibn Athir, but none of them has written that any companion of the Imam went away on this occasion. Those who had to go had already departed on the way when the news about the martyrdom of Muslim bin Aqil, Hāni, Qays bin Mashar and Abdullah bin Yaqtar was received. The Divine Hand had already driven away the cowardly persons from the Holy Imam. The great historians have recorded nothing after the Imam's speech of the Āshura night except the self-sacrifice and steadfastness of the companions of the Imam. All of them write that when the Imam finished his speech and he insisted that they should leave him and escape trouble, his brothers, sons, nephews (sons of his brothers) and the sons of Abdullah bin Ja'far led by Abbas bin Ali said first of all with one voice: "Should we go away to live after you? We pray to Allah that the time may not come when you may be killed and we may remain alive".

Then the Imam turned to the descendants of Aqil and said: "O children of Aqil! It is sufficient that Muslim has been killed. You are now free to go away". They replied: "Allah be praised! If we leave our chief and the best of our cousins and go away and do not fight along with him with arrows, spears and swords and do not know how he and his friends have fared with the enemy, what will the people say? We swear by Allah that we shall do no such thing. On the contrary we shall sacrifice the lives and property of our family in the path of Allah and render you assistance, and shall fight along with you so that we may also acquire the honour of martyrdom. What a shame to live the life which is without you!"

Then Muslim bin Awsaja got on his feet and said: "If we withdraw our support from you and leave you alone what excuse shall we put forward before Allah? I swear by Allah that I shall not go away and shall not leave you. I shall thrust my spear in the chest of your enemies and shall quench the thirst of my sword with their blood as far as possible. And when there are no arms left in my hand to fight with, I shall shower stones upon them. By Allah we shall not leave you, so that Allah may see that in the absence of His Prophet we have honoured the rights of his son. By Allah, even if I come to know that I shall be killed and then burnt in fire and shall be brought to life again and eventually my ashes will be scattered in the air and I die and become alive in this way seventy times, even then I shall not leave you till I lay down my life for your sake. Then why should I not do so when I am going to be killed only once and will thereafter be honoured, happy and exalted, for ever".

When the speech of Muslim bin Awsaja came to an end, Zuhayr bin Qayn Bajali stood up. He was the same man, who was at one time an enemy of Imam Husayn, remained away from him on the route to Iraq, and did not at all wish to meet him. Allah, however, willed that Zuhayr should meet martyrdom in His path in the company of Imam Husayn so that he might be honoured for ever and his good and glorious name should illuminate the history of the tragedy of Āshura. He commenced his speech thus: "By Allah, I wish that I am killed and then brought to life and then killed once again and this act should be repeated a thousand times and this becomes the means of Allah protecting you and the young men of your family, and all of you remain alive".

Others also expressed similar views. The Imam invoked Divine blessings for them and returned to his tent.

Imam Sajjad says: "During the night preceding the day on which my father was martyred I was ill and my aunt Zaynab was nursing me. My father had at that time retired into his own tent and only Jaun bin Jaun, the former slave of Abuzar Ghifāri was with him. Jaun was setting my father's sword right and my father was reciting some couplets. He repeated these poetic verses twice or thrice and I understood what he was saying and what he meant by it. By reciting these verses he referred to the inconstancy and unkindness of the world, which at times smiles like a kind friend, and enchants the people with its pleasing countenance and one feels that the circumstances will always be favourable. However, it suddenly changes its attitude and becomes unkind and unfaithful. It makes bitter with its poison the life which had once been sweet like honey. It drives away the friends, about whom one thinks that they would remain friendly for ever and boasts of their friendship and devotion when the circumstances are favourable; rather it makes most of those friends stand before one in the shape of blood-thirsty and war-like enemies.

No one knows what is going to happen tomorrow, and when he is going to be deprived of the glory, strength and security which has been bestowed upon him. Who is the person, who has not lost the game during his life, and where is the powerful man, whose strength has not been damaged by the vicissitudes of events?

By reciting these verses the Imam meant to say that on the following day many magnanimous persons would meet martyrdom. It is not possible for any person to make someone else take his place to face the events of time. The end of the matter is in the hands of Allah. Every living being must traverse this path. It was not only he and his companions who were faced that day with the unfavourable time. On the contrary the world at one time assumes the same countenance against everyone.

The fourth Imam says: "I understood that my father meant to inform us of his martyrdom, and tears almost choked me, but I controlled myself. I realized that a calamity was about to fall. However, my aunt Zaynab also heard what I had heard, and as she was a woman, and the women are tender-hearted by nature, and lose patience, she could not control herself. She got up suddenly and went before her brother without wearing a veil and said: "Oh! That I should become brotherless! I wish that

I had died earlier. O successor of the deceased and O the refuge of the survivors! It is today that I am going to be left without mother, father and brother". On seeing his sister in a distressed condition Imam Husayn said: "Sister! Be patient lest Satan should make you lose your self-control".

It may be said that these words of the Imam were a lesson for his sister which prepared her to face the difficult situations in Kufa and Damascus later. It was Zaynab who had to assume the leadership of this movement from the time of the Imam's martyrdom till the return of Ahlul Bayt to Madina, and by means of this lesson the Imam was entrusting this Divine trust to her. The Imam said: "Dear sister! Be patient lest Satan should make you lose your self-control". In other words he said: 'Recognize yourself and do not forget your personality and the importance which you enjoy in this great movement. The task which you have to perform is not easier than that which I can perform, and you can discharge your duty only by means of greatness of soul and spirituality which you have acquired and inherited from your parents, Ali and Fatima. If you lose patience today because you have received a hint that your brother will be martyred or you have heard some touching verses, how will you endure the events of tomorrow? At the same time how will you be able to deliver speeches in the bazaars of Kufa and the Islamic capital (i.e. Damascus) with perfect composure, and say what remains to be said, and bring to light what is hidden, and disclose the deceitful acts of the enemies of Ahlul Bayt and apprise the people of true facts in the centre of the caliphate and government of the descendants of Abu Sufyan, and frustrate their unjust propaganda by delivering speeches?'

The Imam in his brief speech gave a significant lesson to his sister. Tears came in his eyes and he said: "Sister! What am I to do? You can see with what condition I am faced and what a large army has gathered to kill me". Zaynab also uttered some touching words and became unconscious.

IMAM HUSAYN CONSOLES LADY ZAYNAB

Imam Husayn made her sister recover her senses and repeatedly requested her to remain patient and persevering. He said:

"Dear sister, be tranquil and patient. It is not that only the inhabitants of the world die. Those in the heavens do not also continue to live. Everything dies except the Almighty, Who has created the people with His power, and will one day bring them to life again, whereas He Himself is Unique. Dear sister! My grandfather was better than me. My father was better than me. My mother and brother were better than me. It is necessary for every Muslim to follow the Prophet of Allah". After these consolatory remarks the Imam said: "Dear sister! I administer an oath to you that you will follow my advice. Do not tear your dress on account of my suffering; do not scratch your face and do not lament".

The night of Āshura came to an end — the night which will never come again in the history of mankind, because the great personalities who had prepared themselves during that night for martyrdom in the path of Allah and were waiting for the morning to repay their debt to the Holy Prophet and Imam Ali cannot make their appearance once again. How can time reproduce such personalities when the conditions in which they appeared and attained so much perfection cannot be repeated.

The night of Āshura and the eleventh night of Muharram can be repeated only if another Qur'an is revealed once again and a prophet as great as the Last Prophet is appointed to the prophetic mission and a father like Ali and a mother like Fatima come into existence, and an atmosphere like that of Ahlul Bayt is present in the world.

That night can reappear only if the conditions are like those in which the seventeen young men of the family of Bani Hashim could return, men, about whom the Imam said that they were matchless on the face of the earth, and the means for the appearance of men like Habib ibn Mazahir Asadi and other companions of the Holy Imam come into existence.

That night can come again only if Islam is threatened by the dangers which it had to face in those days from Bani Umayya, and all the favourable and unfavourable conditions which prevailed in the year 61 A.H. come into existence once again.

MORNING OF ĀSHURA

During the night of Āshura the Imam and his companions

offered prayers, sought Divine forgiveness, and made supplications. The night eventually came to end and the morning of their day of glory arrived. It has been written by Shaykh Mufid in his book entitled al-Irshad and by Tabari in his Tarikh that after dawn prayers the Imam arrayed his companions, out of whom thirty two were mounted and forty were on foot. He entrusted the command of the right wing to Zuhayr bin Qayn and that of left wing to Habib ibn Mazahir and also entrusted the standard to his brother Abbas.

Umar bin Sād also arrayed his forces in the morning of that day. He entrusted the command of the right wing to Amr bin Hajjaj Zubaydi, of the left wing to Shimr bin Jawshan, of the mounted soldiers to Azra bin Qays Ahmadi and of the infantrymen to Shith bin Rabie and gave the standard in the hand of his slave.

On the day of Āshura the Imam addressed the people, and delivered speeches a number of times. However, he commenced the day with supplication and every time before he addressed the enemy he sought strength and guidance from Allah. All the invocations and addresses of the Imam are couched in highly eloquent and expressive language. He addressed the soldiers of the enemy army with a perfectly calm and composed mind as if all of them were his friends and devotees and had gathered together to assist him, although he knew very well that after these addresses those very people would attack him with 30,000 spears and kill him.

These speeches were being delivered by an orator, who was thirsty and did not have even a drop of water to moisten his lips. He was an orator, who knew that after a short time his women and children would be made captives by his impudent and sworn enemies. He was an orator, who had not eaten any food and was also thristy, although on the day of Āshura he did not complain about hunger on account of his lofty character and patience and mentioned thirst only.

Imam Sajjad has said: "The son of the Prophet's daughter was killed when he was thirsty and hungry".

It is really surprising that an orator, who is hungry and thirsty, should speak before thousands of enemies who are ready to kill him. Though there are numerous causes of his anxiety and uneasiness, yet he speaks in such a way that whatever he says is eloquent and expressive. He speaks with perfect peace of mind and courage. Whatever he says is firm and logical. He seldom expresses helplessness and broken-heartedness. As his companions are killed and the place around him becomes vacant his speech becomes all the more eloquent, and he displays more courage and greater peace of mind. Where can one find such an orator in the history of mankind — a helpless and friendless orator, whose speech is not affected by the prevailing conditions and who is perfectly calm and composed, although there is nothing to mitigate his anxiety and mental disturbance.

SUPPLICATION OF IMAM IN THE MORNING OF ĀSHURA

In the morning of the day of Āshura the horsemen of the enemy launched an attack on the ranks of the Imam. The Imam raised his hands in prayer and said: "O Lord! I depend on you in every affliction and am hopeful of Your blessing in every hardship. In every difficulty with which I am faced, You are my only remedy and resort. There have been many embarrassments which weakened my heart and no remedy for it was available. The friends did not assist me and the enemies rejoiced at my misfortune. However, when I ceased to seek assistance from everyone except You and sought the remedy only from You, You provided me solace and relief and removed the difficulty. Every blessing and goodness reaches us from You and everything should be sought from You only".

SERMON OF IMAM TO THE ARMY OF YAZID

Then the Imam mounted his camel and addressed the people with a very loud voice, which could be heard by most of them: "O people of Iraq! Listen to me and do not make haste to kill me so that I may tell you what I must, and appraise you of the reason for my coming to Iraq. If you accept my excuse, believe in what I say, and behave towards me fairly, you will level for yourselves the path of prosperity, and then you will have no reason to kill me. And even if you do not accept my excuse and deviate from the path of justice, you must ponder over the pros and cons of the matter before you kill me, and should not undertake such a delicate task rashly and without deliberation. My supporter is the Almighty Allah Who has revealed the Qur'an. Allah guards His deserving slaves".

When the Imam's speech reached this stage, he heard the wails and lamentations of his sisters and daughters, who were hearing him. Thereupon he said to his brother Abbas and his son Ali: "Go and silence these women, because hereafter they will have to weep much".

When the voice of the ladies of the Holy and impeccable family was no longer heard the Imam praised Allah and invoked blessings for the angels and the prophets. He spoke in more eloquent and expressive words than any orator, who had existed before him, or would come after him, and said to the people of Kufa: "O people! Identify me and see who I am. Then you will come to your senses and reproach yourselves. You should reflect carefully whether it is permissible for you to kill me and to disregard the reverence due to me.

"Am I not the son of your Prophet's daughter? Is the wasi (vicegerent) of your Prophet and his cousin and the first person, who expressed belief in Allah and confirmed what was brought by His Prophet, not my father? Is the Doyen of Martyrs Hamza bin Abdul Muttalib not the uncle of my father? Is the martyr Ja'far bin Abu Talib who has two wings and flies with Allah's angels not my uncle? Have you not heard that the Holy Prophet has said about me and my brother: "These two sons of mine are the chiefs of the young men of Paradise". If you think that whatever I am saying is true so much the better. I swear by Allah that I know Allah hates the liars, and I have never told a lie. And even if you do not believe in my words and refute me, there are still some companions of the Holy Prophet amongst you who, when asked, will apprise you of the facts. Ask Jābir bin Abdullah Ansari, Abu Sa'id Khudari, Nahl bin Sādi, Zayd bin Arqam or Anas bin Mālik, so that they may tell you that they have heard these words from the Holy Prophet about me and my brother. Is this tradition itself not sufficient to restrain you from killing me? If you are doubtful about this tradition can you doubt even this that I am the son of your Prophet's daughter? I swear by Allah that between East and West there is no son of the daughter of a Prophet except me either amongst you or amongst others.

"You should tell honestly whether I have killed anyone from amongst you so that you may take revenge! Is it that I have appropriated your wealth and you are claiming it? Have I injured you for which you have risen to compensate?" None of them, however, came forward to give a reply to what the Imam said.

He was, therefore, obliged to call some of them by their names and addressed them in these words: "O Shabath bin Rabie, Hajjār bin Abjar, Qays bin Ashath and Yazid bin Harith! Did you yourselves not write letters to me saying: "The fruits have become ripe and the lands are green and fresh and the soldiers of Iraq are ready to sacrifice their lives for you and you should, therefore, proceed to Iraq as early as possible?"

Tabari writes that in reply to the Imam they said: "We did not write any letter and are not aware of what you are saying." Truly speaking it is the height of meanness and foul play that the same persons who invited their Imam by means of a large number of letters and had signed those letters, were replying to him with utmost impudence that they had neither written any letters to him nor invited him!

Here we introduce to the readers one of those mean persons so that they may come to know to what extent one can go on account of worldliness and lack of will-power. They appear before the people in one guise today and in another guise tomorrow. One day they draw their swords for the sake of Allah and on another day against Him. If they are friends of Ali on one day they become his enemies on the following day. One day they kill Imam Husayn and on another day they claim to be the avengers of his murder. Shabath bin Rabie i.e. the very person who was the Commander of the Iraqi army on the day of Āshura and one of the killers of the Imam was at one time the mu'azzin of Sajāh and he accepted this office when she claimed to be a prophetess in the tribe of Bani Tamim. However, when Sajāh was disgraced he embraced Islam. He had also a hand in the murder of Uthman. Then he became one of the followers of Ali. Later he revolted against Ali, became one of his opponents and joined the Khawārij. After some time he left the Khawārij also and went in seclusion. In 61 A.H. he participated in killing Imam Husayn and his companions with great savagery. Afterwards when Mukhtār bin Abi Ubayd Thaqafi rose to avenge the murder of Imam Husayn he (Shabath) who himself was one of the murderers of the Imam joined Mukhtār as an avenger of the Imam's murder. Later he became the chief of Kufa police. He had a hand also in the murder of Mukhtār bin Abi Ubayd. He died in about 80 A.H.

How can those persons who do not have the least moral sense benefit from the celestial spirit of Husayn bin Ali and how can their untalented and corrupt souls receive any reflection of the sublime soul of the infallible Imam.

The Imam continued his address till he said: "By Allah I will not swear allegiance to these people like weak and mean persons and will not flee the battlefield like slaves while fighting against the rascals. I seek refuge in Allah from the mischief of you people and of every arrogant person who does not believe in the Day of Judgement".

In the meantime the preliminaries of the battle began to take place gradually. Umar bin Sād drew his bow, shot an arrow towards the companions of Imam Husayn and said: "You should bear witness before Ibn Ziyad (the governor) that I have started the battle earlier than everyone else".

Severe fighting continued till about noon. Most of the companions of the Imam were killed. The Imam offered the noon prayers along with his surviving companions in the form of emergency prayer (Salatul Khawf) i.e. he offered two rakāts. The fighting continued after the prayers till all the young men of Bani Hashim were killed. They met martyrdom one after the other. Even young children and sucklings had also the honour of being martyred. Gradually the moment arrived which changed the course of the history of Islam and recorded the honour of martyrdom for them in the pages of history. It is definitely so and there is no tragedy like the tragedy of Imam Husayn.

The exact number of the persons who were martyred on the day of Āshura is not known. It is usually said that seventy two persons were martyred with Imam Husayn.

Tabari writes that seventy two companions of the Holy Imam were martyred. Shaykh Mufid writes that Amr bin Sād sent the head of Imam Husayn to Ibn Ziyad on the very day of Āshura and ordered the heads of his companions and Ahlul Bayt to be severed from their bodies and these heads were seventy two in number.

Furthermore, in the homage (Ziyārat) which has been quoted in Iqbal of Sayyid bin Tawus the names of 72 martyrs of Karbala have been mentioned. This Ziyārat, the date of issue of which is 252 A.H. from the sacred region of Samarra (Iraq), must have been issued by Imam Hasan Askari and not by Imam Mahdi because in that year i.e. 252 A.H. Imam Mahdi was not born and his father Imam Hasan Askari remained alive for another eight years i.e. till 260 A.H. In this Ziyārat the names of seventeen members of the family of Bani Hashim followed by the names of fifty five other companions of the Imam have been mentioned.

In fact it is necessary to study the performance of these seventy two persons more minutely so that we may understand how this small group could bring this marvellous and eternal movement into existence. If Imam Husayn and his companions had a worldly motive and had they been killed like ordinary persons in order to achieve a material objective it would not have been possible for them to acquire such greatness in the world. Moreover, the very shape of this movement shows that it was not a material rising tainted by worldly and personal motives. The importance which this movement acquired in the history of Islam, rather in the history of the world, was for those very reasons which have already been mentioned and explained i.e. the conditions of the world of Islam of that time had cast a responsibility on the Imam. He assessed that he must rise and sacrifice his life, as the safety of Islam depended upon his rising.

NEGATIVE ATTITUDE TOWARDS THE TRAGEDY OF KARBALA

Imam Husayn rose for the sake of a sublime object. It was not his object that Yazid should cease to wield authority and instead of him he himself should come at the helm of affairs. In other words he had no personal grudge against Yazid. He supported truth in whatever shape it made its appearance and opposed falsehood whether it was headed by Yazid or someone else. These seventy two persons, whose number becomes seventy three with the addition of the Imam himself, rose so that religion might continue to live in history, and if it had not been so they would not have achieved the result from their grand sacrifice. They did not rise so that their sins might be forgiven. Their case was quite different from those who commit sins throughout their lives. They were different from those persons who accumulate wealth by unlawful means and then purify themselves by paying a visit to Karbala or Makkah. They even endow a part of this unlawful wealth so that Allah may overlook the balance amount. These seventy two persons were mostly neither sinners nor debtors. The leader of this movement was the infallible Imam and had not committed any sin throughout his life. The young men of the Bani Hashim family were pious persons and enjoyed an impeccable position. The companions of the Imam were also distinguished persons of their time in the matter of piety.

Did the martyrs, as many persons imagine, met martyrdom so that they might become a haven for the sinners of the ummah? In other words if the Muslims or Shi'ah before the martyrdom of Imam Husayn committed sins with anxiety and concern they may feel relieved, commit sins with impunity, deceive the people in any manner they like and may not feel any fear of accountability before Allah and of Divine punishment, because Imam Husayn was martyred to intercede for the sinners. The Imam met martyrdom so that the sins of the ummah might be forgiven. The people committed sins in the past and will continue to commit sins in future and the Imam made atonement for their sins. Jesus was crucified and the Christian sinners were relieved. Imam Husyan was also killed and guaranteed the salvation of the sinners of the ummah!

We seek refuge in Allah! This explanation and this way of thinking which may perhaps be preferred by most of the common people is exactly opposed to the real object of the Imam in this movement. He rose so that the people might fear Allah more, be on their guard more from the consequences of sin, which they have to endure in this world and in the Hereafter and pay more attention to the performance of their religious duties. He rose to eliminate sin, to restrain the people from doing unlawful things and to revive the spirit of piety in their hearts.

He rose to enjoin the people to do good and to restrain them from evil, to forestall corruption and sins, to strengthen the fear of Allah in their hearts and to draw their attention to Him so that the teachings provided by the Holy Qur'an might be put into practice in the Muslim ummah. Consequently it should be a nation which does not tell lies, does not commit treachery, is honest in whatever it does, is brave and courageous, does not worship anyone except Allah, does not submit to anything except truth, and does not tolerate anything except law and reasonable words.

The Imam was not killed so that he might tell the people: 'After my martyrdom there is no need to tell the truth, to be honest, to worship, to acquire lawful property, to refrain from unlawful acts and to have regard for the rights of the people'. The Imam did not say: 'I have been killed so that my supporters may remain immune from inconveniences and commit sins throughout their lives with perfect peace of mind'. This way of thinking is shameful for the Muslims and pains the sacred souls of the martyrs, who laid down their lives struggling in the path of Allah against sin and impiety. It is not at all possible that a man should be distant from Allah and close to the Imam, and may displease Allah and please the Imam; and may set aside a part of his sins for the Imam so that Allah may not call him to account.

Those people who think on these lines not only betray Islam and the spirit of the movement of Imam Husayn but it may be said that with the capital of the martyrdom of the Imam they have set up an organization of their own against the things declared lawful and unlawful by Allah and the reward and punishment prescribed by Him.

How unlucky is the Muslim, who does not offer prayers or observe fast or respect the rights of the people or does unlawful things or earns his livelihood by means of usury or other unlawful occupations, and then imagines happily that he is a disciple of Imam Husayn. Such a Muslim should be asked: "Why do you claim to be a disciple of Imam Husayn when neither you like his deeds nor he liked yours? He spoke the truth and you tell lies. He was honest and you commit treachery. He asked for extension of time during the night of Āshura so that he might spend that night in offering prayers, supplications, asking Divine forgiveness and reciting the Qur'an, whereas your nights are spent mostly in committing sins and doing undesirable things. He sacrificed in the path of Allah everything which he possessed whereas you cannot dispense with even a small coin for the sake of Allah.

Many persons claim to be the disciples of Imam Husayn and this is due to the fact that they have not recognized him properly and think that they can win his favour by means of usual homages, greetings and compliments. They are exactly like most of the persons who await the appearance of the Imam of the time and do not know that the appearance of the Imam is not profitable for them and the Imam of their imagination will not appear at all, as the Imam who will appear will not distribute money and posts among his disciples.

A person who has a true concept of Prophethood and Imamate does not get involved in such errors and does not attribute anything to the Prophet and Imam opposed to the Divine organization. He knows that the greatness of the Prophet and the Imam is based on obedience to Allah and one cannot benefit from the Prophet and the Imam except through obedience to the Almighty. In spite of all the hardships on the day of Ashura and the fact that the enemies did not agree to postpone fighting for a few moments for the performance of prayers, Imam Husayn offered noon prayers in congregation while fighting was still in progress and made two of his companions namely Zuhayr bin Qayn Bajali and Sa'id bin Abdullah Hanafi stand before him so that they might counteract the attacks of the enemies and enable the Imam to offer his prayers. How can such an Imam be willing that instead of offering prayers one may simply mourn his martyrdom and abandon necessary duties relying on his intercession and favour and commit unlawful acts?

Mourning for the Imam should make the people understand religion. It should bring them nearer to Allah and keep them away from sin. It should make them love religion all the more and revive the spirit of monotheism in them. They should realize that the gatherings held to mourn the martyrdom of Imam Husayn can please Allah and become the means of reward in the Hereafter only when they take place within the limits of obedience to the Almighty Allah and do not consist of falsehood and unlawful acts, because Allah cannot be worshipped by means of sin, and unlawful things cannot be made the basis of worship.

It is so, because Allah accepts only that act which is performed within the limits of piety. It reforms human soul and takes him to a higher spiritual stage. It is not possible that a good deed is done and it has no effect on the soul of man. It is the effect of a good deed which appears in the shape of spiritual reward in the Hereafter and unless a deed has a good effect on human soul it is meaningless to say that it carries spiritual reward. Similarly unless a deed has bad effect on human soul it is meaningless to say that it carries punishment in the Hereafter. Those persons who apparently do good deeds, but do not have the least effect on their souls and do not reform them are sadly mistaken. They remain at the same spiritual stage and still think that they have acquired abundant spiritual reward. Good deeds should provide food for spiritual faculties to man and should improve and reform his inner self. They should eradicate base motives from their mind and should develop good morals in their place and strengthen them. In case good deeds do not produce good effects it should be concluded that the deeds in question were not really good and were not performed properly. For it so happens very often that, contrary to what is imagined, such deeds have bad effects on human soul.

Allah says: *Whoever desires to meet his Lord should strive to do good deeds.* (Surah al-Kahf, 18:110).

TRAGEDY OF KARBALA
REMAINS UNFORGETTABLE

In the month of Muharram 61 A.H. a terrific tragedy took place in Iraq on the bank of the river Euphrates. It seemed in those days to be trivial and insignificant from the historical point of view. A large army which had been mobilized by the Umayyad regime besieged a group of persons numbering less than one hundred and put them under pressure so that they might take the oath of allegiance to the caliph of the time and submit to his authority. As the persons constituting this small group did not swear allegiance and did not surrender, a severe battle took place.

Its duration was very brief. The matter was settled in less than a day's time and all the persons constituting that small group were killed. It appeared at that time that like hundreds of other similar and more important events which continue to take place in human history this historical event would also be recorded in history and forgotten with the lapse of time.

The usual way of life of the Muslims did not change on account of this tragedy and everyone remained engaged in his daily business. The Muslim tradesmen were busy with their occupations. The masjids were frequented as usual. The Muslim preachers spoke about lawful and unlawful things, Paradise and Hell, spiritual reward and punishment and other religious matters from the pulpits. The only thing which was not talked about was this event which was apparently transient and without any effect. It was only the organization of the caliphate which published this event in various regions of the Islamic territories although in a brief and ambiguous manner. This was done with two objects in view; firstly that the people should come to know about the leaders of the movement opposed to the goverment having been killed, and should take a lesson from it, and similar risings should not take place in future; secondly that the caliphate should show itself guiltless and innocent in the matter and the leaders of the movement should be depicted as adventurous and mischievous. Husayn bin Ali who was at the head of the rising was to be introduced as opposed to truth and a liar.

Not only the regime of Bani Umayya and its supporters but even the majority of the Muslims of those days considered this tragedy to have culminated in the success of the killers of Imam Husayn. It was imagined that not only that the Imam and his companions had met martyrdom but thereafter none from amongst *Ahlul Bayt* (the progeny of the Holy Prophet) nor anyone else would pick up courage to oppose Yazid, and the hearts which had been wounded due to the maryrdom of the Imam would also heal up with the passage of time.

Those people were not aware of the true spirit of this tragic event which covered only a few hours. They did not know that with the passage of time the greatness and effect of this sacred campaign against falsehood and tyranny would continue to increase.

At the time of the occurrence of this tragedy there were only a few persons from amongst the Ahlul Bayt, who could assess its value and importance, speak about the effects, which it would have later on the Muslims and relieve them to some extent from the misunderstanding in which they were involved. These were the few persons who could unveil, with their speeches, the wickedness of the prevailing regime and the misunderstanding of the people and draw the attention of the people to the blow, which had been dealt to the enemy by those martyrs who were lying calmly in their graves, and to the tumult those heads would create in history later — the heads, which had been severed and held on the spears. The persons who went to various cities and regions in the capacity of prisoners, changed the thinking of the people and exonerated their sacred martyrs from the charges levelled against them in such a way that the facts of the event became crystal clear.

Here arises a question, which must be looked into and answered. The question is: Why did it so happen that the tragedy of Karbala occupied the central position amongst all the historical events of Islam and all religious risings, and no collective rising, struggle and martyrdom could acquire greatness in the world similar to that of the rising of Imam Husayn?

In the Battle of Uhud which took place near Madina in the month of Shawwal 3 A.H. between the Muslims and the polytheists of Makkah, a group of forty Muslims disobeyed their commander owing to some misunderstanding. Consequently 700 Muslims, who were fighting against 3000 polytheists, were defeated after having gained victory over the enemy. More than 80 persons were martyred. The bodies of most of the martyrs were mutilated in such a way that a sister could not identify the body of her brother except by means of a defect in his finger. Notwithstanding this the Battle of Uhud and the martyrdom of more than 70 to 80 Muslim mujahids has not acquired the grandeur of the tragedy of Karbala.

Another tragical event is that of the martyrs of Fakh, wherein a number of the descendants of the Holy Prophet were martyred near Makkah during the time of Hādi Abbasi.

Another similar event is that of the martyrdom of sixteen Hasani Sayyids who were imprisoned in the Hasimiyya jail of

Kufa under the orders of Mansur Dawāniqi. They died one after the other and Mansur did not allow their dead bodies to be buried. When all of them died he ordered the roof of the jail to be made to fall on the dead bodies of these sons of the Holy Prophet. They were neither bathed, nor shrouded nor buried. These as well as other similar tragedies of the history of Islam cannot equal the tragedy of Karbala and none of these martyrs can be matched with Imam Husayn.

Hamzah bin Abdul Muttalib, the magnanimous uncle of the Prophet of Allah was martyred in Uhud and he received the title of **Doyen of Martyrs** from Allah and His Prophet. However, if even his name is substituted for that of Imam Husayn it cannot be expected to create the same effect.

We do not intend to give and cannot perhaps give a complete and comprehensive answer to this question. It may, however, be said that besides the personality of the leader of this rising which is certainly a reason for its enjoying precedence over other risings, one of the most important and effective factors and causes for the superiority of Imam Husayn's rising was the chapter which was added to the tragedy after the martyrdom of Imam Husayn and his companions. It was a chapter on the creation of which the enemy himself insisted and thus unintentionally provided the means of his own disgrace. The result was that it was through Ahlul Bayt, who had been made prisoners, and also through those who had killed Imam Husayn, the world came to know about the reality and importance of this rising.

The enemies most brutally treated the Ahlul Bayt after the martyrdom of the Holy Imam and termination of fighting. They denuded the martyrs of their belongings, and plundered their dresses. They rushed into the tents, looted the property of Ahlul Bayt and set their tents on fire. They attempted to kill the ailing Imam Sajjad in his bed. They got the dead bodies of the martyrs trampled upon under the hooves of the horses and held their heads on the spears. They behaved harshly towards the bereaved prisoners and struck a stick on the lips and teeth of their Imam.

These heinous acts which recoiled upon the enemy themselves and made the real position known to the people commenced from Karbala and continued up to Damascus. Yazid himself took part in these atrocities and had a share in the consequent disgrace for himself and his associates.

On the contrary the Ahlul Bayt showed perfect greatness and magnanimity and behaved as if nothing had happened and they had experienced no hardship. Most of the people were under the impression that they had been defeated and eliminated, but wherever they went they talked about their own success and the enemy's disgrace. At a time when most of the people thought that the enemy had been victorious, they introduced themselves as exalted and successful, and the proud enemy as unfortunate and disgraced, in history. Contrary to the anticipation of the people they predicted the downfall of Bani Umayya.

If Ibn Sād and Ibn Ziyad, after the martyrdom of Imam Husayn and his companions, had even as a matter of expediency, shown honour and respect to the Ahlul Bayt of the Holy Prophet and offered condolences to them for the tragedy which had been brought about by themselves. They did not prevent the burial of the martyrs but buried them earlier than their own soldiers, and sent the Ahlul Bayt to Madina direct from Karbala with due honour and respect. If the barbarous activities of the enemy on the one hand and the impressive preachings of the Ahlul Bayt on the other, had not taken place, the martyrdom of the Imam and the tragedy of Karbala would certainly not have been reflected in the world in the shape which it assumed, and the enemies of the Imam, too, would not have been disgraced to such an extent. This too was as willed by Allah.

The enemy took the powerful preachers (Ahlul Bayt) forcibly as captives from one city to another and provided them an opportunity to speak to the people, who were mostly spectators of this tragedy, and introduce themselves to them and mentioned the Holy Prophet everywhere as their father or grandfather. The Ahlul Bayt got the first opportunity to display their eloquence on the 12th of Muharram when they were brought into the city of Kufa. Seeing Kufa was very painful for the Ahlul Bayt, because the major part of the Caliphate of Imam Ali had been spent in this city. In 41 A.H. the daughters of Imam Ali had gone from Kufa to Madina along with their brother Imam Hasan and now, after twenty years, they had arrived as prisoners in a city where they had ruled for about four years. The people of Iraq who had been the Nahrawān supporters of Ali in the Battle of the Camel, Siffin and Nahrawān had now killed his son and taken his other descendants captives.

However, it might be said that the orators of Ahlul Bayt had come from Madina and the Hijaz to Kufa and Iraq to address the people and the people assembled in the lanes and bazaars to hear their speeches. They commenced their mission from the very 12th day of Muharram and spoke out to the people without fear. When there was no chance of speaking in the bazaar or at the door and no audience other than the court of Ibn Ziyad was available, they continued their task there also, although it was in the shape of replies to his questions, and then returned to the prison of Kufa. The speeches of these brave and matchless orators extremely impressed the people, stirred their hearts and changed their views. Tears began to trickle from their eyes and they realized their grave error. These speeches roused the sentiments of the people and the value and importance of this event became known to them. The efforts of the enemy to tamper with the facts of this event were frustrated and the tragedy of Karbala was recorded in history in its true shape.

The severe thirst of Ahlul Bayt was confirmed in the pages of history. The misdeeds of the enemy were recorded. History also shows the spiritual eminence of the companions and supporters of the Imam. This sentence of Ali bin Husayn is also recorded in history: "When we are on the right path why should we fear death?" The following words of Qasim bin Hasan also brighten the pages of history: "For me death is sweeter than honey". The devotion and the manner of speech of Muslim bin Awsaja has been embodied in these words: "If we withdraw our support from you and fail in performing this duty what excuse shall we put forward before Allah? I swear by Allah that so long as I live I shall not give up my support to you till I may lay down my life for your sake and am killed earlier than all your other friends".

The Imam had permitted Sa'id bin Abdullah Hanafi to go away. His spiritual greatness, character and courage is summed up in this sentence: "I swear by Allah that even if I am killed and am brought to life again and am then burnt in fire and my ashes are scattered in the air and this process is repeated seventy times I shall not leave you till I am martyred in this path".

The following words have made the name of Bishr bin Amr everlasting in the history of the martyrs of Islam: "O Husayn bin Ali! May the fierce animals of the desert tear me into pieces if I leave you and enquire about your circumstances from others. Why should I withdraw my support to you when you are alone and friendless? I am not at all going to do any such thing". He expressed his devotion in these words: "Is it possible that I should leave the son of the Holy Prophet at the mercy of the enemies and try to save my own life? May Allah not bring such a day".

The following words uttered by other honourable martyrs of Karbala, which show their matchless magnanimity, valour, sincerity and steadfastness are recorded in the pages of history:

Amr bin Qurza Ansari said while he was breathing his last: "O son of the Holy Prophet! Have I been faithful and have I discharged my duty?"

Habib bin Mazahir Asadi said to Muslim bin Awsaja when the latter was about to die: "Muslim! I congratulate you for you are going to Paradise earlier than us".

Muslim who was lying on the ground said in reply: "Habib! I am going, but you must not desert the Imam".

Abu Thamama Sāidi said to the Imam at about noon: "What a good thing it would be if we offer the noon prayers along with you before we are martyred!"

If those speeches which were delivered in Syria had not been there and if the sister and son of Imam Husayn had not got opportunities to speak in the courts of Ibn Ziyad and Yazid, the event of the martyrdom of Imam Husayn and his companions might not have been recorded in history in its present form. History would have ignored the true accounts. Even the sentence uttered by a black slave who said to the Imam: "Do not deprive me of martyrdom and let me acquit myself of my responsibility in spite of my having a black face" would have been forgotten.

Indeed there are very few chapters in history which remained immune from any change to such an extent. Historians often differ about most of the details of historical facts, but it may be said with certainty that the tragedy of the martyrdom of Imam Husayn is one of the most luminous, sublime and the most unique chapters of history. None has been able to tamper with this historical event and to write contrary to the facts. The renowned historians like Shaykh Mufid, Tabari and Abul Faraj Isfahani have unanimously recorded the exact details of this tragedy. As we have already mentioned, its reason was that the enemy made a grave mistake and insisted unintentionally that this tragic event should be related in Kufa — the centre of Iraq, Damascus — the centre of Syria and Madina — the centre of the Hijaz by the Ahlul Bayt, who had been taken prisoners and were eye-witnesses of the happenings on the day of Āshura and who could explain them better than anyone else. Ali bin Husayn related these events to the people one day in the bazaar of Kufa, on another day in the Jamea Masjid of Damascus, and after some time in Madina, in such a way that the position became crystal clear to them as if they themselves had been present in Karbala on the day of Āshura.

At last Yazid felt regretful on account of these developments. He realized correctly that it was a grave mistake to bring the women and children to Kufa and Syria as prisoners and it would have been better if the matter had ended with the martyrdom of Imam Husayn and his companions, and a new chapter had not been opened, and the Ahlul Bayt had not been allowed to speak in the bazaars and before the public gatherings. However, it was then too late. What had been said with the lips could not be returned to the breasts and the scenes seen by the people and the speeches heard by them could not be wiped out from their memory. It was no longer possible that those, who had cried loudly in the bazaars, should once again consider the descendants of the Holy Prophet, about whom the verse of Purification (33:33) was revealed, rebellious and fit to be killed!

When common people are overtaken by a calamity they usually conceal it and do not wish that others should know what has befallen them. Contrary to this the Ahlul Bayt endeavoured that as far as possible they should apprise the people of what they had suffered. It was for this reason that whenever they got an opportunity they mentioned the events of Karbala in detail and even Imam Husayn who possessed the highest human and Islamic virtues was usually mentioned with the title of the martyr.

THE SERMON OF IMAM SAJJAD IN KUFA

The fourth Imam addressed the people of Kufa and delivered a sermon before them. After making a sign to them to keep silent, he said: "O people! Whoever knows me knows me, and he, who does not know me, should know that I am the son of that person, who was dishonoured and whose entire belongings were looted and plundered, and whose women and children were made prisoners .... ".

Of course, if the fourth Imam had not mentioned the plundering and maltreatment by the enemy, and had not revealed openly the details of the event one or two days after it had taken place, when the agents of the regime were still jubilant on account of their apparent success, and did not know that they had dug their grave with their own hands, it was not unlikely that the matter might have been given a different colour in the history of Islam, and it might have been said that the Ahlul Bayt were taken to Kufa and Syria with a view to showing them honour and consoling them, and no constraint or force was involved. However, the fourth Imam depicted the true scene of the tragedy of Karbala in the very first sentence of his sermon and imprinted it on the hearts of the people. Eventually these very speeches and writings were recorded in the third century in reliable Islamic history books and it became impossible even for the succeeding Ummayyad dynasty to change even one line of it, in spite of all their power, or at least to delete from the pages of history the incident of the plundering of the tents and stripping the body of the Imam. They could not make the Muslims forget these shameful deeds.

The *Ahlul Bayt* (family) of the Imam, who had been made prisoners, deprived Bani Umayya of even this power, and performed such a glorious deed that it not only became impossible for the enemy to tamper with the facts, but minute details of the hideous acts of the murderers of the Imam were also recorded in history.

Have not Shaykh Mufid and Tabari written that whatever dress was there on the body of the Imam was plundered after his martyrdom? The Imam's shirt was removed from his body by Ishaq bin Haiwa. His vest was taken away by Bahr bin Kāb Tamimi. His turban was taken by Akhnas bin Marthad. His sword was taken by a man belonging to the tribe of Bani Dārm. Qays bin Ashath bin Qays took possession of his Qatifa (mantle). Qays was later known in Kufa as Qays of Qatifa. The Imam's shoes were removed from his feet by a man named Aswad, who belonged to the tribe of Awd. Then they made a rush on the tents and plundered everything including clothes and camels. They displayed their utmost meanness by removing even the head-dresses of women. Who wrote and recorded these detailed historical facts? It was these very speeches and addresses of Ahlul Bayt which transferred the true facts of Āshura clearly and explicitly to the pages of history. History has not only recorded that Ibn Ziyad gave orders to Ibn Sād to let the body of the Imam be trampled upon by the horses, but has also given full details of this proceeding.

Shaykh Mufid, Tabari and other historians have written that Ibn Sād reached the tents, when some persons wanted to kill the fourth Imam. He, however, ordered that none should molest the ailing person or inconvenience the bereaved women in the tents. And when it was brought to his notice that the tents had been plundered he ordered those who had taken away something from them to return it. However, not a single person returned anything. Then to comply with Ibn Ziyad's orders, Ibn Sād called the volunteers to trample upon the sacred body of the Imam. He was perhaps also cautious in the matter and he did not himself nominate some persons to carry out the orders lest they should decline to undertake such a shameful act. However, this precaution was unnecessary and the possibility was quite remote. As said by great historians ten persons volunteered themselves for the purpose. They mounted their horses with great enthusiasm and performed the job according to his wishes. What is surprising is that the names of these heartless bastards have also been recorded in history and the Islamic historians have mentioned the names and particulars of all of them. Tabari and Mufid have mentioned their names only and recorded that one of the aforesaid ten persons was Ishaq bin Haiwa Hazrami who looted the shirt of the Imam and the other was Akhnas bin Murthad, who took away his turban from his head.

If Imam Sajjad had kept quiet on account of his illness, fatigue caused by the journey, captivity and dejection, and had not proclaimed in the bazaar of Kufa what he had seen on the day of Āshura, and if Umme Kulsum and Zaynab, daughters of Imam Ali and Fatima and daughter of Imam Husayn had also not spoken in the bazaar of Kufa, and had not checked the enemy of an opportunity to tamper with history, how could Bani Umayya permit that the story of their indelible shame and disgrace should form a part of the history of Islam and Bani Hashim should expel their rival for ever from the field of humanity, virtue and piety.

When these speeches were being delivered and these addresses were reaching the ears of the people it was the speakers themselves who knew very well what they were saying and doing, and they made no mistake in assessing the value of their words. Other people could not, however, realize as to what power the speeches of Ahlul Bayt, which were being delivered at times in the bazaars, at the doors and in general gatherings and at times in the masjids, would give to the tragedy of Karbala and to what extent they would change the thinking of the people in the course of time. Most of the people did not understand more than that the persons, whose father had been killed, and who were bereaved, were telling the tale of their woe, crying and shedding tears owing to the calamity which had befallen them. They had no idea that the Ahlul Bayt were in fact performing their part in the Divine mission of this rising.

The task undertaken by the Imam could not be completed without the explanation and interpretation which was being given by them. There was a real danger that this Divine campaign which had been led by the most sacred personalities of Islam might, at a later stage, be made to appear a material movement prompted by worldly motives and the factual position might be concealed from the Muslims and their future generations for ever, leaving them with a few pages of history containing fabricated tales. It was for this reason that Ali bin Husayn ignored his illness and mourning, and lady Zaynab, her sister, and nephew also forgot their captivity and bereavement. Instead of assuming the posture of helpless and bereaved persons or flattering the enemy, they commenced their mission of informing the people of the true facts with perfect determination, and availed of even the smallest opportunity to achieve their end. So much so that even if anyone abused them on account of ignorance or perversion, they considered it to be a valuable opportunity and made it an excuse to talk with him. By this means they changed the heart of the reviler in such a way that he repented immediately, became a supporter of Ahlul Bayt and expressed regret for what he had said.

The Ahlul Bayt acted so intelligently that they benefited even from the abuses hurled upon them. Even if someone addressed them slanderously or tauntingly they considered it an opportunity to talk to him and to remove misunderstandings from the minds of the people.

After mentioning the misconduct of the enemy in a few words which were recorded in history, Imam Sajjad said thus while addressing the people of Kufa: "I am the son of the man who was beheaded on the bank of the Euphrates although he had not shed the blood or usurped the right of anyone. (i.e. he was killed without any offence committed by him). I am the son of the man who was attacked by a huge number of people and martyred when he was no longer capable of fighting and had fallen on the ground owing to weakness. This is sufficient honour for us". By uttering these words the fourth Imam obliged the people to make more investigations about the heart-rending martyrdom of Imam Husayn, because merely being killed cannot be reckoned to be an honour, particularly an honour in the presence of which no other honour should be needed. Imam Zaynul 'Ābidin said: "It is a sufficient honour for us that our blood was shed, our property was looted, we were insulted and our women and children were made prisoners". The Imam wanted the people to ponder as to what the object of this rising was, what its leader desired, and what he did. If he wanted to become the ruler, and as another person had attained to this office he was unhappy, and sacrificed his life and property in an effort to achieve his object, being killed in this way can never be a source of pride, rather it would be a matter of shame. Then how could the fourth Imam feel proud of it and say:

"This honour is sufficient for us?"

On hearing these words the people must have wondered as to how this event could be a source of pride. They might have thought: 'Are people not killed? Are there no casualties in political wars? Is there little loss of property and life in social disturbances? What sort of honour is it that one's property is looted, his tents are set on fire and his near ones are killed. These are afflictions but not a source of pride'. But the words of Imam Sajjad obliged the people to make a deeper study and investigation to assess the importance and value of this rising in the history of Islam and to find out what these persons were saying and what weight their words carried and why they were not calm and quiet like other people and why they were not willing to accept any offer made by the ruler in power.

What was the harm if Imam Husayn had taken the oath of allegiance to Yazid and lived honourably among the Muslims without losing his friends and his own life? These very expressions of the fourth Imam prepared the people to hear, stimulated their thoughts and roused them from slumber. Possibly many persons might have been saying: "It is good that these people have been killed, life has returned to normal, the roads to Iraq which were blocked for some days have been re-opened and the traffic and transportation which had become difficult has returned to its usual course'.

While the people were thinking on these lines the fourth Imam cried suddenly: "They killed us and plundered whatever we had and this is a sufficient honour for us". This interpretation gave a jerk to the people and created in them a desire to make further investigations.

Then Imam Sajjad said: "O people! I put you on your oath to tell me in the name of Allah, whether you know that at one time you wrote letters to my father and then deceived him. You made firm promises with him and then rose to fight against him. May Allah destroy you, may you reap the harvest of your misdeeds in both the worlds, and may you be disgraced for the indecent policy which you have adopted. How will you face the Prophet of Allah when you are brought before him on the Day of Judgement and with which eyes will you look at him? At that time the Holy Prophet will tell you: "You have killed my children and behaved towards me dishonourably. You are not my followers".

These few sentences of the Imam changed the thinking of the people of Kufa and the smiling faces of those persons who had mostly come to see the prisoners blushed with shame. They tried to control themselves but could not do so. At last the groanings and lamentations of the people could be heard from different sides. They began reproaching one another. One of them said: "What an evil thing you have done! You annihilated yourselves". Another replied: "But what can we do now?"

While the people were weeping and sighing the Imam addressed them once again in these words: "May Allah bless those, who accept my advice and put into practice my recommendations about their duty to Allah, the Prophet of Allah and the Progeny of the Prophet, for it is incumbent upon us to follow the Prophet of Allah".

This brief address brought about such a turn in the minds of the people that they cried: "O son of the Prophet of Allah! All of us will hear what you say and obey your orders. We will honour the promises made with you. We will not forsake you and will not side with anyone else. We are ready to act upon whatever you say. We will fight with him, against whom you fight, and will make peace with him, with whom you make peace. We are prepared even to take steps to arrest Yazid. We hate those who oppress you".

It would appear from these statements of the people as quoted by Ibn Tawus that they had not yet understood the object of the Imam. They perhaps thought that he intended to fight and wished to mobilize an army for the purpose. They did not know that part of the movement which involved armed rising and martyrdom had already been completed, and there was no need any longer of warfare and bloodshed. What remained to be accomplished were these very speeches, sermons and addresses which were the only means of reflecting the events of Āshura in the history of Islam and in the minds of the Muslims. Moreover, the promises, which they were making with the fourth Imam, and the assurances, which they were giving him, were not dissimilar to the assurances and promises, which they had held out to Imam Husayn. As such the assurances given by them had no value and could not be relied upon. They fell in the category of the oath of allegiance taken by them to Muslim bin Aqil and the letters written by them to Imam Husayn.

Hence, Imam Sajjad said: "O unfaithful and inconstant people! You will never succeed. Do you want to behave towards me in the same manner in which you behaved towards my forefathers? No, it cannot be so. I swear by Allah that the wounds of my heart have not yet healed up. Yesterday my father and his companions met martyrdom. I have not yet forgotten my being bereaved of the Holy Prophet, my father and my brothers have not overcome this grief. What I want you to do is that you should neither support us nor oppose us. Husayn bin Ali's being martyred is also not surprising. Was not his father Ali better than him and was he not assassinated? O Kufians! It was you, who killed Ali. May I be sacrificed for my father who was martyred on the bank of the Euphrates. The punishment for his killers is Hell".

Then he added: "We shall be perfectly satisfied with you if you give up the practice of siding with us on one day and opposing us on another day".

The fourth Imam did not speak more and could not get an opportunity to speak till the Ahlul Bayt were brought one day before Ibn Ziyad in a public assembly. There also he availed of the opportunity to speak. By uttering a few sentences though they were brief, he impressed the gathering.

IMAM SAJJAD IN THE COURT OF IBN ZIYAD

Imam Sajjad was brought to Ibn Ziyad's court and made to stand before that tyrant. "Who are you?" He asked the Imam. The Imam replied: "I am Ali ibn Husayn". He said: "Did Allah not kill Ali ibn Husayn?" The Imam replied: "I had a brother whose name was also Ali and the people killed him". (The Imam meant to tell Ibn Ziyad not to attribute sin to Allah and not to say something irrelevant, because it was the people and not Allah who killed Ali ibn Husayn in Karbala). Ibn Ziyad said: "It is not so. Allah killed him". In reply to this the Imam recited a verse of the Qur'an: *Allah takes the souls when the time of their death comes*, (Surah al-Zumar, 39:42) but He is not their killer. When Ibn Ziyad saw that the young ailing prisoner had given back replies time and again to what he said he got annoyed and said: "Do you still have courage to resist what I say?" Then he said to his men: "Take him away and chop off his head".

On hearing this lady Zaynab got very much worried and disturbed. However, the only reply which the fourth Imam gave to Ibn Ziyad was this: "If you kill me with whom will you send these women?" Then he added: "After killing me you should send with them a pious Muslim, who should behave towards them according to the orders of Islam".

The fourth Imam did not utter a sentence requesting Ibn Ziyad to spare his life. He only said: "When I am killed do not send with these sacred women a man, who is impious and a non-Muslim".*

In Syria also Imam Sajjad got some such opportunities and availed of them to the maximum possible extent. When Imam Sajjad was a captive in Damascus a man named Ibrahim bin Talha bin Ubaydullah Taymi came before him in the Bazaar and said tauntingly: "O Ali bin Husayn! Who was victorious in this battle?" He meant to say that the Ahlul Bayt suffered a crushing defeat and their enemies won a glorious victory.

The Imam said to him in reply: "Now that the time for prayers is approaching you should pronounce Azān and Iqāmah so that you may come to know and understand clearly as to who has been victorious". The Imam meant to tell him this: 'As you belong to the Taym tribe of Quraysh you are perhaps happy for some reasons that Bani Hashim have suffered defeat. However, so long as you are a Muslim it is necessary for you to pronounce in Azān as well as Iqāmah: "I testify that Muhammad is the Prophet of Allah". We and not others are the descendants and heirs of Prophet Muhammad without mentioning whose name and invoking Divine blessings for him the prayers of any Muslim are not acceptable. Hence, so long as Islam exists the honour and glory belonging to us, the descendants of Muhammad, will also remain established and confirmed'.

*The author of Luhuf says: "When Ibn Ziyad ordered that Ali ibn Husayn should be killed. . . . Lady Zaynab said: "O son of Ziyad! If you want to kill him kill me along with him". The Imam, however, said: "Dear aunt! Be calm. I shall give him a reply myself". Then he said: "O son of Ziyad! Do you threaten to kill me? Don't you know that being killed is our legacy and martyrdom is an honour for us".

The Imam uttered these brief but fascinating words in reply to one person and perhaps uttered it in a low tone, but these very words uttered in low tones continue to resound in history. At times it so happens that only one sentence becomes the cause of coming into existence of many important books, speeches and articles. At that time neither Ibrahim, nor Talha nor anyone else could assess the importance of these brief words and pay attention to its essence overlooking its form, but the Imam knew that even if he had come to Syria to utter only this brief sentence and to say nothing else during this journey, it would be sufficient to achieve the object he had in view, and those who could not make the requisite assessment at that time would shortly later applaud the plan chalked out by Imam Husayn and his companions and Ahlul Bayt.

Imam Sajjad got another opportunity when the Ahlul Bayt were made to stand by the gate of the Masjid of Damascus, the place where the prisoners were usually kept. An old man, who was a Syrian, came there and said: "I thank Allah that He has killed and destroyed you and annihilated seditious people like you". Then he began abusing the Ahlul Bayt. The fourth Imam kept quiet and let him speak on till he became silent. In his reply, however, he did not say any improper thing nor complained to the old man of using abusive language. At that time the fourth Imam was ill and was also a traveller and had experienced the hardships of the journey from Kufa to Damascus. He was also bereaved and afflicted. Furthermore, he had arrived in a city which was at that time the centre of the enemy of Ahlul Bayt. The Syrian used abusive language, expressed pleasure and thanked Allah for what had happened. When all these causes of annoyance and fury are present who can keep calm and not lose temper or give a harsh reply? It is not possible for a person to control himself in such circumstances, whoever he may be. However, the Imam behaved towards the old Syrian like a kind and sympathetic teacher, as if he had experienced nothing from him except kindness and respect and asked him mildly: "Have you read the Qur'an?" He replied "Yes, why not?" Thereupon the Imam said: "Have you not read the verse: *Say, O Muhammad! I do not want from you any recompense for my preaching to you except that you should love my kin.* (Surah al-Shura, 42:23)

The man replied: "Yes, I have". The Imam said: "I swear by Allah that we are the kinsmen of the Holy Prophet".

It may be said with certainty that this very question must have created a tumult in the mind of the man. Then he asked the man: "Have you not read this verse: *People of the house, Allah wants to remove all kinds of uncleanliness from you and to purify you thoroughly*". (Surah al-Ahzab, 33:33) He replied: "Yes. I have". The Imam said: "We are the people of the Household whose infallibility has been testified by Allah". The Syrian thereupon raised his hands in prayer and said thrice: "O Allah! I repent and am regretful for what I have done. O Lord! I am disgusted with those who are the enemies of the progeny of the Holy Prophet and who have killed them. I do not know how it so happened; I have read the Qur'an but did not pay attention to these verses".

The fourth Imam got another such opportunity in the court of Yazid when the Ahlul Bayt were brought before him for the first time. The Imam who had been chained during his journey from Kufa to Damascus said to Yazid: "O Yazid! I put you on oath, in the name of Allah, just to imagine how the Holy Prophet will feel if he sees us in this condition?" These words proved to be very effective. All those who were present there, began to weep and Yazid ordered the fetters to be removed from the body of the fourth Imam. Another important thing was that the Imam addressed Yazid by name and did not call him, the Commander of the Faithful, as was customary. It was thus recorded in history that the Ahlul Bayt did not call Yazid, the Commander of the Faithful, even when they were chained and made captives and did not recognize him to be the successor and caliph of the Holy Prophet. History of Islam bears witness to the fact that none of the Ahlul Bayt who had been made prisoners addressed Yazid except by his name.

SERMON OF IMAM SAJJAD
IN THE MOSQUE OF DAMASCUS

The fourth Imam got the best opportunity on the day on which the official preacher mounted the pulpit and abused Imam Ali and his children and eloquently praised Mu'awiya and his descendants, and thereupon the Imam said to Yazid: "Do you permit me also to ascend these pieces of wood and to say a few things which may please Allah and also become the means of the hearers earning spiritual reward". This brief statement of the Imam is very subtle. It may be said that it contains the gist of what the Imam wanted to say. He did not call the pulpit in question a pulpit but said to Yazid: "Permit me to ascend these pieces of wood". What he meant to say was 'that everything which is given the shape of a pulpit, on which someone ascends and then delivers a speech, is not a pulpit. These pieces of wood are the means for destroying the pulpits. This preacher has sold his faith for material benefits, because he has consented to please the people and to oppose Allah, and consequently his destination is Hell. In other words he said that what the preacher was saying was the cause of Divine wrath, because it is not possible to please Allah by abusing a man like Ali ibn Abi Talib'.

When Imam Sajjad said: "I want to say a few things which may be the means of the hearers earning spiritual reward"; he meant that what the preacher was saying could only involve the people in sin and adversity and could not produce any result except the perversion of the people. The people insisted that Yazid should accord the Imam permission, but he declined persistently. At last he (Yazid) said: "These are the people, who were fed on knowledge and wisdom while the others were sucklings and children. If I permit him to speak he will disgrace me in the eyes of the people". Eventually, however, he had to accede to the demand of the people and the fourth Imam mounted the pulpit. He said things which made a serious impact on the minds of the people and they began to cry and lament.

During the course of his address Imam Sajjad specified the place of Ahlul Bayt in the realm of Islam and said: "O people! Allah has given us six things and our superiority to others is based on seven pillars. The six things which He has given us are: knowledge, forbearance, generosity and mercy, eloquence, valour and heartfelt love of the believers i.e. people cannot be forced to become our friends, devotees and adherents. Allah has so willed that the faithful people should love us and it is not possible to prevent this by any means and to do something as a consequence of which people may love others and hate us. Our superiority to others is also based on these seven pillars

Muhammad, the Prophet of Allah, his successor, Ali ibn Abi Talib, the Doyen of the Martyrs Hamza, Ja'far Tayyar, Hasan and Husayn, the two grandsons of the Holy Prophet of this nation, and Mehdi, the saviour (of the oppressed and deprived people of the world) of this nation and the Imam of the last age. All these are from our Holy Family".

Imam Sajjad, the fourth Imam, meant to say that Yazid should in the first instance deprive the Ahlul Bayt of these honours and transfer the same to himself and then quarrel with them. Otherwise, so long as these honours of Islam belonged to the Ahlul Bayt how could they be disgraced and ignored, how could their rights be given to others and how could the hearts devoted to them be turned towards others!

The Imam introduced himself and the matters took such a turn that Yazid and his supporters were obliged to disrupt his speech. They asked the mu'azzin to pronounce Azān. Naturally the Imam, too, had to become silent but at the same time he availed of another opportunity. When the mu'azzin said: "I testify that Muhammad is the Prophet of Allah" he took off his turban and said: "O mu'azzin! I beseech you in the name of this very Muhammad to keep quiet". Then he turned to Yazid and said: "Is this great and magnanimous Prophet your grandfather or our grandfather? If you say that he is your grandfather all of them know that you will be telling a lie. And if you say that he is my grandfather why did you kill my father and plundered his property and made his women captives?" Then he stretched his hand and tore his collar and continued to speak till the people were deeply moved and dispersed in a state of distress.

JOURNEY OF AHLUL BAYT
TO KUFA AND DAMASCUS

The history of the sacred movement and rising of Imam Husayn is one of the most glorious chapters of the history of Islam. Although this period of less than a year was very short and transient from the point of view of length of time, it was very forcible and everlasting from the point of view of quality and the results which it produced. This short historical period may be reckoned to have commenced in the last days of the month of Rajab of 60 A.H. i.e. with Imam Husayn's departure from Madina to Makkah and may also be treated to have ended with the return of the Ahlul Bayt to Madina, although the date of the arrival of the Ahlul Bayt to their house is not known and we are not aware for how many months they stayed in Damascus, when they left Syria for Madina, and how much time was spent in their journey from Syria to Madina. In short, it may be said with certainty that a year had not yet passed since the departure of Ahlul Bayt from Madina in the month of Rajab when the fourth Imam returned to Madina along with his Holy Family after spending the period of captivity. They came from Damascus to Madina direct or via Karbala.

However, as regards the incident that Ahlul Bayt came from Syria to Iraq and reached Karbala on the 20th of Safar is entirely incredible and no reliable evidence is available to support this historical myth. The Ahlul Bayt went from Madina to Makkah in the month of Rajab of the year 60 A.H. and proceeded from Makkah to Iraq in the same year in the month of Zil Haj. In the month of Muharram of the year 61 A.H. they were taken to Kufa as prisoners after the martyrdom of Imam Husayn and his illustrious companions. After they had remained in Kufa for quite some time they were sent to Syria in compliance with the orders received from Yazid. They remained there for a period which is not exactly known, and then returned to Madina.

The fact is that the dates of the departure of Ahlul Bayt from Kufa for Syria, their arrival in Damascus, the period of their stay in the capital of Yazid, the dates of their departure from Damascus and arrival in Madina are not exactly known. It may, however, be said on the basis of probability and guess and not with certainty that after the family of Imam Husayn arrived in Kufa on the 12th of Muharram of the year 61 A.H. they remained imprisoned in Kufa for about a month i.e. till after the middle of the month of Safar and were sent to Syria a day or two before the 40th day of the martyrdom of Imam Husayn and his companions. As written by some historians they reached Damascus in about the middle of the month of Rabiul Awwal. It cannot be said as to how long they remained in Damascus; when they departed from there and on which date they arrived in Madina. If reliable evidence had been available to the effect that the Ahlul Bayt came to Karbala at the time of the Arba'in (40th day) of the martyrdom of Imam Husayn, it could be said that this happened when they went to Syria and not at the time of their return from there. This is so because if, as stated by some historians, the Ahlul Bayt were sent to Syria, on receipt of orders from Yazid, within about three days after the first half of the month of Safar, it does not seem impossible that they went via Karbala where they paid homage to the sacred resting places of their dear ones and martyrs on the 20th of Safar and then proceeded to Damascus. However, we do not have any reliable evidence even for this statement and only some sporadic evidences in this behalf can be culled from history.

It is not possible to believe that the Ahlul Bayt reached Syria on the day of Arba'in or left Damascus for Madina or reached Madina on such a day. It is, therefore, advisable that such baseless matters should not be mentioned in connection with Āshura and Arba'in and one should content oneself with only those things which are reported from reliable sources. Neither Imam Sajjad came from Syria to Iraq, nor the Ahlul Bayt came to Karbala on their return from Syria, nor did Jabir bin Abdullah Ansari and Atiyya bin Sād bin Junada Awfi meet the fourth Imam and the Ahlul Bayt when they went to perform pilgrimage to Karbala on the day of Arba'in. In the narrations related to homage by Jabir and Atiyya it has not at all been mentioned that they met Imam Sajjad or Ahlul Bayt. This story has been invented by the story-tellers.

Only Sayyid bin Tawus has written in Luhuf, contrary to the historical and geographical evidence, that on return from Damascus the Ahlul Bayt proceeded to Iraq when they reached the parting of the ways to Iraq and the Hijaz (a place which is not identified even by the geographers) and on the 40th day of the Āshura they reached Karbala. Sayyid bin Tawus was, no doubt, a great person. Allama Hilli has acknowledged that he performed unusual feats and there is no denying the fact that he enjoyed high status. However, it is not possible to attach any value to this statement of his from the historical viewpoint and it is not known whether he himself believed in this narration which is not based on any authority.

In any case this matter needs investigation and research.

As a matter of principle it is opposed to common sense that everything should be accepted without any investigation, study and comment. Even if Sayyid bin Tawus had been our contemporary we would not have approached that great scholar in this particular matter, and his remark in a book, which according to the researchers was written in his youth, would not have carried any historical value for us. It is a vulgar and foolish way of thinking that whatever is said by anyone or is written in any book should be accepted as correct and free from errors. The path of research and criticism is always open to the intelligent persons and research scholars of history. According to the Muslims of the world in general there is only one person whose remarks cannot be erroneous in the least and he is the Holy Prophet. According to the Shi'ah school, however, this distinction is enjoyed by the Holy Prophet as well as by lady Fatima Zahra and the twelve Imams whose infallibility is proved by reason as well as by narrations.

EVENTS OF KARBALA
REMAINED SAFE FROM DISTORTION

Notwithstanding all that has been said above it should be kept in mind that the tragic event of Karbala has remained more safe and immune from distortion as campared with most of the other historical events, and this event was so clear, explicit and unexpected that even the enemies of Imam Ali ibn Abi Talib and Imam Hasan bowed their heads before it in respect and praised it. Whoever has written on this subject, whether he be the historian Tabari or Abul Faraj Isahani or Ibn Wāzeh Kātib or Shaykh Mufid, the great Shi'ah scholar of the later part of the fourth century, has written nothing except the greatness, valour, frankness, courage, liberty and manliness of Imam Husayn — the leader of this rising.

In the year 60 — 61 A.H. the campaign by Imam Husayn was accomplished in such circumstances that it may be said that even those persons who did not hesitate from making any distortion in history could not pick up courage to tamper with this sacred chapter of history and to tarnish the brilliant face of the movement of Imam Husayn. Those persons, who tamper with historical events or show a personality contrary to what it actually is, do so only when they find the circumstances favourable for this purpose, and are able to lead the people into error. However, it often happens that even the adversaries cannot help admitting and praising one's greatness, purity and piety.

In 7 A.H. the hostility of the Umayyad Abu Sufyan demanded that he should have spoken ill of the Holy Prophet before the Roman Emperor as far as possible, concealed his honesty, magnanimity, and truthfulness and introduced him as an avaricious person and a liar. However, he could not find an opportunity to do so. Contrary to his own inclination and policy he praised the Holy Prophet and mentioned his greatness and magnanimity in a much better way than even a friend of the Holy Prophet could do.

In the beginning of 7 A.H. the Holy Prophet wrote letters to the Kings and rulers of the territories adjoining the Arabian peninsula inviting them to embrace Islam. As written by the author of Tabaqāt six messengers of the Holy Prophet left Madina in the month of Muharram of 7 A.H. with six letters. Amr bin Umayya Zamari proceeded with a letter to the Negus, the Emperor of Ethiopia, Dahyah bin Khalifa Kalbi with a letter for Caesar, the ruler of the Eastern Roman Empire, Abdullah bin Huzayfa Sahmi with a letter to Khusro Perviz, the King of Iran, Hātib bin Abi Baltā with a letter to the King of Alexandria (Egypt), Shujā bin Wahab Asadi with a letter for Harith bin Abi Shamir Ghassāni, the King of Syria, and Salit bin Amr with a letter to Hawza bin Alayya Hasani, the King of Yamamah.

ABU SUFAYAN ADMITS THE GREATNESS OF THE HOLY PROPHET

According to Insānul Uyun, Seera-e Nabawiyya, Tarikh-e Tabari and Kāmil Ibn Athir, when the Caesar received the Holy Prophet's letter he became curious and ordered a man from the Hijaz to be found out and brought to him so that he might make investigations about Muhammad. By chance at that time Abu Sufyan and some other Qurayshites had gone to Syria for the purpose of trade. They were taken to Jerusalam and were presented at the Caesar's court. He asked them: "Who amongst you is most closely related to the man who claims to be the Prophet of Allah?" Abu Sufyan replied: "I am more closely related to him than all others". It was a fact because none of the Qurayshites in the caravan, except Abu Sufyan, was a descendant of Abd Munāf. Caesar said: "What is your relationship with Muhammad?" Abu Sufyan replied: "He is the son of my uncle". Caesar said: "Come nearer". After this he ordered the companions of Abu Sufyan to stand behind him. Then he turned to the interpreter and said: "Tell the companions of Abu Sufyan that I have made him sit before them so that I may question him about the man who claims to be the Prophet of Allah and I have made them sit behind him so that if he tells a lie they may not feel ashamed on account of looking him in the face and may contradict him. Abu Sufyan used to say later: "I swear by Allah that if I had not been afraid that if I told a lie those persons would contradict me, I would have told a lie. However, I felt ashamed and spoke the truth against my wish".

The following conversation took place between the Caesar and Abu Sufyan:

Caesar: To what sort of family does this proclaimer of prophethood belong?
Abu Sufyan: He belongs to a noble family.
Caesar: Did anyone amongst you make such a claim earlier?
Abu Sufyan: No.
Caesar: Did he ever tell a lie before he claimed to be a Prophet?
Abu Sufyan: No.
Caesar: Has there been any king among his ancestors?
Abu Sufyan: No.
Caesar: How is his wisdom, understanding and intelligence?
Abu Sufyan: We have not observed any defect in his wisdom, understanding and intelligence.
Caesar: What kind of people have embraced this religion — the nobles and aristocrats or the middle class and the poor?
Abu Sufyan: The middle class and the poor.
Caesar: Are his followers increasing or decreasing?
Abu Sufyan: They are increasing day after day.
Caesar: Does it so happen that someone of them may hate the religion of Islam and apostatize?
Abu Sufyan: No.
Caesar: Does Muhammad break promises?
Abu Sufyan: We have not seen any such thing from him so far.

We have since concluded a covenant with him and do not know how he will act in future (Abu Sufyan meant the 10-year's covenant concluded at Hudaybiya).
Caesar: Have you fought any battle against him so far?
Abu Sufyan: Yes.
Caesar: What was the result of your fighting?
Abu Sufyan: Sometimes we won and sometimes he was victorious. In the Battle of Badr he was successful against us, but I did not participate in that battle. A year later, (i.e. in the Battle of Uhud) we launched an attack on his city and split the bellies and cut off the ears and noses of the people.
Caesar: What does he order you to do?
Abu Sufyan: He orders us to worship Allah and not to associate anything with Him in the matter of authority. He forbids us to worship the idols which have been worshipped by our ancestors. He asks us to offer prayers, give alms, speak the truth, observe chastity, honour the promises and covenants and not to commit breach of trust".

The Caesar considered the investigation sufficient about the personality of the Holy Prophet. He, therefore, said to Abu Sufyan: I asked you about his ancestry and you replied that he comes from a noble family. All the Prophets of Allah are of noble birth in their tribes. I asked you whether someone from amongst you claimed to be a prophet earlier and you replied in the negative. Of course, if someone from amongst you had made such a claim it might be said that he was imitating what had been said earlier. Then I asked you whether he had been telling lies before he claimed to be a prophet and you yourself admitted that there had been no such thing and he had never lied to the people. I then concluded that there was no reason why a person who did not lie to the people should calumniate Allah. I sked you whether there had been any king among his ancestors and you replied in the negative. Of course, if there had been any king among his ancestors it might be said that he too had risen to regain kingship. Then I asked you whether the aristocrats and powerful persons or the poor had embraced his religion and you replied that they were the poor people. And the followers of the Prophets of God are always these poor people (i.e. the penniless and not those, who accumulate wealth by fair and foul means in the prevailing conditions, and oppose everyone, who aims at bringing about a revolution to reform the society).

The Caesar continued: "Thereafter I asked you whether the number of the followers of Muhammad was increasing or decreasing gradually and you replied that their number was increasing day after day. Faith in God and His true Prophets produces such results i.e. it attracts more adherents day after day till it attains perfection. I also asked you whether it so happened that someone from amongst the Muslims has shown hatred against Islam or has turned apostate and you said that there had been no such case. This is the case with faith, because when one's heart acquires relief and comfort by means of faith it does not feel sad. Then I asked you whether you had ever fought with him and you replied that battles had taken place between you and him, and in some of them you were successful whereas in others he was victorious. That is what happens to the Prophets of God. At times they get into difficulties but eventually their advancement and success is certain. Then I asked you what he ordered you to do and you replied that he ordered you to offer prayers, give alms, observe piety and chastity, honour your promises and not to commit breach of trust. You have admitted that he has never been dishonest, deceitful and unfaithful. This is how the Prophets of God behave. They are not dishonest, deceitful and unfaithful. In the light of these enquiries I am certain that he is the Prophet of God".

This was an example of how an enemy becomes helpless and humble before a sublime personality and cannot muster up his courage to tamper with the realities.

EXHORTATION OF IMAM ALI

Imam Ali says: "O people! Your behaviour with people should be in such a way that if you die and depart from the world others should mourn your death and weep on account of your absence and in case you are alive and exist amongst the people, they should be enamoured of you and love you" i.e. by means of good behaviour and sociability based on good morals one can win the favour and affection of the people.

"It is only by means of goodness and decent behaviour that one can attract the people to oneself and captivate their hearts".

Who could act better on this sublime moral precept of Imam Ali than his honourable son Imam Husayn and who could succeed like him in making the people love him during life and after martyrdom?

In the month of Muharram 61 A.H. an event took place in Iraq on the bank of the Euphrates and some highly magnanimous and virtuous persons were martyred. Most of the people in those days did not consider this event to be greater than other historical events. They perhaps imagined that after the passage of a few years this event would also be buried in the inner folds of history books and find its place along with hundreds of other old and forgotten historical events and none would remember it except as a story and an adventure. However, they were not aware that the personality of Husayn bin Ali would assume an immortal position. His rising would also be an eternal event of history and would not become old or get obliterated with the passage of time.

Perhaps most of the people in those days considered that the murderers of the Imam had succeeded in achieving their object and not only the event relating to these martyrs had been settled but none would be able to oppose Bani Umayya in future, and the name of Imam Ali and his descendants would no longer he mentioned in the history of Islam with glory and respect. It was also imagined that with the passage of time the wounds sustained by the friends of Ahlul Bayt owing to the martyrdom of the Imam and his honourable companions would heal up and this calamity would also be forgotten like many other historical tragedies. However, history proved later that most of the people were mistaken. They considered the event of Karbala as an ordinary political campaign and did not understand the sacred object which the Imam had in view in this rising, and were not acquainted with its spirit.

The difficulty which usually misleads the people is that they cannot differentiate between similar words and deeds although they may be quite different from each other. People have seen very often that some persons rise in the name of truth and also make sacrifices but eventually the step taken by them leaves no impression whatsoever, or some persons preach forcefully, support truth and side with the oppressed, and ask the people to remember Allah and the Day of Judgement, but neither the people nor history have recognized them as good and pious persons.

It is for the reason that very often the people consider the words and deeds of the godly persons also to be prompted by personal and material interest and do not pay heed to their Divine motives. They cannot differentiate between those who rise for the sake of Allah and those who are preoccupied with personal interests and carnal desires. However, it is a matter of great pleasure that if the people make mistakes history does not, and the passage of time eliminates the causes of misunderstanding. It is history which has recorded the sayings of Imam Ali as the best religious counsels, but has ignored and forgotten the lengthy and insipid lectures of may other caliphs. As an example of this we draw the attention of the readers to the counsels recorded by an Abbasid ruler named Mansur Dawāniqi for his son Mahdi Abbasi. Ibn Wazeh Ya'qubi has narrated it thus: "After the death of Abu Ja'far Mansur his son Mahdi read out his will before the people. The following is the will:

In the name of Allah, the Beneficent, the Merciful.

This is the will of the slave of Allah the Commander of the Faithful, for his son Muhammad Mahdi, the crown prince of the Muslims. The Commander of the Faithful has nominated him as his wasi and successor over all the Muslims, the Zimmis, the sanctuary of Allah and the public treasury. The land belongs to Allah and He makes its heir whomsoever He likes and the virtuous people have a good future. The Commander of the Faithful recommends it to you that wherever you may be you should be pious and should carry out Allah's orders pertaining to His slaves. He warns you against the regret, remorse and disgrace on the Day of Judgement, before the time of your death arrives and before you say: "O Lord! Why have you given me so short a time?" Never! When the time of your death has come you will not be given any respite. And he also wanrs you (before you say): "O Lord! Send me back to the world. It is possible that I may perform good deeds". At that time your family will forsake you and only your deeds will be with you. Then you will see what you have done with your hands and to what place you have gone with your feet, and what you have said with your tongue and how your limbs have assisted you in your actions; and what your eyes have seen and also what has entered your brain. Thereafter you will be fully rewarded for your good deeds and punished for the bad ones. Hence, you should always fear Allah and obey His orders. Ask Allah for His assistance in the matter of piety and seek His proximity by means of faith. Call your self to account and do not surrender yourself to passions and desires. Do not insist on doing bad deeds. None is more heavily burdened, more sinful, more afflicted and more mournful than you, because your sins have accumulated and your acts have been stored. As Allah has made you the guardian of your subjects so that you may arbitrate between them, even in respect of an atom, He will call you to account, and you will be punished for the misdeeds of your oppressive agents. Allah says: *You will die and others too will die and then all of you will quarrel with one another in the presence of your Lord. It seems as if I can see that you have been detained before the Omnipotent Lord.*

Your friends have deserted you. Your adherents have surrendered you to accountability and punishment. Your offences are lying at your door and your sins have involved you into difficulties. Fear has taken hold of you and weakness and helplessness have ruined you. Your logic has been spoiled and you have lost the remedy. The people have taken their rights from you and have avenged themselves. All this will happen on the day which will be very dreadful and hard. It will be a day on which the eyes will be dazzled, the hearts filled with anger will reach the throats and the oppressors will have neither a relative nor an intercessor who might hear their entreaties. What will then be your position on the day on which the people will quarrel with you and their rights will be demanded from you!

It will be the time when there will be no relatives to assist or support you. It will be the day on which all deeds will be rewarded; intercession will not be accepted; the balance of justice will be set up and final orders will be given.

Allah has said that on that day injustice will not be done to anyone and He will settle the accounts of all very soon. It is necessary for you to get ready for that day and endeavour to achieve deliverance. Free yourself from sins. Make the most of the opportunity available at present and fear the Day of

Judgement. Keep the world away from you, for it is deceitful and will destory you. You should keep your mind directed towards Allah and seek the fulfilment of your needs from Him. It is necessary that your justice is extensive and wide spread. The people should be immune from injustice. Arbitrate between your subjects on the basis of equality and make efforts to please Allah. Select your friends and associates from amongst the pious persons. Give the Muslims their due share from their wealth. Give them without stint that to which they are entitled out of the revenue and the booty. Pay them their pension regularly and pay their monthly and annual dues immediately at the proper time. Develop the cities and regions by reducing the taxes. Reform the people by means of good behaviour and sound policy.

The most important task for you is to protect your surroundings and guard the frontiers. You should despatch the army immediately when necessary. Seek Allah's assistance in the path of jihad and for the defence of His religion and destruction of His enemies. It is Allah who grants victory to the Muslims and makes them free and contented with the religion. You should sacrifice your life, dignity and wealth in this path. Look after your army constantly and keep information about the military station of horsemen and the camps of the soldiers. You should know that refuge, movement, and power, are from Allah and you should depend on Him only, because it is He Who is sufficient for you, Who makes you independent and helps you, and His help and support is enough".

This is a specimen of the didactic sayings and writings of an Abbasid ruler. It is very expressive and eloquent from the point of view of phraseology and style. However, it cannot be counted among the religious sermons and celestial wisdom. In spite of all their wealth and power Bani Umayya and Bani Abbas could not compile a **Nahjul Balaghah** or a **Sahifa Sajjadiya** with the help of such insipid testaments and speeches, nor could they prepare a book like **Tuhaful 'Uqûl** which is a collection of the sermons delivered by the Holy Prophet and the Imams.

On account of the special power and insight which history possesses to assess the personalities and their words it makes some sermons, speeches and letters ever lasting, whereas it ignores some other speeches which apparently resemble them but have no worth at all. This is the task which is performed by history with the passage of time and not by the contemporary persons who cannot usually make a correct assessment of the facts.

TRAGEDY OF KARBALA REMAINS IMMORTAL

At the time of the occurrence of the tragedy of Karbala there were a very limited number of Ahlul Bayt and the Shi‘ah who could evaluate the importance of this event, speak about the effect which it was likely to have on future history and remove the misunderstanding of the people.

With the grace of Allah we shall study the event in which seventy three persons sacrificed their lives and the part played by their mournful and bereaved women and children. We shall see how the addresses and speeches of the brave and eloquent speakers belonging to the Ahlul Bayt created a tumult in the spirit of the people, shook their hearts, removed their misunderstanding, completely changed the thinking of the people, invited them to realize the value of this sacred rising and deprived the enemy of an opportunity to alter the facts of this historical event. Whatever the enemy said or wrote and whatever meanness was shown by him was recorded in history. It was the addresses and speeches of Imam Husayn delivered in Masjid Harām and at the halting-places on his way from the Hijaz to Iraq, and on the day of the Āshura, and the addresses of the fourth Imam and other members of Ahlul Bayt during their journey in the capacity of prisoners, which depicted the event of Āshura so explicitly on the pages of history. Of course, when these memorable and everlasting words were being uttered, very few people could realize their value and impact. It was only the speakers who knew well what they were saying and doing and what result they would get from it. It was Imam Husayn who knew well from the very moment he left Madina what he was doing and where he was going and what result his movement and rising would produce for the world of Islam. The Shi‘ah men and women and the Ahlul Bayt who had been made captives possessed perfect insight with regard to the task undertaken by them and in spite of all their mental sufferings and unlimited dejection they spoke very eloquently whenever they felt that it was necessary for them to speak, laid the facts bare before the people and deprived their enemies from altering history.

However, as we have already said it is certain that most of the people in those days were not aware of the depth of these speeches. Very often it so happened that if they heard lady Zaynab, the daughter of Imam Ali speaking in the city of Damascus they thought that she was a mournful and bereaved woman whose sentiments had been aroused and she was speaking on account of grief and suffering, but later when she would become calm and forget her sufferings she would be forgotten by history. These short-sighted persons, who could not understand the realty, were not aware that the powerful pen of history was ready to write down and record every word uttered by her and was recording her speeches very minutely without expecting any reward for performing this task. The pen of history did not record only what the daughter of Imam Ali said but also recorded the poetic verses of the ruler of the time and handed them over to history.

Indeed, even if the enemies of Ahlul Bayt did not fear Allah and were not ashamed before the Holy Prophet they should have feared at least history and should have kept in mind that history would record everything and hand it over to the future generations, and keep it carefully in the libraries of the world, and if they wanted to eliminate even one speech of the fourth Imam or lady Zaynab, it would not be possible to do so unless all the libraries were demolished and all the books were destroyed. History is the dossier of all the past and future generations. History is a mirror which shows the face of every person as it has been. Persons depart from the scene and the nations are displaced but history stays at its place and cleverly supervises the good and bad deeds of the individuals and the coming and going of the nations. History does not confuse the accounts of the people, and does not hold on person responsible for the crimes of another. Contrary to what is imagined by most of the people that with the passage of time history forgets the historical accounts and conceals the facts, it actually reveals the realities as the time passes and removes for the future comers the impediments which are experienced by the contemporaries so that they may become more fully acquainted with the historical realities. The passage of time not only does not create any impediments in the path of study and research of the events but also removes the existing ones and makes the path of research and study shorter and clearer for the unbiased researchers. And the study of the history of the Āshura of Imam Husyan is easier for us who are more than thirteen centuries distant from that historical event as compared with those who lived in 61 A.H. We do not experience those difficulties which they experienced in the matter of research and investigation about this event and hereafter also the passage of time and the laspe of centuries and ages will not create any impediment in the path of research about it.

SELF-SACRIFICING LADIES

One should not, however, be oblivious of the fact that during the course of this everlasting and important event which took place in 61 A.H. some great and magnanimous women also participated and made sacrifices. So much so that some of them were even martyred in this path and their honourable names have been mentioned in the glorious history of the rising of Imam Husayn with honour and respect.

We now mention here the names of each of these great women in the historical order and the role played by them.

Lady Dulham: The first whose name deserves to be remembered with honour and respect was the wife of Zuhayr bin Qayn Bajali. She was the woman who acquired the most honourable position in the history of Islam for all times to come.

A man belonging to the tribe of Bani Fazara says: "We were returning from Makkah along with Zuhayr bin Qayn Bajali and were proceeding to Iraq. At that time Husayn bin Ali was also on his way to Iraq. However, we did not wish to halt at the same halting-place at which Husayn halted. Hence as and when Imam Husayn departed from a place, we halted there and when he halted at a place we moved on. However, on one occasion it so happened that we were obliged to halt at the same place at which Husayn bin Ali halted. We pitched our tents on one side and he pitched his on the other. While we were taking our meals there suddenly came a messenger of the Imam. He saluted us and said: "O Zuhayr bin Qayn! Husayn bin Ali has called you".

We disliked this message so much that we put down the morsels which we had in our hands and all of us were perplexed. However, Dulham, the daughter of Amr who was the wife of Zuhayr said to him: "The son of the Holy Prophet of Allah has sent someone to you and called you; are you not prepared to go to him? Allah be praised! What is the harm if you go and see him, hear what he has to say and then return!" The words of this woman had the desired effect and she placed her husband in the category of the greatest martyrs of Islam. Zuhayr was impressed by the words of his wife and presented himself before the Imam. After some time he returned with a face beaming with happiness and ordered his tent to be pitched adjacent to the camp of the Holy Imam.

Indeed, Allah is the guardian of those who believe. He takes them out of darkness into light. (Surah al-Baqarah, 2:257)

Zuhayr went with the Imam and met martyrdom, and his wife returned to her relatives.

Another honour which is recorded in history about this woman has been mentioned in the book entitled Tazkira-e Sibt. According to it when Zuhayr was martyred his wife said to his slave: "Go and shroud your master". The slave came and saw the Imam without a shroud. He said to himself: "Should I shroud my master and leave the Imam without a shroud? By Allah I will do no such thing". He, therefore, shrouded the sacred body of the Imam first and then he shrouded his master.

Lady Umme Wahab: The second lady who deserves to be praised for her lofty character and sacrifice was the wife of Abdullah bin Umayr Kalbi. Abdullah bin Umayr was a resident of Kufa and belonged to the tribe of Bani Ulaym. One day he saw that a large army had gathered in the date-palm garden of Kufa. He enquired about the army. He was informed that those people were going to fight against Husayn, son of Fatima, the daughter of the Holy Prophet. Abdullah said: "Allah knows that I have been keen to fight against the polytheists for His sake. However, I now hope that the spiritual reward for fighting against these people who are going to kill the grandson of the Holy Prophet will be not less than that for fighting against the polytheists. Abdullah decided to leave and informed his wife Umme Wahab, daughter of Abdullah about his intention. His wife said: "It is an excellent idea. May Allah guide you in all circumstances. Please take me also with you". Both of them left Kufa at night and perhaps reached Karbala during the night of the 8th of Muharram. When fighting was started by the enemy in the morning of Āshura two slaves of Ubaydullah ibn Ziyad came forward for a single combat. Habib bin Mazahir Asadi and Burayr bin Khuzayr Hamdani got ready to fight with them, but the Imam asked them to wait. At this moment Abdullah bin Umayr sought the Imam's permission to fight. He faced both the enemies alone and killed them.

When the woman observed her husband fighting with them she also picked up the stick of a tent and entered the battlefield. She said to her husband: "May my parents be your ransom! Sacrifice your life for the sake of the children of the Holy Prophet". The Imam said to her: "May Allah give you a good reward! May Allah bless you! Return towards the women and stay with them in the tent, because women are not required to perform jihad". Abdullah was the second person to be martyred on the day of Āshura, the first being Muslim bin Awsaja.

Lady Rubāb : The third lady whose illustrious name has been recorded in the history of Āshura was Rubāb, daughter of Imraul Qays, a wife of the Holy Imam. She was the only wife of the Imam who accompanied him during his journey to Karbala.

As regards Shehr Bānu, the daughter of Yazd Gard, the last King of Persia and the mother of the fourth Imam, she had died about 24 years earlier than the tragedy of Karbala.

The name of Layla, daughter of Abi Murrah bin Urwah bin Mas'ud Thaqafi, the mother of Ali Akbar, has also not been mentioned in connection with this tragedy and it is not known whether or not she was alive at that time. No mention has also been made of the mother of Ja'far bin Husayn, who belonged to the tribe of Quzā'ā. There is also no mention in the event of Āshura of the mother of Fatima, daughter of Husayn i.e. Umme Ishaq daughter of Talha bin Ubaydullah Taymi. Her daughter Fatima was, however, present in Karbala. She also went to Kufa and Syria.

The Imam's only wife who was with him during this journey was, therefore, the said honourable lady viz. Rubāb, daughter of Imraul Qays Kalbi. Imraul Qays was a Christian.

During the period of the Caliphate of Umar he embraced Islam. From the very first day the caliph made him the chief of the tribe of Quzā'ā. Besides the honour of becoming a Muslim and an Islamic chief he also acquired another distinction. He had three daughters and he gave one of them in marriage to Ali the second to Hasan and the youngest namely Rubāb to Imam Husayn. Thus he became the father-in-law of three Imams.

Lady Rubāb had one daughter and one son from Imam Husayn who were named Sukayna and Abdullah respectively. The son who was a suckling was killed on the day of Āshura and she herself as well as her daughter Sukayna were made prisoners. The name of this lady, however, has not been mentioned in connection with the events of the day of Āshura.

The fourth lady whose name may be mentioned in connection with the events of the afternoon of the day of Āshura belonged to the tribe of Bakr bin Wā'il. She enjoys an eminent position in depicting the tragedy of Karbala. She has recorded on the pages of history a precise picture of the meanness of the enemy in a few words.

She was with her husband in the army of Ibn Sād. However, when she saw that the soldiers of Kufa had made a rush on the tents of the children of Imam Husayn and were looting even the dresses of the ladies she picked up a sword, proceeded towards the tents of Imam Husayn and shouted: "O children of Bakr bin Wā'il! You are alive and in spite of this these people are plundering the tents of the daughters of the Holy Prophet. Allah is the only Arbitrator. Come on, and avenge the bloodshed". By means of these brief words she showed to what extent the enemy had become mean. It seems as if the cry of this lady is still resounding at the doors of the tents of Imam Husayn.

While studying the history of Āshura we come across the names of many magnanimous women who rose to support truth and the godly persons with perfect sincerity and they are not the only four women mentioned above. However, just as none of the martyrs, whether Hashimite or non-Hashimite, in spite of their greatness, magnanimity and self-sacrifice, can attain to the position of Imam Husyan, who was the leader of this revolution, none of these great women who displayed an eminent performance at the time of the martyrdom of the martyrs or during captivity, could acquire a position equal to that of lady Zaynab, the eldest daughter of Imam Ali. It was she who could truly take the place of her brother during captivity and followed the same movement from the afternoon of the day of Āshura till her arrival in Madina. She truly followed what her brother said: "Abjectness and humiliation are far removed from us, the Ahlul Bayt". She thus discharged the responsibility devolved upon her. We may say that it was due to the education given to her by her mother, lady Fatima Zahra. She ought to have been as patient in the path of faith as her mother Fatima and her grandmother Khadija had been. Was it not lady Khadija who was the first to believe in the Prophethood of the Prophet of Allah, and who made greater sacrifices than anyone else for the advancement of his religion and supported him in all difficulties and hardships for about ten years i.e. from the first year of his prophetic mission till the tenth year when she died?

Was lady Zaynab not the grand-daughter of the same lady Khadija and was the path pursued by Imam Husayn any other path than the advancement of religion and the revival of the call of the Holy Prophet? Hence, in case it was necessary that, for the sake of the true religion of Islam and for the Holy Qur'an, women should become captives and as a consequence of this should address the people in the bazaars and the streets so as to nullify the unjustified propaganda of the enemy and to make the reality known to the people, who could be more suited for this task than the daughter of Imam Ali, who had inherited self-sacrifice from Khadija, the greatest self-sacrificing lady of Islam, and Imam Ali, the greatest supporter of the Prophet of Allah. Lady Zaynab, who was the daughter of Ali ibn Abi Talib and also the grand-daughter of Khadija addressed the people in the bazaar of Kufa and spoke eloquently like her father. It might be said that she was speaking with the tongue of Imam Ali. By making a sign to the people she made them quiet as if they had ceased to breathe, and suppressed the tumult.

Ahmad bin Tāhir Baghdadi (d. 280 A.H.) has given three versions of her address in his book entitled Balāghatun Nisa, one of which is reported to have come down from Imam Sadiq.

Umme Kulsum, the sister of Zaynab also addressed the people in the bazaar of Kufa. Both the sisters severely reproached the Kufians who were touched so much that they began to weep and lament.

Fatima, the daughter of Imam Husayn also addressed the people in the bazaar of Kufa and invited their attention to the great sin which they had committed and the bad luck and adversity in which they had involved themselves.

The task of Ahlul Bayt in the bazaar of Kufa came to an end, and then they got an opportunity to speak in the court of Ibn Ziyad. The daughter of Imam Ali came in the court in a very simple dress. She was encircled by her slave-girls. She went and sat down in a corner of the palace. Ibn Ziyad asked: "Who is the woman who has gone and sat down in a corner along with her slave-girls?" None gave him a reply. He then repeated his question. Thereupon one of the slave-girls of lady Zaynab said: "It is Zaynab and she is the daughter of the same Fatima who was the daughter of the Prophet of Allah".

At this moment a heavy responsibility devolved upon Zaynab. It was necessary that she should excercise self-control. She should also give a reply to Ibn Ziyad and should not give him a chance to let the matter be ambiguous in the eyes of the people.

Ibn Ziyad said: "I thank Allah that He has disgraced you and killed you and made the people aware of your fresh lies". Ibn Ziyad uttered three blasphemous words on account of his being arrogant of his victory. Otherwise what fresh lie had Bani Hashim told? Was it a fresh lie on their part that they said, "Muhammad is the Prophet of Allah", or did they tell any other lie? In any case lady Zaynab said immediately in reply to Ibn Ziyad: "Allah be thanked that He has honoured us by means of His Prophet Muhammad and purified us of every impurity. You have said that we have been disgraced but it is a libertine who is disgraced; and you have said that we have lied but lies are told by the wicked. And I thank Allah once again that others and not we are the libertines and the wicked".

In spite of this prompt reply by the daughter of Imam Ali, Ibn Ziyad said again: "Have you seen what Allah has done with your family?" It appears that by saying this Ibn Ziyad wanted to remind her of those who had been martyred two days earlier so that she might be moved and possibly say some-

151

thing according to his wishes or make some requests. He was, however, oblivious of the fact that the Ahlul Bayt did everything very intelligently and did not utter even a word which was not worthy of their position, and whatever they said was well calculated and according to a plan, so that the object which they had in view might be achieved.

In reply to Ibn Ziyad's question: "Have you seen what Allah has done with your family?" Zaynab replied: "Nothing new has happened. These martyrs of our family were persons for whom Allah had destined martyrdom, and they achieved this blessing, and embraced martyrdom. However, a day will come soon when Allah will summon you and them for the settlement of accounts and there you will grapple and dispute with each other". On hearing this Ibn Ziyad was so much disturbed and annoyed that if Amr bin Harith had not reproached him, it was possible that he might have ordered the sister of the Imam to be killed. However, of what use could it be to him? Zaynab had already said what she had to say. She had also identified the libertines and the wicked and introduced the pure and sacred family of the Holy Prophet.

After a month or a few days more had passed, the daughter of Imam Ali arrived in a more important and more delicate assembly. Here also it was her duty to speak more clearly. As compared with the Kufians the Syrians were more mistaken and more unacquainted with the Ahlul Bayt. It was, therefore, necessary that she should mention the reality and introduce the Ahlul Bayt more emphatically. This assembly was organized in Damascus, the Islamic capital. Here, too, lady Zaynab addressed the people and spoke to them. This speech has also been mentioned by Ahmad bin Tāhir Baghdadi in Balāghatun Nisa. He says: "When Yazid saw the prisoners belonging to Ahlul Bayt and found them standing before him he ordered the head of Imam Husayn to be brought in a tray. He hit the teeth of Imam Husayn with a stick which he had in his hand and recited some poetic verses which are summarized thus: "I wish that my ancestors, who were killed in Badr, had been alive today so that they might see the present condition of the descendants of Muhammad and had rejoiced and said: 'O Yazid! May your hands never ache". He added: "May I not be a descendant of my ancestors if I don't take revenge upon the children of Muhammad".

When the matters took such a turn, and Yazid, who killed Imam Husayn, now rose to oppose and take revenge upon the Holy Prophet. Was then lady Zaynab justified in ignoring his words and deeds and in keeping quiet before one who claimed to be the successor of the Holy Prophet and ruled in that capacity, and killed the most pious persons of Islam avenging the murder of the polytheists of Makkah, who were killed by the Prophet in the Battle of Badr? Could she remain silent when she saw that the Syrians had accepted the words of Yazid as true and believed them? Evidently Lady Zaynab could not keep quiet at this stage. Whatever she said was her duty which she performed. Allah also preserved her speech and it was not eliminated like many other religious documents. We should be thankful to the Almighty Allah for this blessing.

HISTORY IS VERY POWERFUL

We have already said that the speeches and addresses of the Ahlul Bayt remained prescribed and were free from distortion. They have been recorded in books and documents and have reached us through reliable sources.

Today it is possible to narrate the event of Karbala in detail by means of the speeches which Imam Husayn and the Ahlul Bayt delivered in Makkah and on their way from the Hijaz to Iraq and at Karbala, Kufa, Syria and Madina, by means of the replies given by them to the questions asked by various persons, by means of the epic verses recited by the Imam himself and his companions before the enemy on the day of Āshura and which are recorded and preserved in reliable resources, and by means of the letters which were exchanged between the Imam and the people of Kufa and Basra as well as the letter written by Yazid to Ibn Ziyad and the letters written by Ibn Ziyad and Umar bin Sād to Ibn Ziyad and the letters by Ibn Ziyad to the Governor of Madina, all of which are recorded in reliable history books and will reach the hands of future generations and remain safe for ever. In the presence of these sources there remains no need for any other source or document for the compilation of the history of Āshura.

When Yazid wrote a letter to Ibn Ziyad appointing him the Governor of Kufa and Basra, he also wrote to him about Muslim bin Aqil saying: "I understand that Muslim has come to Kufa to create differences between the Muslims". And when Muslim was arrested and brought before Ibn Ziyad the latter said to him harshly "O son of Aqil! The people of this city were living in peace and then you came and created differences between them and made them bitter enemies of one another". It was the same thing which Yazid had written about Muslim, and Ibn Ziyad did not add anything to it and repeated it to Muslim and this too was recorded in history. Muslim said in reply: "It is not so. I have not come to this city of my own accord and have also not come to disturb the people and to create differences and discord between them. On the contrary it is evident from the letters written by them to us that your father Ziyad killed their good persons, and shed their blood, and behaved towards them like unjust persons and the tyrants. We have, therefore, come to establish justice and to invite the people to obey the commands of the Holy Qur'an".

Evidently how could it be possible that what Yazid and Ibn Ziyad wrote and said should have found its place in history whereas the brief reply given by Muslim wherein he pointed out the mal-administration during the rule of Ziyad, who was one of the tyrants of Iraq, should have been omitted from history and none should have heard it or written about it? In that event the future generations would have remained unaware of it and would have believed that Muslim was seditious, cruel, mischievous, and one, who created differences between the people; and this was not possible. Yazid could kill the Imam and his companions, and could also make his Ahlul Bayt prisoners. He could not, however, alter the verdict of history and create for himself a place in it other than that which he possesses.

In order to inform the people formally about the tragedy of Karbala Ibn Ziyad went to the Jame'ā Masjid of Kufa and said such things that if he had not done so Husayn bin Ali would have been mentioned in the history of Islam as a liar. In the presence of a few thousand Iraqi Muslims he mounted the pulpit of the Jame'ā Masjid of Kufa and said: "Allah be thanked that he made truth and the truthful victorious and helped the

Commander of the Faithful Yazid and his party, and killed the liar son of the liar i.e. Husyan bin Ali and his supporters".

Truly speaking if history had favoured Ibn Ziyad at this stage to some extent he would not have been given a reply in that assembly and by the side of that very pulpit. It was possible that this speech, which was delivered in the Masjid of the Muslims and before the Muslims by the ruler of the Muslims, might have created doubts in the minds of some persons for some time, and it might have been thought, although by persons lacking intelligence and the spirit of investigation that maybe that was the reality and those persons were telling the truth and the man who had mounted the pulpit and was thanking Allah for this occurrence so firmly in His own House was right, and it appeared that it was really good that Husayn bin Ali had been killed. However, before even one person had left the Masjid, a Muslim was courageous enough to give a reply to that foolish remark and it was recorded in history. Shaykh Mufid and Tabari write that before Ubaydullah ended his speech Abdullah bin Afif Azadi Ghāmidi* rose from his place. (When the nonsense talk of Ibn Ziyad crossed the limits) Abdullah sprang up from his place and said: "O Ibn Marjāna! Liar, son of the liar are you, your father, and he who has sent you as ruler of Iraq, and his father. Do you pretend to advocate truthfulness after killing the children of the Holy Prophet?"

Ibn Ziyad, who imagined that he ruled over history as well, said: "Bring him before me". There was a tumult and what this enlightened man had said could no longer be ignored. This brave person sacrificed his life for the sake of his truthful words and was sent to the gallows under the orders of Ibn Ziyad. However, his words recorded his name in the history of Ashura with his blood.

When Ibn Ziyad looked at the sacred head of the Imam, he laughed and struck a stick, which he held in his hand, on the

---

*He was one of the supporters of Imam Ali. He lost his left eye in the Battle of the Camel and also lost his right eye in the Battle of Siffin and thus became blind. He used to come to the Masjid Kufa every day in the morning where he remained busy in prayers and supplications and returned home at night.

teeth of the Imam. Zayd bin Arqam, a companion of the Holy Prophet who was then very old turned towards Ibn Ziyad and said: "Keep your stick off these two lips for I swear by Allah besides whom there is no god that I have seen innumerable times that the Holy Prophet placed his lips on these lips". He uttered these words and began to weep and lament. Perhaps Ibn Ziyad was under the impression that a person might be a Muslim and might also kill the children of the Holy Prophet, he might consider the guardians of Islam to be liars and still remain a Muslim and he might shed the blood of the dear ones of Islam and still appear as a Muslim in the history of Islam.

SERMON OF LADY ZAYNAB
IN THE COURT OF YAZID

Now we propose to study the sermon of lady Zaynab which she delivered in the court of Yazid and which is recorded in a book written in the third century A.H.*

Yazid recited the blasphemous poetic verses of Abdullah bin Zab'ari Sahmi which he had composed while he was an unbeliever and also added some poetic verses of his own and said openly that he wanted to take revenge upon the descendants of Muhammad because Muhammad and his companions had killed his polytheist ancestors. Zaynab, the daughter of Ali rose and began speaking. She added a new chapter to the history of the Caliphate of Yazid which covered a period of three years and a few months, and said: "O Yazid! Allah and His Prophet have said that committing sins and considering the signs of Allah to be false is ridiculing them", i.e. deny the sign of Allah today and hold them in derision and have become happy, and recite poetic verses on account of the martyrdom of the children of the Holy Prophet just as the polytheists of Makkah became happy and sang songs because of the martyrdom of some Muslims in the Battle of Uhud, and talk about taking revenge upon the Holy Prophet. This is how you become like them and how you have reached this stage? You have reached this stage because you have committed too many sins. Whoever treads the path of sin and persists in committing sins will, according to the

*Balāghatun Nisā', Abul Fazl Ahmad bin Abi Tāhir, (208 — 280 A.H.).

verdict of the Qur'an, deny the signs of Allah one day and eventually will ridicule them and then deserve Divine punishment.

She added: "O Yazid! Do you think that we have become humble and despicable owing to the martyrdom of our people and our own captivity? As you have blocked all the paths for us, and we have been made captives and are being taken from one place to another, do you think that Allah has taken away his blessings from us? Do you think that by killing the godly persons you have become great and respectable and the Almighty looks at you with special grace and kindness? For this reason and on account of this wrong thinking you have become elated and arrogant. You have become boastful because you have seen that the matters have taken a turn in your favour. You have, however, forgotten what Allah says: *The disbelievers must not think that Our respite is for their good. We only give them time to let them increase their sins. For them there will be a humiliating torment.*" (Surah Ale Imran, 3:178)

Then lady Zaynab reminded Yazid that on the day of the conquest of Makkah which took place in 8 A.H. the Holy Prophet did favour to all the men and women of Makkah and set them free. Yazid himself was a descendant of those very freed persons. His father Mu'awiya, his grandfather Abu Sufyan and Mu'awiya's mother were among those who were set free at the time of the conquest of Makkah. On that day the Holy Prophet very magnanimously set all of them free irrespective of what they had done in the past and said: "Go, for all of you are free".

In the second part of her speech the daughter of Imam Ali made the conquest of Makkah her topic and said: "O son of the freed ones! Is it justice that you keep your women and slave-girls in seclusion but have made the helpless daughters of the Holy Prophet ride on swift camels and given them in the hands of their enemies so that they may take them from one city to another".

Then she said: "Why should'nt Yazid be spiteful against us; it is he, who looks at us with hostility. You say with perfect intrepidity and without imagining that you are committing a sin: 'I wish that my ancestors who were killed in Badr had been present here today'. Then you strike Imam Husayn in his teeth with a stick in your hand! Why should'nt you be like this, although you have done what you wanted to do and have pulled out the roots of piety and virtue! You have shed the blood of the sons of the Holy Prophet and have hidden the brilliant stars on the earth from amongst the descendants of Abdul Muttalib under the clouds of oppression and injustice. However, you shall go before Allah soon. You shall meet your ancestors and shall also be taken to their place. At that time you will wish that you had been blind and dumb and had not said that it was a day of rejoicing for your ancestors".

At this stage the daughter of Imam Ali prayed to Allah and said: "O Lord! Procure our right and take revenge upon those who have oppressed us". Then she turned to Yazid and said: "By Allah you have pulled off your skin and cut off your flesh. You will soon go before the Prophet of Allah and will see with your own eyes that his children are in Paradise. It will be the day when Allah will deliver the descendants of the Holy Prophet from the state of being scattered and will bring all of them together in Paradise. This is the promise which Allah has made in the Holy Qur'an. He says: *Do not think of those who are slain for the cause of Allah as dead. They are alive with their Lord and receive sustenance from Him.* (Surah Ale Imran, 3:169)

O Yazid! On the day when Allah will be the Judge and Muhammad will be the petitioner, and your limbs will give evidence against you, your father, who made you the ruler of the Muslims, will receive His punishment. On that day it will become known what reward the oppressors earn, whose position is worse and whose party is more humble. O enemy of Allah and O son of the enemy of Allah! I swear by Allah that I consider you to be humble and not fit even to be reprimanded and reproached. But what am I to do? Our eyes are shedding tears, our hearts are burning, and our martyrs cannot come to life by our reprimanding and reproaching you. My Husayn has been killed and the partisans of Satan are taking us to the fools so that they may get their reward for insulting Allah. Our blood is dripping from their hands and our flesh is falling down from their mouths. The sacred bodies of the martyrs have been placed at the disposal of the wolves and other carnivorous animals of the jungle. If you have gained something today by shedding blood, you will certainly be a loser on the Day of Judgement. On that day nothing but your deeds will count. On that day you will curse Ibn Marjāna and he will curse you. On that day you and your followers will quarrel with one another by the side of the Divine scale of Justice. On that day you will see that the best provision which your father made for you was that he enabled you to kill the children of the Prophet of Allah. I swear by Allah that I do not fear anyone except Him and do not complain to anyone else. You may employ your deceit and cunning efforts, but I swear by Allah that the shame and disgrace which you have earned by the treatment meted out to us cannot be eradicated". The daughter of Fatima Zahra ended her speech with offering thanks to Allah. She said: "I thank Allah Who has concluded the task of the chiefs of the youths of Paradise with prosperity and forgiveness and accommodated them in Paradise. I pray to Allah that He may elevate their ranks and favour them more with His kindness, for Allah is Omnipotent".

BENEFITS OF HISTORY

The Almighty Allah says: *That nation, (Children of Ibrahim) is gone. They have reaped what they sowed, and the same applies to you. You are not responsible for their deeds.* (Surah al-Baqarah, 2:134)

This verse has occurred in Surah al-Baqarah with identical wording at two places. At one place it occurs after 2:133. It says: *Were you present when death came to Ya'qub and when he said to his sons: What will you worship after me? They said: We shall worship your God, the God of your fathers, Ibrahim and Ismail and Ishaq, One Allah, and to Him do we surrender.* Then it says: *Those are a people who have passed away; they shall have what they have earned and you shall have what you earn, and you shall not be called upon to answer what they did.*

At other place it occurs after 2:140. It runs as follows: *Do you say that Ibrahim, Ismail, and Ishaq, and Ya'qub and the twelve descendants of Bani Israil were Jews or Christian? O Prophet of Allah say: "Do you know best, or does Allah? And who is more unjust than he who hides a testimony which he has received from Allah? Allah is not unaware of what you do".*

Here also after this verse the Qur'an says: *Those are a people who have passed away* (i.e. the Children of Prophet Ibrahim) and his sons were neither Jews nor Christians and they lived before Prophet Musa and Isa. Secondly whatever they were and whatever faith they possessed and whatever good or evil deeds they did cannot benefit or harm you. If they were good people and did good deeds how does it concern you, and if they were evil-doers why should you be worried for their bad deeds? Is it possible that on the Day of Judgement you will be held responsible for their bad deeds?

While studying the history of Āshura we have mentioned in the foregoing pages the names of some good, brave, self-sacrificing, faithful and pious persons, and have also spoken about their good deeds and valour in the path of Allah as well as their steadfastness, virtues and good morals. Similarly we have mentioned the names of some bad, sinful, rebellious and oppressive persons and referred to their bad and cowardly deeds. Keeping in view the good and bad deeds of the people we have extolled and praised those who were good and decent persons and cursed those who were mean and ignoble. However, notwithstanding the fact that honouring and sending greetings to the souls of the martyrs and the devotees who sacrifice their lives for the sake of Allah, and cursing those, who oppose truth and draw their swords against the godly people, and eliminate the virtuous and pious persons, who are the best capital of every nation, is a good and proper act, it cannot guarantee the prosperity of man unless he thinks and acts like good persons and shuns the practices of evil-doers. Otherwise the position will be the same as mentioned by the Almighty Allah thus: *Those are a people who have passed away; they have reaped what they sowed.*

The good and pious persons and the wicked ones formed a nation which went its own way. Whatever goodness and virtue they had is for themselves and whatever sins and oppressions they committed are also a burden on them. You will neither be rewarded for their good deeds nor held responsible for their bad deeds.

The object of repeating this verse in Surah al-Baqarah with a distance of less than ten verses is to invite the attention of the people to a very important point. One should not feel contented only by saying that Imam Husayn and his companions were great and magnanimous persons and Ibn Ziyad, Yazid and their collaborators were bad and deviated, because very often it is possible that there may be people who send greetings to the sacred soul of Imam Husayn but choose to follow Ibn Ziyad in the matter of thinking, actions and way of doing things. There are many persons who criticize and revile the bad people of the past and wish that they may be awarded severe punishment, but as far as their deeds and conduct are concerned they choose these very persons as their leaders and guides.

There is no doubt about the fact that supporting truth and the truthful people and opposing the bad persons and the bad deeds, in whatever manner it may be, is something good in itself but it does not place man in the category of good and virtuous people and does not bring him out of the circle of the bad and wicked persons, except when one follows the ways of the former and shuns those of the latter. It is only in this event that a person may be justified in saying that he supports and favours the good and opposes the bad and the wicked persons. The Holy Qur'an has paid special attention to the narration of the history of the past nations and the stories of the Prophets and of those who opposed them, and a large part of the verses and Surahs of the Qur'an has been specially devoted to this very subjet i.e. the history of the ancients. However, the object of these narrations of the Qur'an is not only that the Muslims should know that Prophet Musa was a good man and Phroah was a bad man or that the tribes named Ād and Thamud were bad and deviated whereas the people belonging to other nations were good. How do Muslims stand to gain or lose because of the goodness of Prophet Musa and other Prophets and the goodness of the Christians of Najrān, who were killed at the hands of Zu Nuwās, the King of Yemen or the badness of Zu Nuwās? The object of the narration of the history of the ancients is that the Muslims should ponder over the factors for the advancement, glory and good name of a nation and for the adversity, humility and downfall of another nation, and do things which make nations advanced and respectable, and shun those things which have in the past been the cause of the downfall, adversity,

Divine punishment and extinction of the nations. They should understand that the Divine Sunnah (Divine Path) does not undergo a change. If a nation becomes honourable in the world for some reason, that reason will always be the means of glory, and if a nation becomes degraded and humble for some reason, that reason will always be the source of its misfortune and humiliation.

DIVINE LAW IS UNALTERABLE

Whenever the word *Sunnah* has been used in the Holy Qur'an it has been used in this very literal meaning i.e. the manner in which Allah has treated the past nations. And whenever Allah says that His *Sunnah* is unalterable it means that there is a path for attaining to dignity and honour and He does not change it, and there is also a path and ground which leads to adversity and helplessness and that, too, is unalterable.

Allah says: *That was the law of Allah in the case of those who lived before and there will never be any change in the law of Allah.* (Surah al-Ahzab, 33:63)

It means that it has been the practice of Allah in the case of the sinners and the hypocrites that in order to serve an ultimatum upon them, He in the first instance sends the Prophets to them and makes goodness and badness and truth and falsehood perfectly clear to them. Thereafter He destroys and makes extinct those who do not believe, but persist in their infidelity. As regards those who try to deceive Allah and His Prophet and behave hypocritically, side with Allah as well as with His enemies, and on the one hand take from the Prophet a share out of the war booty and other benefits due to the Muslims, and on the other hand take remuneration from the enemies for spying for them and creating trouble, He disgraces them, deprives them from gaining from either side and drives them hither and thither. This Sunnah of Allah is unalterable and it should not be expected that deceit and hypocrisy can be the cause of shame and disgrace on one day and the means of honour and good name on another day.

The same thing has been said in the Holy Qur'an in these words: *(Such was Our) system in the case of those whom We sent before you (to mankind), and you will never find change in*

Our system. (Surah Bani Israil, 17:77)

In the following verse also the word *Sunnah* has been used in this very sense: *Tell the unbelievers, 'If you give up your evil behaviour, Allah will forgive whatever you have done in the past. But if you transgress again, your fate will be the same as that of those (unbelievers) who lived before you',* (Surah al-Anfal, 8:38) i.e. Allah declares 'We shall employ the same method in their case which We employed in the case of the past people and shall destroy these deviated people in the same way in which We destroyed them'. The same thing has been said in the Holy Qur'an thus: *They do not believe in truth and they exactly follow the Sunnah (tradition) of the past people;* (Surah al-Hijr, 15:13) i.e. there is no hope that these infidels of Makkah who persist in their enmity and grudge against the Prophet of Allah will believe. They do not believe but their matter is quite clear and Our Sunnah (method) with regard to those who lived before them and persisted in their infidelity is known. We shall deal with them in the same way in which We dealt with those persons.

Allah say: *Had the disbelievers fought against you, they would take to flight and would have found no guardian or helper. This is the Sunnah (law) of Allah which existed before you, and you will never find any change in Allah's system,* (Surah al-Fath, 48:23) i.e. if the polytheists of Makkah had fought against you in Hudaibiya they would not have gained anything and would have taken to flight and thereafter they would not have found any refuge or helper. This is the way in which Allah has dealt with the unbelievers earlier and the law and the Sunnah of Allah do not change. It means that one of the laws of Allah is that faith is the source of victory and domination over the enemy and it is not only you and the polytheists of Makkah but out of every two parties which grapple with each other Allah grants victory to that party which joins the battle with the stimulant of faith.

Allah says: *Evil plots only affect the plotters. Do they expect anything other than (Allah's) law (torment) with those who lived before? You will never find any change in the tradition of Allah nor will you find any alteration in it.* (Surah al-Fatir, 35:43) i.e. These people who do not give up idol-worship and make evil plots so as to hinder the advancement of Islam should know that evil plots eventually recoil on those who make them. And if they expect that We shall treat them in a way other than that in which We treated the people of the past, it is an inopportune expectation because Allah's Sunnah does not change and deceit and fraud can never be the source of honour and advancement.

Allah says: *Their faith could not avail against Our punishment. Such is Allah's prevailing Sunnah (law) among His servants in the past. Thus the disbelievers are ruined.* (Surah Mumin, 40:85) i.e. When We subjected to torture those who denied and ridiculed Our Prophets and they experienced the severity of Our punishment they appealed to Us for help and said: "We forsake infidelity and polytheism and believe only in Allah". This faith which was the consequence of pressure of torture did not do them any good and this is the Divine Sunnah (law) which has ever prevailed over the people. Consequently the disbelievers sustained loss.

When all the verses quoted above are taken together it appears that the Divine law does not change for the sake of anyone. He does not make one honoured or humble without cause. He has not created any nation to dominate and rule others, nor has He created any nation to remain afflicted, indigent and backward. Those who have acquired wealth and authority in the world have acquired it according to a Divine law, and similar is the case of those, who have been subjected to humiliation and disgrace.

IMAM ALI'S SERMON ON DIVINE LAW

Imam Ali has said: "By Allah I think that these enemies of yours will soon gain a victory over you because in spite of their falsehood they are united whereas you, in spite of your being right, are dispersed and separate from one another. They obey their leader in the false path whereas you disobey your ruler in the path of Truth. They behave towards their leader honestly whereas you are treacherous towards your leader. They safeguard the interests of their land and do not do anything which may be harmful to it whereas you do harm to your own country and commit crimes. How can I work with you people, for if I entrust a wooden bowl to anyone of you I really fear that he would remove its handle". (Nahjul Balagha)

It may be said that with these words Imam Ali explained all these Qur'anic verses and pointed out that it is not possible to disobey the Divine laws and traditions. Imam Ali wanted to tell his companions: 'You will not be victorious only because your Imam is Ali and your opponents will not be defeated only because a bad man rules them. This has not been the Divine law in the matter of victory and defeat of the nations. It is not so that every party whose leader is a good and just person should be victorious and successful, although its members may not be united, may disobey their leader,* commit treachery with him and commit crimes in their land. It is also not the Divine law that the group of persons whose leader is oppressive should not succeed and should not achieve their object and come into power although they may obey their leader and behave towards him sincerely and may be good, useful and honest in their mutual dealings. According to the Divine system the first group would be defeated in spite of their good leader and lose their power and sovereignty because it is not possible to maintain these things in the presence of dispersion, differences, disobedience, treachery and dishonesty. And in spite of their oppressive leader the second group would succeed and snatch power from the hands of others, because according to the Divine law advancement, victory, domination and acquisition of power are the necessary outcome of unity, obedience, submission, sincerity and honesty".

Ali did not want to elate his companions and tell them falsely: "Because of your having an Imam like Ali you should remain contented, for in any case the present as well as the next world belong to you. It does not matter that you are not united, because your Imam is Imam Ali. There is no harm if you are treacherous because your Imam is Ali. There is nothing to worry even if you do not obey your Imam and do not listen to

---

*For example the Muslims were defeated in the Battle of Uhud owing to the disobedience of some persons (although they were Muslims and they believed in Allah, the Prophet, Islam and the Qur'an and their opponents were the enemies of Allah and His Prophet).

his words, because you have an Imam like Ali. If you are bad persons in your mutual relations and as the citizens of your city and country, and pull down your house with your own hands, and are mischievous and corrupt, no harm will come to you, because an Imam like Ali is your ruler. On the contrary as your enemies are ruled by a tyrant they will always remain wretched and humble and will always be defeated by you even though they may be more united and more honest than you and may be more obedient to their ruler and more useful for themselves and their country than you are. Imam Ali did not tell his companions and his followers any such false things all of which are against the Divine law, and reminded them on all occasions that Allah's laws are unalterable. However, the supporters of Imam Ali said these false things to themselves and possibly most of them imagined and still imagine that in fact the system and methods of Allah can be changed and it is possibly to derive good results from those things from which all other human beings have derived bad results, and to become honourable, powerful and happy by doing things which have made others base, humble and degraded and ruined their honour, power and happiness.

In another sermon Imam Ali says about jihad: "If a person turns away from jihad considering it to be disagreeable, Allah humiliates him. He is overtaken by calamities. He loses authority and does not receive justice".

Here also Imam Ali has not spoken about the spiritual reward for performing jihad for the sake of Allah and defending the frontiers of one's country and one's religion. He has also not said that, if a person does not perform jihad and a nation forgets the duty of jihad and defence of the country and sits quietly till the enemy launches an attack, will be awarded such and such punishment in the next world. He wants to draw the attention of the people to one of the Divine laws and methods i.e. when a nation abandons the duty of jihad and defence and does not care to protect its frontiers from the attacks of the enemy, it will become humble and degraded, and will suffer affliction and abjectness even though its Prophet may be the last of the Prophets and its Imam may be Imam Ali. Its people will lose wisdom and intelligence. As a result of the abandonment of the duty of jihad and defence they forfeit their right, and authority is transferred to others. Such a nation is branded with disgrace and no one deals justly and equitably with it. It appears that considering that the people could not be prompted to perform jihad by rousing their religious sentiments, Imam Ali appealed to their national sentiments and said to them that if they did not perform jihad to earn spiritual reward and did not fear the punishment to be awarded in the Hereafter on account of giving up jihad they should at least fear its evil effects on their present life and should beware of the Divine laws which are unalterable. In other words he said to them: 'Even if you are not desirous of spiritual reward in the Hereafter you should at least get up to preserve your honour and independence and should protect the frontiers of your country from the attacks of the enemy. You should not jeopardize your position and honour amidst the various nations and should not make yourselves afflicted and helpless by remaining confined to your homes and providing an opportunity to the enemy'.

Then Imam Ali says: "I have been telling you openly and in private during day and night to fight against the people of Syria and your enemies and to attack those rebels, and advance before they invade you and come upon you unawares, because there has never been a nation which sits in its house till the enemy makes a rush on it and plunders its frontiers one after the other and then fighting takes place in the centre of the country of that nation and it is not humiliated and defeated. However, you ignored what I said, on one pretext or another, and discouraged one another in the matter of jihad. Consequently, according to the Divine system, the enemy crossed your frontiers and plundered and snatched away a region from you every day". (Nahjul Balagha)

The Holy Qur'an has said repeatedly that Allah does not alter His system for anyone and there are many verses in it which make this fact clear. The Holy Qur'an says thus about the Jews who were contemporary with and inimical towards the Holy Prophet: *They (the Jews) say: 'Even if we go to Hell we shall not remain there save for a certain number of days'. (O Prophet of Allah) ask them: 'Have you received a covenant from Allah? Then truly He will not break His covenant; or do you speak against Allah that which you know not?* (Surah al-Baqarah, 2:80) i.e. 'Has Allah given you an undertaking that when the deeds of the people are taken into account on the Day of Judgement, He will deal with you differently as compared with other sinners and whereas they will remain in Hell for ever, you will be subjected to torture for a few days only? Has Allah really made such a confidential promise with you or are you associating with Allah that of which you are not aware?'

Then the Holy Qur'an refers to the aforesaid Divine law and says: *Certainly, the evil-doers who are engulfed in sins are the companions of Hell-Fire wherein they will live for ever.* (Surah al-Baqarah, 2:81)

Here the Jews have been told that they, too, will be punished according to the general law and that law is that whosoever is involved in sin and polytheism and does not leave it till his death shall remain in Hell for ever.

In the following verse the same thing has been said in a more clear and comprehensive manner: *'It* (i.e. reward and punishment and good and bad consequences of deeds) *will not be in accordance with your desires* (i.e. desires of the Muslims) *nor the desires of the people of the Scripture'* i.e. the Divine law will not be changed either for the Muslims or for the people of the Scripture and that law is: *Whoever commits evil will be punished accordingly and no one besides Allah will be his guardian or helper. And whoever does good deeds, whether male or female, and is a believer will enter Paradise and they will not be wronged in the least.* (Surah an-Nisa, 4:123 – 124)

INVITATION OF THE PROPHET TO HIS KIN

On the very first day when the Holy Prophet made his call public according to the Command of Allah and was commissioned by the revelation: *Warn your near relatives* (Surah Ash-Shuara, 26:214) to invite them to the true religion of Islam he said to his near relatives time and again: "Do not deviate from the path of Allah relying on my relationship with you. You should understand it clearly that the matter is not in my hands and I cannot do you any good or save you from any loss contrary to the Divine law. If you can gain something it is by the same method which has been specified by Allah, and if you sustain a loss it will be according to the same law, which has been prescribed by Him. None should imagine that the accounts will be nullified for the sake of Quraysh or Bani Hashim or Bani Abd Munāf or Bani Abdul Muttalib or my daughter Fatima or my aunt Safia and their misdeeds will be overlooked".

After the revelation of the aforesaid verse the Holy Prophet called Quraysh together and said: "O Quraysh! Save yourselves from the Fire of Hell, because your profit and loss is not in my hands" i.e. there is a law for profit and loss and reward and punishment. If you do good deeds you will benefit and gain spiritual reward, but if you do evil deeds you will sustain loss and will be awarded punishment. O Bani Kāb bin Lu'ee! Deliver yourselves from the Fire, for your profit and loss is not in my hands. O Bani Qusay! Deliver yourselves from the Fire, because I cannot provide you spiritual reward nor can I turn away punishment from you. 'O Bani Abd Munāf! You yourselves should procure means to save yourselves from Divine punishment, for I cannot do anything for you i.e. if you are pious you will go to Paradise but if you are polytheists you will go to Hell. I have not been given a key to take my polytheist relatives to Paradise through a back-door and I have also not been given an authority to exempt my friends and relatives from the responsibilities imposed upon them by Allah. O Bani Zohra bin Kilāb! Deliver yourselves from Divine punishment.

O Bani Abdul Muttalib! You should act in such a way that Allah may not punish you, and you should know that I cannot help you in the matter. O Bani Murra bin Kāb! O Bani Hashim! O Bani Abdush-Shams! Deliver yourselves from the torture on account of polytheism by worshipping Allah, for I cannot do anything for you in this regard. O Abbas, (uncle of the Prophet)! You, too, should free yourself from Divine torture. O Safia, (aunt of Muhammad)! You too should think of your freedom and deliverance for I cannot do anything for you. Neither your profit in this world nor your share in the Hereafter is in my hands. So you must believe in Allah and say: "There is no deity but Allah". O Fatima daughter of Muhammad! You must also endeavour to save yourself from Divine punishment because your father cannot help you in the matter and has no control over your gain and loss. Of course, you are my relatives and I shall discharge the duties which devolve on me on that account".

If relationship with the Holy Prophet cannot take the place of faith and pious deeds, and the daughter of the Holy Prophet must also follow the same path for her good future which it is necessary for other persons to follow, and not only for the daughter of the Holy Prophet but for the Holy Prophet himself, there should be no means to acquire Divine pleasure except faith and good deeds. Then how can it be possible that after the martyrdom of Imam Husayn all these Qur'anic verses, reports, traditions and the sermons of Nahjul Balagha should be treated as of no consequence and some method other than faith and good deeds should be found to enter Paradise? Can it be so that before the tragedy of Karbala the Muslims were in need of truthfulness, honesty and uprightness and paying attention to articles of worship and religious duties and abstinence from telling lies, drinking wine, usury and acquisition of wealth by unlawful means, but now these things are not needed to that extent? It is now possible that a man may get ahead of the murderers of Imam Husayn in the matter of cruelty but may at the same time be contented by sending greetings to the Imam and his magnanimous friends and may also be associated with the Imam and his friends on the Day of Judgement! The friends of Imam Husayn were an embodiment of greatness of soul, sincerity, faith and truthfulness. It is by studying about the sacrifices performed by them that we understand the true meaning of support. The friends of Imam Husayn have explained to us the meanings of the words love, faith, support and self-sacrifice. Even the epic verses which they recited before the enemies on the day of Āshura reflect their personality and spiritual greatness so that one who says *Yā Lay Tani Kuntu Ma'akum* (I wish that I too had been with you and had been honoured and exalted with you) should reflect a little and judge fairly whether this sentence of his will fall under the category of truth or falsehood, and whether he really wishes that he had been with Ābis bin Abi Shabib Shākiri and had, at the time of stoning by the enemy, removed his coat of mail from his body, and his helmet from his head like him, whose body had been smashed with stones in support of truth! Or he wishes to have been their companion, because he has never pondered as to what grand sacrifices the companions of the Imam offered and what blows of the enemy they faced with firmness. Consequently he utters things which are contrary to reality and perhaps hopes that his words will be treated to be at par with those of the companions of the Imam. The companions of the Imam had, however, reached such a stage of purity and faith that the light of conviction was reflected even in what they said to console the Imam.

CONFIDENT COMPANIONS OF IMAM HUSAYN

Tabari writes that after the Imam had offered the noon prayers, Zuhyar bin Qayn engaged the enemy. While fighting he continued to say: "I am Zuhayr bin Qayn. I drive the enemies away from my Imam with my sword".

Then he placed his hand on the shoulder of the Holy Imam and said: "Step forward and do not be worried. You are our Divine guide. Why should you be anxious in connection with this occurrence? Is it anything other than that today you will see your grandfather, the Prophet of Allah, your brother, your father Ali, your uncle Hamza, the Doyen of Martyrs, and become happy?

What a high position Zuhayr had attained in the matter of faith and spiritual insight! He consoled the Imam and said: "Do not be worried on account of what has happened, because there is no need for anxiety and regret". It would not be surprising if, as written in some books, Imam Ali is reported to have said: "Even if the curtain is lifted and the hidden realities are manifested it will add nothing to my faith". Whether Ali did or did not say this he definitely enjoyed this position and did possess such a sublime faith. It is not some thing unexpected and nothing else could be expected from Imam Ali. What is surprising is that Zuhayr bin Qayn also enjoyed this position to some extent. What he said to the Imam shows that he was telling him: "I who am Zuhayr and one of the devotees of the son of the Commander of the Faithful have arrived at such a position after attending upon the Imam for some days that even if the curtain is removed from my eyes nothing will be added to my faith". This very faith and clear sightedness kept the friends of the Imam on the right path in all circumstances and they did no stumble in the least.

Nāfe' bin Hilāl Jamali, one of the companions of the Imam, was shooting down the enemies with arrows and was reciting the following epic verse: "I am Hilāl Jamāli. I follow the path of Ali" i.e. even when fighting was in progress he was advocating the cause of Ali and was mentioning his name and praising his faith. He killed twelve men of Umar bin Sād and also wounded some others. Eventually, however, his arms were broken and he was disabled and arrested. When he was brought before Ibn Sād he asked him: "O Nāfe', why have you subjected yourself to this calamity?" Umar was perhaps expecting that like many others he would regret his action and apologize. However, Nāfe' said: "Allah is aware of my intention with regard to what I have done"; and while blood was flowing down from his beard he added: "I swear by Allah that I have killed twelve of your men and also wounded some others. I do not regret my action and if I had not broken my shoulders and arms you could not have arrested me". Nāfe' was the first of the companions of the Imam to be arrested and executed.

At the time of his death also he furnished a clear proof of his faith and correct assessment, and history, too, recorded it with perfect honesty. When the sword was raised to cut off his head he said: "I thank Allah that I am going to be killed at the hands of the worst people".

This was the spiritual condition of the persons to whom we send greetings and then say with boldness: "We wish that we too had been with you and had been honoured and exalted like you". Why don't we ever say: "Thank Allah that we were not present on that day and did not get involved in such a test and did not participate in shedding the blood of the pure and virtuous persons like you". Was that day nearer to reality and truth or is this thanksgiving and rejoicing?

MARTYRS OF ĀLE ABI TALIB IN KARBALA

In the year 61 A.H. Imam Husayn went from Madina to Makkah and from there he reached near Kufa. At all these places he invited the people to assist him and to defend truth and reality, and delivered various speeches. This campaign lasted for more than six months but as it is well-known he did not find more than seventy two sincere supporters. Out of them seventeen belonged to his own family. Two of them were his own sons namely Ali Akbar and Ali Asghar — the suckling child of the Imam. There were the sons of his brother Imam Hasan viz. Qāsim, Abdullah and Abu Bakr. There were also five brothers of the Imam namely Abbas, Abdullah, Ja'far and Uthman, sons of Ummul Baneen, and Muhammad bin Ali. There were also two sons of Abdullah bin Ja'far named Awn and Muhammad. Besides them there were five descendants of Aqil viz. Ja'far bin Aqil, Abdur Rahman bin Aqil, Abdullah and Muhammad sons of Muslim bin Aqil and Muhammad bin Abi Sa'id bin Aqil. The names of these seventeen persons have been mentioned in Ziyārat-i Nāhiya.

As regards others not more than fifty five accompanied the Imam. Even if some more persons have accompanied him in the beginning they deserted him when they became aware of the political conditions in Kufa and Iraq. However, if the supporters of the Imam in these days are counted they will be found to be innumerable. The question, therefore, arises: Were the people in those days very bad and do those belonging to the present age excel them in the matter of recognition of the Imam and self-sacrifice? No. That is not so. During those days also until the people were put to test and Muslim and Hāni were hanged, there were innumerable devotees of Imam Husayn and he was greeted vociferously from all sides. In fact it may be said that it was a very good time because by means of his eloquence, personality and the antecedents peculiar to him, Imam Husayn was able to find, during the period of his six month's journey from Madina to Makkah and then to Iraq, seventy two enlightened and sincere supporters and he did not really need any more. He had not gone with the object of conquest so that he might have needed a larger army. For the purpose of achievement of the object which the Imam had in view these seventy two great and honourable men and children were sufficient. Besides them were the brave and magnanimous ladies who said in all conditions what they had to say. They informed the people about the true facts and the great services rendered by their self-sacrificing men. They related the events of Āshura in every town where

173

they were taken, and told the people about the enemy stopping the supply of water, making the horses trample the bodies of the martyrs and killing the suckling child. They performed a great duty in Syria when they changed the ideas of the people of Damascus and its suburbs who had been misled by anti-Ahlul Bayt propaganda for a period of forty two years. In the bazaar of Damascus they told the people that the Verse of Purification had been revealed about them and also explained the rights of the relatives of the Holy Prophet. Notwithstanding the fact that they were bereaved and mournful they eventually returned to Madina with a relieved mind.

It is possible that some followers of the Ahlul Bayt may not relish our saying that they returned to Madina with a disburdened and relieved mind. However, if we deliberate upon what has been said so far and take into account the definite successes which the Ahlul Bayt achieved during this journey, we shall have to admit that their sentiments cannot be interpreted in any other way. We have before us the same interpretation of the daughter of Imam Ali and we have only followed that great lady about whose bravery and magnanimity we have definite proof with us.

As narrated by Ibn Tawus, when Ibn Ziyad said to lady Zaynab: "Have you seen what Allah has done to your family?" She replied: "I have not seen anything bad. They were destined to be martyred and, therefore, went to Paradise. Soon Allah will bring you and them together. Then the matter will be settled and we shall see in whose favour the decision is taken. O Ibn Marjāna! May your mother weep for you".

Enormous blessings be upon you, O great lady, who were made prisoner and that too by one who had inherited grudge for the Ahlul Bayt from his father, but in spite of that you spoke so explicitly and frankly. In our opinion this example of the courage and bravery of the daughter of Imam Ali is more explicit and valuable than even the speeches which she delivered in Kufa and Syria.

Can there be found in the history of mankind any other woman, whose six or seven brothers were martyred, whose son was martyred, whose ten nephews and cousins were martyred and who was made prisoner also along with her sisters and the children of her brothers, and even in the state of captivity who defended herself and her martyrs and that too in a city which was her father's capital at one time and where she had stayed for about four years during the time of her father's caliphate? However, in this condition and in the presence of all causes of worry and dejection she should not complain about what she had to suffer but should say with perfect frankness: "We have not experienced anything contrary to our liking and inclination. If our men have met martyrdom they had come for this very purpose. If this had not happened it would have been a matter of worry and uneasiness. Now that they have performed this Divine duty decently and acquired the honour of martyrdom it is only approapriate that we should thank Allah for this success".

ROLE OF ISLAMIC TRAINING

It has been narrated by Wāqidi that during the Battle of Uhud when many Muslims met martyrdom and even the martyrdom of the Holy Prophet was rumoured in Madina, an Ansari woman named Hinda daughter of Amr bin Hizām and aunt of Jabir bin Abdullah Ansari, came to Uhud and collected the corpses of three of her martyrs viz. her son Khallad, her husband Amr bin Jumuh and her brother Abdullah bin Amr. She loaded them on a camel and proceeded to Madina with the intention of burying them there. While on her way she met the wives of the Holy Prophet who were going to Uhud to obtain news about the welfare of the Holy Prophet and were worried. One of the wives of the Holy Prophet asked Hinda: "What is the news?" She replied: "There is good news. The Holy Prophet is alive and safe and whatever other calamity may have befallen the people is immaterial."

Hinda who was carrying the corpses of her dear ones to Madina to bury them there said with a feeling of strong devotion, courage and faith: "When the Prophet of Allah is alive why should we be sad and when this good news is there what other news can make us unhappy?" Then she said: "I have brought other good news also from Uhud. Firstly, Allah has honoured some of our faithful men with martyrdom and secondly the following verse has been revealed: *Allah repulsed the disbelievers in their wrath; they gained no good. Allah sufficed the believers in fighting. Allah is Mighty.* (Surah al-Ahzab, 33:25)

She was asked: "What have you loaded on the camel?" She replied: "My brother, son and husband have met martyrdom and I am now carrying their corpses to Madina".

As narrated by Ibn Ishaq the husband, brother and father of a woman belonging to Bani Dinar tribe were martyred in the Battle of Uhud. When she received the news of the martyrdom of her dear ones, she enquired about the Holy Prophet and was told that he was quite well and was not exposed to any danger. She, however, said: "I must go and see the Holy Prophet myself". When she saw him and knew that he was safe, she said: "Now that I have seen you alive and in good health every other calamity that may have befallen us is of no consequence".

Indeed if Islamic teachings and training of the Holy Prophet could make a woman, who was previously an unbeliever and idol-worshipper, so faithful, sincere and self-sacrificing in the path of Allah that finding the Prophet alive made her tolerate every other grief, and she considered every other affliction to be immaterial it deserves consideration as to what a deep impression this training and these teachings must have made on the daughter of Ali and Fatima and what an enormous faith, sincerity and devotion they must have created in her. If the Muslim women belonging to the Aws and Khazraj tribes could display so much spiritual greatness, lady Zaynab must have acquired a much higher stage of spiritual greatness and it was on this account that in spite of all that she had to suffer she said with perfect calmness and peace of mind: "I have seen nothing except goodness". This was the secret of the greatness and the rapid and astonishing advancement of the Muslims. It was the sublime faith which dazzled the eyes of the enemy and made him humble and helpless.

It is possible that some persons may say and it is also perhaps written in many books that the Muslims had to suffer heavy losses in the Battle of Uhud and many of their dear ones were martyred. However, the Battle of Badr was very fruitful. Many men of the enemy were killed and some of them were also taken prisoners and excepting those who were freed without ransom, 1000 to 4000 dirhams per head were realized to redeem them. However, this way of thinking i.e. to consider the Battle of Badr more beneficial for the advancement of Islam as compared with the Battle of Uhud, shows that proper attention has not been paid to the results which were gained from the Battle of Uhud and which could not be produced from the Battle of Badr. In Badr the Muslims displayed such physical strength that the enemy realized that even if they (the Muslims) were 313 in number and had only six coats of mail and seven swords they could rout 950 armed men, kill some of them, make some of them captives and put the remaining ones to flight. However, Quraysh could not yet imagine that if one day the dear ones of the residents of Madina met martyrdom for the sake of the Prophet of Allah and their women lost even their husbands, brothers and sons they would still be happy on account of the Prophet being safe. And when the Holy Prophet asked them to pursue the enemy, those wounded in the battle would collect their baggage and make haste to pursue the enemy as if they had not sustained any wound. The Battle of Uhud was more effective in terrifying the enemy than the Battle of Badr and the test on this day was more fruitful than the test on that day.

There are many people who show enthusiasm at the time of gaining victory, taking the enemies prisoners and acquiring war booty, but become weak, abject and demoralized when they have to suffer affliction and hardship and are faced with death or are taken prisoners. After the Battle of Badr Quraysh were confident that if they gained victory over the Muslims one day and killed the dear ones of the Ansar and the residents of Madina, their enthusiasm to support the Prophet would cool down and they would be discouraged and would desert him. They could not imagine that it made no difference to the Muslims whether the Holy Prophet returned to Madina with seventy prisoners and a large booty or with wounded companions with amputated limbs after more than seventy of them had been martyred.

The prisoners of Karbala made the same impression on the mentality of the enemy during their journey to Kufa and Syria as the bereaved women and men of the Ansar had made after the Battle of Uhud. The conduct of Ahlul Bayt during this journey could not be predicted. It could not be imagined that after all their sufferings they would be able to stand erect, deliver speeches everywhere, bring the victorious and powerful enemy to his knees and change the public opinion so much that even the prevailing regime would be affected by it and say, on the very first day, to the prisoners belonging to Ahlul Bayt: "May Allah curse the son of Marjāna. If there had been any relationship between you and him he would not have treated you in this manner and would not have sent you to Syria in this terrible plight".

ALLEGIANCE OF THE MADINITES TO THE PROPHET

We have already mentioned that in the thirteenth year of the Prophet's mission the elders of Madina took the oath of allegiance to him in the valley of Mina, and Abbas bin Abdul Muttalib took a promise from them that they would not fail to assist the Holy Prophet. Some historians say that Abbas addressed them thus: "O people of Khazraj! Now that you are inviting Muhammad to come to your city you should know that he is honoured and enjoys amongst us a position about which you are well aware. I swear by Allah that we, Bani Hashim, who have expressed belief in him as well as those who have not done so, are prepared to sacrifice our lives for him and will defend him as a matter of faith and also as a matter of family honour. Muhammad is respected and honoured in his own city as well as in his own family. Now that out of all the people he has chosen to go with you, you should think over the matter very carefully. If you feel that you will remain faithful to him and support him against his enemies and are strong, brave and experienced in warfare and able to withstand the enmity of all the Arabs who will rise collectively to fight against you, only then you should pursue the task which you have undertaken to accomplish. In case, however, you are afraid that after taking him to your city you will withhold support from him and leave him friendless, you should leave him alone just now, because he is respectable and powerful amongst his relatives and in his city. You should consult one another and take a decision in the matter and should not disperse without a final decision, because the best words are those which are more true".

After Abbas had spoken, Bara bin Marur, one of the

distinguished companions of the Prophet, said: "We have heard what you have said. By Allah if we had thought of something other than that mentioned by you, we would have spoken about it. However, we are determined to support the Prophet sincerely and not to spare even our lives in the path of Allah and His Prophet".

Abbas bin Ubada said: "O people of Khazraj tribe! Do you know on what matter you are taking the oath of allegiance to this man?" They replied in the affirmative. Thereupon he said: "You are taking the oath of allegiance to him with the intention that you will fight for his sake with the red and the black people. In case, therefore, you feel that you will desert him when you are required to spend your wealth for his sake or when your elders are killed you should abandon the idea of taking the oath of allegiance just now, because by Allah such an action is the cause of disgrace in this world as well as in the Hereafter. However, if you feel that even after spending wealth and in spite of your nobles and elders being killed you will remain faithful to him, you must not forsake him, because I swear by Allah that in this lies the happiness of both the worlds. Thereupon all of them said with one voice: "We are ready to take the oath of allegiance notwithstanding the fact that we have to sacrifice our wealth and our elders are killed". Then they asked the Holy Prophet: "What shall we gain if we remain faithful?" He replied: "The Paradise". They said: "Then stretch forth your hand so that we may take the oath of allegiance to you". According to Ibn Ishaq the Holy Prophet commenced his discourse by reciting the Holy Qur'an, inviting them to Allah and encouraging them to embrace Islam. He then said: "I accept your allegiance on the condition that you will support me in the same manner in which you support your women and children".

Barā bin Mārur held the hand of the Holy Prophet and said: "I swear by Allah who has sent you as the true Prophet that we will certainly defend you in the same manner in which we defend our women and our honour. O Prophet of Allah! Do accept our oath of allegiance. By Allah we are well-versed in fighting and are ready to fight. In fact we have inherited warfare as our way of life from generation to generation".

At this stage Abul Haitham bin Tayhān who was one of

the elders of the Ansar and the martyrs of Siffin interrupted Barā bin Mārur and said: "O Prophet of Allah! There are relations between the Jews and us and we are going to sever them now. Let it not be that we should leave our confederates and later when Allah makes you successful you should return to your people and leave us helpless". The Holy Prophet smiled and said: "This will never happen. On the contrary your blood is my blood and my honour is your honour. I belong to you and you belong to me. I will fight against anyone who fights against you, and will be at peace with him who is at peace with you". Upon this the Ansar declared: "We accept the invitation of the Holy Prophet and take the oath of allegiance to him and are prepared to give our wealth and property in this path, even though our elders may be killed".

Abbas bin Abdul Muttalib who was holding the hand of the Holy Prophet said: "Speak in low tones because spies have been appointed to keep a watch on us. Keep your aged persons in the front so that we may talk with them and you should disperse after taking the oath of allegiance and everyone of you should return to his own place". The first person who took the oath of allegiance to the Holy Prophet was Barā bin Mārur. According to another narration it was Abul Haitham ibn Tayhān and according to still another narration it was As'ad bin Zurāra. Thereafter the remaining seventy persons put their hands in the hand of the Holy Prophet and took the oath of allegiance. Then twelve persons were selected from amongst them as *Naqib* (guards) and made responsible to look after the affairs of their people. In this way Yathrib i.e. the city which was named *Madinatur Rasul* (the city of the Prophet) after the Holy Prophet's migration, became the greatest centre of Islamic propagation.

The migration of the Muslims to Madina began in the month of Zil Haj of the thirteenth year of the Holy Prophet's mission, because after the return of the seventy five persons to Madina, who took the second oath of allegiance at Aqaba and the Quraysh having come to know that the tribes of Aws and Khazraj had made a pact with the Holy Prophet and taken the oath of allegiance to him, the persecution of the Muslims by them became severer. They began abusing and torturing them more than before and life became unbearable for the Muslims in

Makkah. They, therefore, sought the Holy Prophet's permission to migrate and the Holy Prophet permitted them to go to Madina and join their brethren, the Ansar, and said to them: "The Almighty Allah has made Yathrib, a place of peace for you and its residents your brothers". The Muslims proceeded from Makkah to Madina in groups and the Holy Prophet also awaited the Command of his Lord telling him to migrate from Makkah and go to Madina. The Quraysh, too, conspired to kill the Prophet of Allah and drew a plan in this behalf with great precision. They did not, however, know that Allah intended to take out His Prophet from the city of his relatives and kin, and place him amongst the people who were more kind and devoted than any father or brother and ready to support him and make sacrifices for his sake. The idolaters were planning to kill the Holy Prophet and Allah also willed to protect him for the advancement of Islam as a universal religion.

Allah says: *The unbelievers planned to imprison, murder or expel you (Muhammad) from your city. They make evil plans, but Allah too plans and Allah's plans are the best.* (Surah al-Anfal, 8:30)

The Prophet of Allah left Makkah during the first night of the month of Rabiul Awwal of the fourteenth year of his mission. After remaining hidden for three nights in the cave of Thaur he proceeded to Madina accompanied by two Muslims as well as a polytheist, who had been hired as a guide. On the 12th of Rabiul Awwal he arrived in Quba, a place in Madina. The people of Madina accorded him a hearty welcome and the gay voices of the people were resounding in the city. They recited the poetic verses thus: "The full moon has risen from Thāniyatul Widā (name of a place). So long as one prays to Allah it is necessary for us to thank the Almighty for this blessing. O you, who have been raised amongst us by Allah! You have come and arrived amongst us in such circumstances that we are prepared to obey all your orders".

HISTORICAL DAYS OF MADINA

In those days the city of Madina was witnessing important historical events. There was a day when in the Battle of Badr, which took place in the month of Ramazan 2 A.H., 313 Muslims gained a victory over 950 polytheists. They killed more than seventy of them and made more than seventy of them prisoners. The good news of this victory reached Madina and the Holy Prophet and his companions returned to their homes successful and victorious. Then there was the day when the Muslims fought against 3000 polytheists of Makkah in the Battle of Uhud in the month of Shawwal 3 A.H. In that battle more than seventy distinguished Muslims met martyrdom and the Holy Prophet and the Muslim Mujahids returned to Madina mournful and bereaved. There was a day in 4 A.H. when the news of the martyrdom of forty or seventy distinguished Muslims at Bayr Mauna reached Madina. In that very year the news of the martyrdom of nine companions of the Holy Prophet in the Sarya (battle) of Rajie spread in Madina. In 5 A.H. 3000 Muslims gained victory in the Battle of the Ditch over an army of 12,000 or as stated by Masudi in al-Tanbih wal Ashrāf 24,000 polytheists. Allah helped His Prophet and made the enemies return disgraced and defeated. In the 2nd, 4th and 5th A.H. the Jews belonging to the tribes of Bani Qaynuqā, Bani Nazir and Bani Qurayza received the punishment which they deserved and the surroundings of Madina were cleared of these treacherous people. In 7 A.H. the Muslims gained victory over the Jews of Khayber and the news of this great victory reached Madina. When Ja'far bin Abi Talib and many others who had migrated to the Christian State of Ethiopia, thirteen years earlier, returned safely to Madina and the Holy Prophet was so pleased on their arrival that he said: "I do not know what makes me more happy today the conquest of Khayber or the return of Ja'far from Ethiopia". In the year 8 A.H. the news of the martyrdom of Ja'far bin Abu Talib, Zayd bin Harith and Abdullah bin Rawaha at Mota (Syria) reached Madina. The Holy Prophet and 30,000 Muslims returned to Madina safely from the Battle of Tabuk. It was indeed a very dangerous occasion. In the month of Ramazan 8 A.H. the Holy Prophet conquered Makkah and entered the city accompanied by 12,000 armed men. The good news of this great victory spread in Madina and idol-worship came to an end in the Arabian peninsula for ever. In the early part of the 11 A.H. the Holy Prophet breathed his last. This great tragedy made all the residents of Madina mournful and bereaved. After his demise also the city of Madina witnessed many important historical events everyone of which had effect to some extent on the political and social life of the Muslims till 61 A.H. arrived and after Bani Hashim and the Muslims of Madina had experienced severe sufferings for about six months the news of the martyrdom of Imam Husayn and his devoted companions reached this city. This event reflected once again the situation which was created on the day of the demise of the Holy Prophet.

Shaykh Mufid and Tabari write that when Imam Husayn was martyred and his head was brought before Ubaydullah ibn Ziyad he summoned Abdul Malik bin Abil Hârith Salami and said to him: "Proceed to Madina and convey to Umar bin Sa'id bin As, the Governor of Madina, the good news of Husayn bin Ali's assassination".

It is, of course, surprising that within a short period of fifty years after the demise of the Holy Prophet the Muslims became so ungrateful that the news of the murder of his children and dear ones was conveyed as "good and great tidings" to the Governor of the city of Madina i.e. the place where the Holy Prophet migrated and where he was buried. Abdul Malik bin Abi Hârith was reluctant to convey that news to Madina, the place of habitation of Bani Hashim and the kith and kin of the Imam and felt ashamed to undertake that task. He, therefore, requested Ubaydullah to excuse him from performing that duty. However, Ubaydullah who wielded authority and had become more severe after killing the Imam threatened Abdul Malik and said to him: "You must go and convey this happy news to the Governor of Madina and it should not reach Madina before you". He also gave him some money and said: "Do not coin excuses and depart as early as possible. If your camel ceases to be fit to perform the journey arrange for another camel and abandon the first one". Ibn Ziyad did not yet realize that all that insistence was harmful to him and when the details about the martyrdom of the Imam would reach the ears of the people they would become a part of history and the source of disgrace for him and Yazid and it would not do any harm to the Imam. The Imam would have stood to lose (if this interpretation be correct) if the tragedy of his martyrdom had not become public and the immorality and corruption of the enemy had not been recorded in the history, the contemporary and future Muslims had remained ignorant of the true facts. Ibn Ziyad was one of those persons who dig their grave with their own hands, insist on their own foolishness and publish their disgrace everywhere.

Almighty Allah says: *They think to beguile Allah, and the believers; in fact they beguile none save themselves, but they perceive not.* (Surah al-Baqarah, 2:9)

The more they insist on these indecent acts and take pride in them the more they provide a document in the hands of their enemy and block the way of their escape from the court of justice of history. Ibn Ziyad did not know with what disgrace his name would be mentioned in the history of Islam and what would be the judgement of history about him. He was also not aware in what manner the brilliant names of Imam Husayn and his companions would manifest themselves and shine in the history of Islam and how his religious movement and Divine rising would find its place amongst the greatest and most important risings of mankind.

Anyhow, as Abdul Malik Salami was not in a position to oppose Ibn Ziyad he proceeded hastily to the Hijaz in compliance with his orders and reached Madina. When the people saw that a messenger had come from Iraq they concluded that he must have brought news about the happening there. A man from amongst Quraysh whose name has not been mentioned in history saw Abdul Malik and having come to know that he had come from Iraq asked him with great anxiety: "What news have you brought from Iraq?" What he wanted to know was how the conflict between Husayn bin Ali ended and what was the result of the rising of the Kufians against the caliph. Abdul Malik said only this in reply: "Whatever the news may be it is with the Governor of Madina" i.e. he would communicate the news to the governor and the people would learn it through him. This brief reply was sufficient for the intelligent people to realize the position. They understood that when the information about the developments in Iraq was being furnished to a governor who had been appointed by Yazid and was himself an Umayyad it meant that Husayn bin Ali had been removed from the stage of caliphate and politics and the rulership of Yazid and the family of Abu Sufyan had been established. On hearing the brief reply the said Qurayshite understood what had happened and said: "We are from Allah and to Him we have to return. It appears that Husayn bin Ali has been slain".

Abdul Malik says: "When I met Amr bin Sa'id bin Ās Umawi he too was unaware of the state of affairs in Iraq. He, therefore, asked me anxiously as to what news I had brought from Iraq. I replied that I had brought news which would make the Governor of Madina happy and that news was that Husayn bin Ali had been killed and thereby the conflict had come to an end. On hearing this news Amr bin Sa'id bin As became extremely happy and said: "Go and inform the people that he has been slain". I went out and proclaimed to the people that Husayn bin Ali had been martyred in Iraq. I swear by Allah that on hearing this the ladies of Bani Hashim began to lament in a manner which I had never witnessed before. When Amr bin Sa'id heard the lamentations of the Hashimite women for the Holy Imam he laughed and said: "The women of Bani Ziyad lamented in the same manner in which our women lamented in the Battle of Urnab".*

Then he said: "The present lamentation of Hashimite women should be compared with the lamentations of Umayyad women who were bereaved and who mourned over the murder of Uthman". Amr bin Sa'id was also under a false impression like Yazid and Ibn Ziyad and imagined that it was possible to confuse and mislead history. He wanted to connect the killing of Imam Husayn with that of Uthman and to show that Imam Ali and his sons had taken part in it, although the fact is that when Uthman was in trouble their role consisted of advice, love and benevolence. They did not take any part in Uthman's murder. On the contrary they had done their best to make the disturbance subside and had also carried water for him during the days of siege. Amr did not know that these falsehood, calumnies and idle talks could not produce any result except disgrace for those who uttered them. He arrived in the Masjid

---

*This is the poetic verse of Umar bin Ma'd Yakrab Zubaydi. The Battle of Urnab took place between Bani Zubayd and Bani Ziyad and Bani Ziyad bin Harith bin Ka'b were defeated by Raht Abdul Madan.

of Madina, mounted the pulpit and announced that the Imam had been killed. However, as the women and men belonging to Ahlul Bayt had entrusted a document to history on each occasion and expressed reality in reply to the nonsensical talk of the enemy, a lady belonging to the Holy family also gave a reply to the idle words of the Governor of Madina on this occasion. It has also been recorded in the pages of history. It has been written that at this time a girl belonging to the family of Aqil bin Abi Talib came out of her house along with the ladies of Bani Hashim, proceeded to the sacred grave of the Holy Prophet, embraced the grave and while wailing, uttered the two poetic verses translated below. In them she has summarized the history of Āshura:

"The Day of Judgement will come. The grandfather of this very Husayn bin Ali whom you have killed and whose martyrdom is being mentioned by you as a happy news will come face to face with you and will ask: 'What did you, who were the best of the communities, do and how did you behave towards my children and the members of my family after my death? You killed their men and made them welter in their blood and made their women and children prisoners".

HOLY FAMILY RETURNS TO MADINA

The people of Madina came to know about the martyrdom of the Imam in this way and awaited the return of the Ahlul Bayt who had been made prisoners. At last Imam Sajjad and his companions reached Madina. He dismounted near Madina and made the ladies descend. He then sent a man to Madina to inform the people about his arrival. The messenger says that when he arrived in Madina he went to the Masjid of the Prophet of Allah. There he wept loudly and said: "O people of Yathrib! With what hope can one continue to live in this city? Husayn bin Ali has been martyred and the eyes of the people are shedding tears for him".

The Imam's messenger could content himself with saying this. However, he did not consider it sufficient to explain his own object as well as that of his Imam. He did not desire that people should weep and lament much. However, he wanted to add a document to the documents about the tragedy of Karbala so that the study of the event might become easier for those who came later. It was not the only object of the rising of Imam Husyan that spiritual reward should be earned by arranging meetings for mourning his martyrdom and it should not always be made the subject matter of religious discourses from the pulpit as a touching event which provokes tears. The event of the rising of Imam Husayn is in itself a very important event and has a vital significance in the history of Islam which should be studied keeping in view its own value and worth. It is more valuable than that it should be mentioned lightly while studying other matters.

In the second poetic verse recited by the messenger of the Imam he disgraced the Umayyad dynasty for ever. Standing by the grave of the Holy Prophet he said: "These faithless people killed the son of their Prophet, besmeared his body with dust and blood and hoisted his head on the spear".

Then he informed the people about the arrival of the Holy family and added that they had at that time dismounted outside the city of Madina.

The people started going out of the city and the roads were blocked. Madina assumed an unusual appearance. When Imam Sajjad saw himself face to face with the people of Madina he made a sign to the people to remain quiet. At this moment he considered it necessary to inform the Muslims of Madina about the events which had taken place during the journey covering a number of months. The details of his speech on this occasion will be given later.

When the Ahlul Bayt left for Madina they were, notwithstanding their being bereaved and mournful, fully confident about their own victory and the helplessness of the enemy. While they were still in Syria the signs of Yazid's helplessness began to appear. As we have alluded earlier the Ahlul Bayt were released from imprisonment soon and were transferred to the capital as ordered by the caliph. There they were treated by the people of Damascus with honour and respect. As written by Tabari the women of the family of Mu'awiya went, without exception, to the ladies of Bani Hashim to offer condolences. They mourned the martyrdom of Imam Husayn and a gathering to mourn for the martyrs of Bani Hashim was held in the palace of the caliph for three days. Yazid did not spend the morning and the evening except in the company of Imam Sajjad. It was on one of those days when a child of Imam Hasan or Imam Husayn had accompanied the fourth Imam and during the course of conversation Yazid said to him: "Are you prepared to fight with my son Khalid?" He replied: "No, except that you may give a knife to me and a knife to him and then we may fight with each other". Yazid was deeply impressed by the bravery and frankness, especially of a child who had suffered so many hardships. He embraced him and said words which means: "The cub of a lion is also a lion".

NUAMĀN BIN BASHIR

Nuamān bin Bashir was ordered to make arrangements for the return of Ahlul Bayt and to send a reliable and honest person with them. According to Shaykh Mufid Nuamān himself was ordered to go with them. It is written in Akhbārud Duwal that Nuamān bin Bashir accompanied Ahlul Bayt from Syria to Madina along with thirty other men and served them throughout the journey. Nuamān treated them so respectfully that Fatima daughter of Imam Ali who was one of the ladies who had been made prisoners said to her sister lady Zaynab: "This man has behaved towards us very gently and it is proper that we may give him a reward". However, Nuamān did not accept the reward and said: "If I have rendered any service it has been for the sake of Allah and on account of your relationship with the Prophet of Allah".

Nuamān bin Bashir and his father both were the companions of the Holy Prophet. His father Bashir bin Sād Khazraji was the first person who took the oath of allegiance to Abu Bakr in Saqifa bani Sā'idah. It has been written that his object in taking this oath was not to please Allah, but he took it lest Sād bin Ubada Khazraji should attain to the caliphate. As he envied Sād and did not wish that any Khazraji except him should become caliph he made haste in taking the oath of allegiance to Abu Bakr and took it even before the distinguished Muhajirs did so. Nuamān himself was one of those persons who did not take the oath of allegiance to Imam Ali. He was a supporter of Mu'awiya and was inimical towards the people of Kufa on account of their friendship for Ali. After Uthman was killed and Imam Ali became caliph he (Nuamān) went away to Syria and in the Battle of Siffin none from amongst the Ansar (i.e. the Muslims who were the companions of the Holy Prophet and belonged to Madina) except Nuamān and Salma bin Mukhlad accompanied Mu'awiya. Nuamān was alive till 65 A.H. In that year he thought of becoming the caliph and some persons gathered round him. However, he was defeated by Marwan bin Hakam and killed. In any case, during the journey of Ahlul Bayt from Syria to Madina Nuamān behaved towards them with great respect, and every Muslim appreciates his good behaviour.

The Ahlul Bayt, however, reached near Madina. It was the same Madina which had been inhabited by the Holy Prophet and his descendants and for which they had great attachment. From the time of the Holy Prophet's migration i.e. from 1 A.H. the people of Madina i.e. the Ansar and the Muslims of the tribes of Aws and Khazraj had made extreme sacrifices for the sake of the Holy Prophet. It was the same city which received the Prophet of Islam with devotion and sincerity and opened its gates before him when all other gates were closed for him, and also provided quarters to the Muhajirs and homeless Muslims who migrated from Makkah and othe regions of the Hijaz. The Prophet, too, who had at one time migrated to this place only to comply with the Command of Allah, developed so much love for it that even after the conquest of Makkah in 8 A.H. he did not choose to reside in Makkah and returned to Madina after the Battles of Hunayn and Tāif were over, and spent the remaining part of his life there. He went to Makkah only in 10 A.H. to perform Haj and to teach the Muslims the ceremonies connected therewith and even then he returned to Madina after performing Haj.

Madina was the birth-place of Imam Husayn and most of his brothers and sisters. Fifty seven years of his life had been spent in Madina excluding the period of four years and four months of the caliphate of his father and his brother Imam Hasan when he remained in Iraq. Madina was the city which provided favourable atmosphere for the Prophet's call to Islam and at a time when Makkah had virtually become a prison for him it was this city which made his message reach the people of the world.

Imam Ali hints in one of his sermons at the facilities which Madina provided for the spread of Islam. He says: "The Prophet of Allah was born in Makkah but migrated to Madina. It was from there that he communicated the message of Islam to different parts of the world".* The near relations of the Prophet of Allah were hostile to him. They fought against him and made him leave his home. However, the two tribes of Aws and Khazraj accepted him, brought him to their city and sacrificed their lives and wealth to spread his call. This is the fact which Ali has mentioned in one of his aphorisms; he says: "When the relatives and near ones of a person desert him and do not render him assistance, others come forward to help him and Allah prepares them to take the place of his near relations". The same thing happened in the case of the Prophet of Allah. There were twenty five families of Quraysh, who were all related to the Holy Prophet and were the descendants of Prophet Ibrahim, Adnān and Nazar bin Kanāna were the honourable fore-fathers of the Holy Prophet. All these families who were Isamaili and Adnāni Arabas rose in opposition to the Prophet of Allah and, so long as he was in Makkah, prevented the expansion of Islam by all possible means. They tortured the followers of the Holy Prophet and killed some of them in a most tragic manner. They used abusive and unbecoming language for the Holy Prophet till he was obliged to migrate from Makkah. And even when he went to another city they did not leave him alone but started hostilities, created trouble, killed his supporters as and when it was possible and instigated the Jews of Madina to fight against him and violate the pacts made with him. They sent their eloquent poets to the Bedouin Arabs and instigated them also to rise against the Prophet of Allah till in 5 A.H. they were able to gather together about 12,000 persons against the Muslims from amongst the polytheists of Makkah, the Bedouins and the Jews. All this was done by the near relations of the Prophet of Allah. These ungrateful Quraysh remained inimical towards him before as well as after migration and did not change their attitude till Makkah was conquered and they were no longer in a position to oppose him.

*Nahjul Balaghah (Sermon 156).

Imam Ali wrote to Muawiya: "Our people i.e. our relatives and the families of Quraysh, all of whom were our uncles and cousins determined to kill our Prophet and annihilate us. They took decisions and also acted to destroy us. They deprived us of the amenities of life and subjected us to all inconveniences and fear. They made us so helpless that we had to take refuge in an uneven mountain i.e. for three years and a few months we were besieged in one of the valleys of Makkah called Shib Abi Talib and spent our lives there in constant fear. Apart from what they did in Makkah, when we abandoned our home and went to other cities, they did not let us live in peace there also, but sparked off war and created mischief".* In these few sentences Imam Ali has referred to the activities of the relatives of the Holy Prophet against the Prophet. He briefly mentions every stage at which he was opposed by them and refers to Quraysh all the difficulties and impediments that he had to surmount. Such was the behaviour of the relatives of the Holy Prophet towards him and this is a specimen of their enmity and unkindness towards a man whose fame, and the spread of whose call, and whose recognition by the people as their chief, would have been more than anything else a means of their own honour and pride. However, as against these unkind and ungrateful people of Quraysh, who, it might be said, were opposed to their own dignity and honour, two groups, who were the descendants of the Qahtāni tribes of Yemen, got ready to accept and support the Prophet of Allah and made more sacrifices for the advancement of the Prophet's call than could be expected of the near ones. They were not Adnāni or Ismaili Arabs and had no relationship with Quraysh or the families of Hashim and Abdul Muttalib. However, with the preliminaries which Allah provided, hundreds of years before the birth of the Prophet of Islam. He made them migrate from South Arabia and Yemen to North Arabia and the Wādiul Qura in the Hijaz and the city of Yathrib.

TRIBES OF AWS AND KHAZRAJ

After the destruction of the Ma'ārib dam of Yemen a large part of the lands of Yemen became uncultivable. The

*Nahjul Balaghah (Letter No. 9).

opening of the sea route of the Red Sea and the deterioration of the economic importance of Yemen was the pretext for their migration, and it is possible that each of these two things had an effect on the scattering of the Qahtāni tribes of Yemen. In any case on whatever pretext it might have been, the Almighty Allah brought these two tribes of Yemen to Yathrib and made them settle there, and eventually when it became intolerable for the Holy Prophet to continue to live in Makkah amongst his relations, these two tribes received him and his immigrant companions, gave them place in their houses and preferred them even to themselves.

From the day these two tribes called Aws and Khazraj came to Yathrib and settled there, they were continuously fighting with each other till they were fed up with this state of affairs and realized that if they continued to fight they would be annihilated and the Jews of Yathrib belonging to the tribes of Bani Nazir etc. would prevail over them. Some of them were, therefore, obliged to go to Makkah to seek assistance from Quraysh so that they might become exalted and powerful. However, Quraysh put forward certain conditions which were not acceptable to them. Then they went to Tāif and sought the assistance of the tribe of Thaqif. However, they also dilly-dallied and the persons from Yathrib returned home without achieving any result. In the meantime the Holy Prophet had made his call public in the 4th year of his mission. For ten years continuously he contacted the people in the bazaars of Arabia like ukkāz and Zul Hijāz and the pilgrims during Haj season at Mina, Makkah etc. and invited them to Islam. He asked them to assist him and support his Divine mission so that they might be rewarded with Paradise. He approached various tribes one after the other and said to them: "O people! Say that there is no deity but Allah so that you may be delivered, rule over the Arabs and non-Arabs and become the chiefs in Paradise as a result of your faith. None of the Arab tribes except Aws and Khazraj of Yathrib agreed to receive the afflicted homeless Muslims. It was only this sacred city which could embrace the Holy Prophet of Allah for ever. As a consequence of the demise of Abu Talib and Khadijah in the 10th year of the Holy Prophet's mission it became very difficult for him to stay on in Makkah.

The city of Tāif also did not accept him. In the circumstances he made greater efforts to contact the various tribes. After having one or two brief contacts with the people of Yathrib he met a group of persons belonging to that city in the vicinity of Mina in Haj days in the 11th year of his mission and asked them: "Who are you?" They replied: "We belong to the tribe of Khazraj". The Holy Prophet said: "Are you confederates of the Jews?" They replied: "Yes". The Prophet asked: "Won't you sit with me so that I may have a talk with you?" They replied: "Certainly". They then sat down with the Prophet of Allah and he invited them to Islam and recited verses of the Holy Qur'an for them. After hearing the Holy Prophet the people belonging to Yathrib said to one another: "By Allah this is that very Prophet about whose prophethood the Jews used to warn us. These persons who were six in number and belonged to the tribe of Khazraj accepted the invitation of the Holy Prophet. All of them embraced Islam on the spot and said: "We have courted our people's enmity and are at the juncture of warfare. We hope that the Almighty Allah will create mutual love in them through you. We are now returning to Yathrib and shall invite them by means of this religion. In that event you will become very honoured and powerful among us. At this time the Qahtānis of Yemen i.e. the tribes of Aws and Khazraj were accepting the Holy Prophet's invitation to Islam, providing preliminaries for his migration to their city and discerning in him ability to unite their two tribes, which had been fighting with each other for many years. Meanwhile the relatives of the Holy Prophet and the distinguished persons amongst Quraysh were planning to kill him and did not consider any thing more necessary to achieve their prosperity and good luck than to put an end to his life.

These six persons belonging to the Khazraj tribe returned to Madina, informed the people about their meeting and conversation with the Holy Prophet as an important news. It was an important matter and a harbinger of honour and prosperity for them. They invited the people to embrace Islam. Islam began to spread soon in the favourable atmosphere of Madina and there was not a single house of Aws and Khazraj where the Prophet of Allah was not talked about. The number of the Ansari Muslims who were the first to embrace Islam has been reported by some writers to be two and by others to be eight.

In the following year i.e. in the 12th year of the Holy Prophet's mission twelve persons belonging to Madina took the oath of allegiance to him in Aqabah (Mina) during Haj season. These persons consisted of five out of the six persons who had taken the oath in the previous year and seven others. They swore that they would not associate anyone else with Allah, would not commit theft and adultery, would not kill their children, would not beget illegitimate children and would not disobey the Prophet of Allah and would perform good deeds. The Holy Prophet also promised them that if they remained faithful they would be sent to Paradise. He also told them that if they committed any of these evil acts and were punished for it, the punishment would constitute atonement for it. In case, however, the crime remained undetected till the Day of Judgement the decision would rest with Allah. He might punish them for it, or might forgive them".

The twelve persons returned to Yathrib and the Prophet of Allah sent Mus'ab bin Umayr Abdari along with them so that he might teach the Qur'an and invite everyone to embrace Islam. Mus'ab invited the people to Islam with so much zeal that this religion spread very rapidly and Muslim men and women could be found in every quarter of the city inhabited by Aws and Khazraj. In the 13th year of the prophetic mission seventy five persons consisting of men and women met the Holy Prophet near Mina and took the oath of allegiance to him in the presence of his uncle Abbas. This oath was taken at midnight after the Haj ceremonies. Abbas had not embraced Islam till then but was present at that time because he was interested in the safety of his nephew. He took a promise from them that they would abide by their words and would not make the Prophet of Allah leave his home unnecessarily.

Ya'qubi writes: "They requested the Prophet of Allah to accompany them to Madina and undertook to defend him against his own people as well as against the strangers and the black-skinned as well as the red-skined people. Abbas bin Abdul Muttalib then said: "May may parents be your ransom! Let me obtain a promise from them". The Prophet of Allah entrusted this task to his uncle and Abbas obtained a promise from them that they would support the Prophet of Allah and his people just as they supported their own people and children, would fight against the black-skinned and the red-skinned people for his sake and would assist him against his relatives as well as against the strangers. The Holy Prophet also promised that he would honour this pact and added that their place would be in Paradise".

AUTHORITIES ON THE EVENT OF KARBALA

The event of the tragedy of Karbala is nearing completion. It however seems desirable to mention some important authorities and authentic references which have not been stated up till now.

One of those valuable authorities is the sermon which Imam Sajjad, the fourth Imam delivered in Damascus, the capital of the Islamic caliphate, in the year 61 A.H. He acquired a very suitable opportunity, which he availed of in the most sublime manner.

Indeed, it may be said that the best opportunity which Imam Sajjad got during his journey as a captive was on the day when the official preacher of the caliph mounted the pulpit and began to vilify Imam Ali and his children and to praise Mu'awiya and his children. Of course, this stage was designed by Yazid himself. It was he who ordered a preacher to mount the pulpit and inform the people of Syria about the evil deeds (God forbid!) of Imam Husayn and his father, Imam Ali. This drama, like many other dramas in history, was also staged against truth and the truthful people. Those who staged it did not, however, realize that truth can utilize every development to its own advantage and every plan which is chalked out to destroy it increases its strength. Imam Sajjad's addressing the people in these cities was especially necessary because from the day on which the city of Damascus was conquered till the day on which the Ahlul Bayt who had been made captives arrived there (i.e. for about 46 years) it had been continuously under the influence of Bani Umayya and the Islamic Government there was administered by the Umayyads who had been old enemies of Ahlul Bayt (the progeny of the Holy Prophet) during the Age of Ignorance as well as after their embracing Islam.

In 13 A.H., four days before the death of Abu Bakr, the

Muslim mujahids besieged Damascus under the command of Khalid bin Walid. When Abu Bakr died and Umar succeeded him as caliph he removed Khalid from the Commandership and Abu Ubayda took his place. The Muslims continued the siege of Damascus for one year and a few days and were able to conquer it in the month of Rajab of 14 A.H. For some time Yazid bin Abu Sufyan was the Governor of Damascus and when he died of plague in 17 A.H. Umar appointed his brother Mu'awiya in his place. Mu'awiya held this office from 17 A.H. till the beginning of the Caliphate of Imam Ali in 35 A.H. During the time of the Caliphate of Imam Ali and Imam Hasan, which lasted for about five years, Mu'awiya held Syria under his control and Damascus remained the base of enmity against Ahlul Bayt. After Imam Hasan renounced the caliphate in 41 A.H. this city became the capital of the caliphate and Islamic Government and till 61 A.H. i.e. for about twenty years was more than ever a centre of hostility against Bani Hashim and especially against Imam Ali. In 61 A.H. Imam Sajjad arrived in this city and got an opportunity to address its inhabitants and to unveil the realities which had remained hidden from them for a period of forty-six years. Of course, Imam Sajjad did not get this opportunity to address the people easily and had to face numerous difficulties and inconveniences to acquire it, but even then it was something very valuable. What could be better than that Imam Sajjad, the grandson of Imam Ali and the son of Imam Husayn, should have come to Damascus on the insistence of the caliph himself, where he mounted the pulpit which had been set for vilifying his honourable ancestors, set at naught the forty-six year old propaganda of Bani Umayya and enlightened with one speech those people, who had been ignorant of truth for years. In this way their hostility against Ahlul Bayt immediately converted into friendship and they became acquainted with the sacred names which they had seldom heard before.

We think that till that time most of the people of Syria did not know that the Doyen of the Martyrs was Hamza bin Abdul Muttalib or that the Holy Prophet had said about Imam Hasan and Husayn that they were the chiefs of the young men of Paradise. It cannot, therefore, be imagined that if Imam Sajjad and his aunt lady Zaynab had not got such an opportunity or had not availed of one which had been bestowed upon them by Allah it would have been possible for anyone till the end of the caliphate of Bani Umayya in 132 A.H. to utter a word, in the unfavourable atmosphere of Damascus, about the magnanimity and greatness of the persons belonging to Ahlul Bayt or to introduce them as the honourable personalities of Islam. After these speeches, however, the position became such that although during the period of 1000 month rule of Bani Umayya, Bani Hashim and Ahlul Bayt and the followers of Imam Ali were tormented and persecuted, the effect of these speeches also remained firm and established. In fact, the efforts of the distinguished companion, Abuzar Ghifari, had already created a favourable atmosphere for the success of these speeches and with the arrival of Ahlul Bayt in Syria and with what the people of Damascus heard from them, the memory of Abuzar, who had firmly and openly opposed the deviations of Mu'awiya, was revived. (Refer to Abuzar Ghifari, ISP, 1984)

Abuzar was a very out-spoken, religious and brave person and as soon as he realized that the Islamic Caliphate had deviated from its proper course he opposed and criticized it in the presence of the caliph as well as in the streets and the bazaars. He may be considered to be the founder of such Islamic risings and movements, because he was a companion of the Holy Prophet and enjoyed precedence over others in the chronological order. Of course, Abuzar was exiled, suffered hardships and died in Rabaza in a state of helplessness, but in spite of all this he never sat still and continued to invite the people to good and to restrain them from evil.

After Mu'awiya came in power some other persons continued the task of Abuzar. Abuzar departed from the world but Hujr bin Ady Kindi took his place and said what ought to have been said. He opposed with great boldness the regime which had declared in the name of Islam the vilification of Imam Ali to be a religious duty and even a condition for the acceptance of worship, and laid down his life in pursuance of this task. Hujr did not reach Damascus and was killed at Marj Uzrā, a place situated near that city, but even there he continued to say what he had to say and to defend Imam Ali's right. However, the words of Abuzar and Hujr bin Ady and his friends could not constitute a sufficient reply to the unjust propaganda of the Umayyad dynasty and caliphate which extended over a period of more than forty years. It was, therefore, necessary that persons belonging to Ahlul Bayt should have met the people of this city themselves and removed their misunderstanding. They should have furnished a living proof of the services rendered by the distinguished members of the family of Bani Hashim to Islam and the Muslims of the world and also made public the shameful past of Bani Umayya consisting of enmity with the Prophet of Allah and the Muslims. It was for this reason that Imam Sajjad considered the availability of the pulpit and an assembly to be something very valuable and joined that assembly notwithstanding the fact that it had been arranged to vilify Imam Husayn and his father Imam Ali.

The preacher appointed by Mu'awiya mounted the pulpit and praised Allah. Then he abused Imam Ali and Imam Husayn and at the same time praised Mu'awiya and Yazid lavishly and associated every goodness with them as if these father and son were the fountain-head of all noble acts and good morals and whatever the people possessed had been given to them by the descendants of Abu Sufyan. They had to depend on them for their prosperity in this world and in the Hereafter and the only source to gain Divine pleasure was to obey and follow them.

It was on this occasion that Imam Sajjad said loudly without any fear or apprehension: "Woe be to you O speaker! Why in order to please the people are you courting Allah's wrath? You should know that your destination is Hell".

The remark of the Imam was aimed at the preacher of Damascus who annoyed Allah to please Yazid and thus chose the path to Hell, but actually it contains advice for every speaker and warns him against things which displease Allah and please His creatures. All the Muslim speakers have thus been instructed to keep in view only the Divine pleasure in whatever they say, and should communicate Allah's message to the people without any addition or distortion. They should not say anything which displeases Allah so as to please people and should have firm faith in what Allah has said in this regard in the Holy Qur'an: *Certainly We created man, and We know what his soul whispers to him. We are closer to him than his jugular vein. Since the two scribes are placed on each of his shoulders, man does not utter a word which is not recorded immediately by the watchful scribes.* (Surah Qaf, 50:16 — 18)

These are the words of Allah which find their place in the Holy Qur'an. Imam Sajjad was also inviting the attention of the ignorant preacher to this very thing and warning him that every good or bad act of man is recorded and one should not ignore the wrath of Allah to please one of His creatures and should not forget that a day will come when the persons whom he considered powerful will not be able to do anything for him.

After reproaching the caliph's preacher and admonishing him for his extravagant talk, Imam Sajjad (Zaynul Abidin) turned to Yazid and said: "Do you permit me as well to ascend these pieces of wood and say something which may please Allah and become a means of spiritual reward for the listeners?"

A very fascinating wit is hidden in these few words of Imam Sajjad and it might be said that he summarized in a few words what he wanted to say. Firstly he did not seek permission to ascend the pulpit but the piece of wood. He meant to say that everything which is given the shape of a pulpit and someone mounts and delivers a speech from there, cannot be called a pulpit. On the contrary these pieces of wood are a means to destroy the pulpits. Anybody who assumes the guise of a preacher cannot be called the promoter and preacher of religion. He also meant to say that the preacher who had delivered the speech had sold his faith for the sake of worldly gains and had agreed to please the people and to displease Allah and his destination was, therefore, Hell. Then Imam Sajjad said: "I want to say things which may please Allah". He meant to say that what the preacher was saying was the cause of inviting Divine wrath and it was not possible to earn Allah's pleasure by abusing a man like Imam Ali and by praising a man like Yazid. He himself, therefore, wanted to say things through which the listeners might earn spiritual reward i.e. what the preacher was saying could not produce any result other than sinfulness and adversity for the people and their deviating from the right path.

The people insisted that Yazid should permit the Imam to speak but he declined vehemently to do so and said at last:

"These are people brought up in the atmosphere of knowledge and wisdom and if I allow him to speak he will put me to shame". However, insistence of the people prevailed and Imam Sajjad mounted the pulpit. He spoke in such a way that the people were moved and began to weep and cry. The son of Imam Husayn indicated the position of Ahlul Bayt in the Islamic society and made their merits and virtues known to the people. He also put forward a logical verdict which is accepted by all wise men. He said: "Whoever wishes to lead and guide the people must be superior to them and be chosen for their leadership on account of that very superiority. The Holy Qur'an says about this very logical verdict: *Is one who guides to the truth a proper guide or one who himself cannot find guidance unless he is guided? What is wrong with you that you judge so unjustly?* (Surah Yunus, 10:36)

This verse is not used as an argument, rather the attention of the people has been invited to the very logical verdict that only that person who is more knowledgeable, can guide the people and not others, and whoever himself needs guidance cannot guide others. Although the polytheists of Makkah did not believe in the prophethood of the Holy Prophet of Allah, they accepted the logical verdict that if a prophet was to be appointed by Allah a great man of the nation should have been chosen for this task. They were, however, mistaken about the means of greatness and source of superiority and thought that greatness depended on a large amount of wealth or many sons and kinsmen or power. They, therefore, used to say: "If Allah desired to send a prophet for us, the people of the Hijaz, why did he not appoint to this office the great man of Makkah i.e. Walid bin Mughira Makhzumi or the great man of Taif i.e. Urwa bin Masud Thaqafi?" The Holy Qur'an says: *They say why this Qur'an had not been revealed to a great man from either of the two towns.* (Surah Zukhruf, 43:32)

The polytheists of Makkah were correct in saying that the Divine Book should have been revealed to one of the great men of the Hijaz. They were, however, mistaken in attributing the quality of greatness to Walid or Urwa. This was so because they treated wealth and material power and distinction to be the criterion of greatness and superiority but did not attach any importance to knowledge, good morals and other human virtues They could not, therefore, believe that the great man of not only the Hijaz but of the entire world was Muhammad, the Prophet of Allah and not Walid or Urwah.

In his sermon Imam Sajjad mentioned the merits by which an individual could excel another individual and a nation could become superior to another nation. He also made it clear that the Holy family of the Prophet enjoyed superiority over others and others are not of the same rank, because Allah has made them superior to others and chosen them for the guidance and training of the Muslims. Imam Sajjad said explicitly and with great boldness: "O people! Allah has given us six things and our superiority over others rests on seven pillars. We have been given knowledge which is the basic condition for the superiority of an individual over an individual or of a nation over a nation. We have been given forbearance which is very important for the reformation and guidance of the people. Generosity which is useful for the Islamic rulers is our habit. Eloquence which is extremely necessary for the guidance of the people and enjoining them to do good and restraining them from evil and enlightening and stimulating them for jihad. And self-sacrifice is our family distinction. Bravery on which leadership and rulership rest has been given to us. Friendship and affection of the faithful people which is the secret of rulership and sovereignty has been given to us i.e. it is not possible to acquire the friendship and attachment of the people by force". By uttering these words he meant to say: "O Yazid! Allah has desired that the faithful people should love us and it is not possible to restrain them from doing so, and not do anything whereby they may become friendly towards others and inimical towards us".

Then Imam Sajjad said: "Our superiority over others, whoever they may be, rests on these distinctions: Muhammad, the Prophet of Allah, his successor Ali bin Abi Talib, Hamza bin Abdul Muttalib, the heavenly flyer, Ja'far bin Abi Talib, Hasan and Husayn, the two grandsons of the Prophet of this nation, and the Mahdi (the saviour of the oppressed) viz. the twelfth Imam they all belong to us. That being so Yazid should in the first instance take away these distinctions from us, if possible, and attribute the same to himself. In other words he should distort the facts of history, if he can, so that it may give him what belongs to us, overlook his shameful and evil deeds and re-allocate the positions. Yazid should grapple with us only if he can do this. Otherwise, how can it be possible to make us obscure or to defame us or to give our right to others or to turn towards others the hearts attached to us, till the day the distinctions of Islam are with us and the members of the family of Bani Hashim like Abu Talib and his brother Hamza and his sons Ali and Ja'far and the sons of Imam Ali i.e. Hasan and Husayn are recorded in history as the most sincere servants of Allah and especially when the Prophet of Allah also belongs to the family of Bani Hashim". Then Imam Sajjad introduced himself and the condition became such that Yazid was obliged to interrupt him and in order to achieve his end he asked the mu'azzin to pronounce the call to prayers. The Imam also became silent as a mark of respect to the name of the Almighty Lord. However, he got another opportunity soon and availed of it fully i.e. when the mu'azzin said: "I testify that Muhammad is the Prophet of Allah", Imam Sajjad took off his turban and said: "O mu'azzin! I ask you to keep quiet for the sake of the very Prophet whose name you have just taken". Then he turned towards Yazid and said: "Is this Holy Prophet your grandfather or mine? If you say that he is your grandfather all know that you will be telling a lie. And if you say that he is my grandfather why did you kill my father, plunder his property and make his women captives?" Then he tore the collar of his shirt and continued to speak till the people were deeply moved and the gathering dispersed in a state of confusion and disorder.

EXPLANATION OF THE SERMON
OF IMAM SAJJAD IN DAMASCUS

In the foregoing pages we have reproduced the sermon delivered by Imam Sajjad in Damascus. Every word of that sermon confirms the frankness, bravery and spiritual greatness of the Imam and incidentally the value and necessity of such sermons and speeches delivered in the circumstances then prevailing become clear. It has also become evident that these sermons and addresses were not such that they should have been delivered as a consequence of sentiments, spiritual uneasiness and pressure of hardships. Whatever the men and women of Ahlul Bayt said during the journey, which culminated in their martyrdom and captivity, and has been recorded in history, consists of speeches which were delivered, as and when it was appropriate and necessary, in accordance with a minute and properly chalked out plan. Just as Imam Husayn knew well as to what he was doing and where he was going and what the result of his activities would be, other members of the Holy Prophet's family also possessed perfect insight, and whenever they felt it necessary to speak they ignored all their mental sufferings and depressions, and revealed the realities in such a way that it was no longer possible to tamper with them. It is, however, certain that at that time most of the people were not aware of the importance of their speeches and the depth of their object. Very often they thought about this very sermon of the fourth Imam that a bereaved person was crying and lamenting as his sentiments had been aroused and with the passage of time he would become calm and forget all that he was saying. However, history not only recorded the sermon delivered by the fourth Imam but also recorded the words and poetic verses of Yazid and handed them over to the posterity, and placed them side by side with each other so that on one page of history the people should read that Imam Sajjad said in the city of Damascus with great dignity: "I am the son of Makkah and Mina. I am the son of Zamzam and Safa. I am the son of the Prophet of Allah", and on the next page of history they should find that Yazid said: "There was nothing like revelation or prophethood. On this pretext Bani Hashim wished to befool the people and to rule over them". Indeed, even if Yazid did not fear Allah and did not feel ashamed before the Holy Prophet why did he not fear the power of history and why was he not afraid that whatever he was saying would be recorded?

Individuals come in the world and depart and the nations are dislocated. However, the rise and fall of the nations and the change in governments does not affect history. It continues to occupy its place and carefully supervises the good and evil deeds of the individuals and the traffic of the nations. It does not confuse the account of one person with that of another and does not make anyone responsible for another's sin.

The Holy Qur'an says: *Those are a people who have passed away. Theirs is that which they earned, and yours is that which you earn. You will not be asked of what they used to do.* (Surah al-Baqarah, 2:134)

History records the behaviour of the people to maintain accounts in this world and the angels write them for accountability in the Hereafter.

In the second part of the speech delivered by lady Zaynab, daughter of Imam Ali in Damascus, (its first part has already been dealt with in the foregoing pages), she warned Yazid firstly of the accountability in the Hereafter and secondly of the accountability before history and the world. It was in this very part that she said to him: "O Yazid! On the day when Allah will be the judge and Prophet Muhammad will plead for justice and your limbs will give evidence against you, your father, who made you dominate the Muslims, will receive the punishment due to him. On that day it will become known what reward the oppressors get and whose place is worse and whose party is humble. (O enemy of Allah and O enemy of the son of the Prophet of Allah!) I swear by Allah that I consider you quite mean and incorrigible. However, what can I do? Our eyes weep and our bosoms burn and our martyrs cannot come to life by reproaching or reprimanding you. Our Husayn has been killed and the partisans of Satan take us to the fools and take from Allah's wealth remuneration for showing disrespect to Allah. Our blood trickles from their hands and our flesh falls from their mouths and the pure bodies of our martyrs have been placed at the disposal of the wolves and the rapacious animals of the jungle. If you think that you stand to gain today by killing us, you will suffer for it on the Day of Judgement. It will be the day on which you will possess nothing except your deeds. It will be the day on which you will shout at the son of Marjāna and he will shout at you. It will be the day on which you and your followers will quarrel with one another by the side of the scale of Divine Justice. It will be the day on which you will learn that the best provision which your father made for you was that you should kill the descendants of the Prophet of Allah. I swear by Allah that I do not fear anyone except Him and do not complain before anyone else".

So far the daughter of Imam Ali warned Yazid of Divine punishment and accountability on the Day of Judgement. Then she invited his attention to his being accountable to history and told him that even if he did not fear Allah and did not believe in the Day of Judgement or had lost his faith on account of his sins, he should fear history which would disgrace him. It was with this object in view that the daughter of Ali said: "O Yazid! Practise deceit, pursue your vicious plans and do whatever you can. I swear by Allah that the stain of disgrace which has been stamped on your name owing to the treatment meted out by you to us cannot be obliterated and this ignominy can never be converted to goodness". The daughter of lady fatima Zahra invited the attention of Yazid to the might of history and warned him against shame and disgrace. However, Yazid who, it might be said, had lost intelligence did not benefit from lady Zaynab's words and could not foresee the future of history. On this occasion the following tradition of the Holy Prophet quoted by Suyuti in his book Jāmi'us Saghir was applicable to Yazid: "When Allah wishes to execute His Decree He takes away intelligence from the intelligent people so that He may do with them what He likes. And, when what He wills is accomplished, He restores their intelligence to them and then they regret very much what they have done". If Yazid had not been deprived of his intelligence he should have realized that after killing the son of the Prophet of Allah and his near ones, it would not be possible for him to rule the Muslims and to ignore this great Islamic tragedy. And even if he could not understand this fact he should have at least so much sense that he should not have attacked the very basis of Islam in his poetic verses and should not have announced openly his decision to take revenge upon the children of the Prophet of Allah and should not have denied the Divine revelation and the Prophethood of the Holy Prophet Muhammad.

Lady Zaynab, the daughter of Fatima Zahra concluded her speech with thanks to Allah and said: "Allah be thanked Who ended the task of the chiefs of the young men of Paradise with benevolence and made Paradise their resting place. I pray to Allah that He may raise their ranks and shower His blessings on them, for Allah is Almighty, All-Powerful".

It was this very speech which obliged Yazid to pretend disgust for Ibn Ziyad and to curse him. It has been written that while sending the Ahlul Bayt to Madina Yazid called Imam Sajjad and said to him: "May Allah curse the son of Marjāna. By Allah, if I had met your father I would have agreed to whatever he had suggested and asked for, and would not have allowed, as far as possible, that he should have been killed. However, whatever has happened had been destined. I wish that you may write to me from Madina for all your requirements". Yazid did not say this to seek Divine pleasure. He was grateful to Ibn Ziyad that he had killed Imam Husayn and his companions and in reply to his letter seeking instructions about the Ahlul Bayt who had been made prisoners he (Yazid) had himself written that they should be sent to Syria. Yazid's cursing Ibn Ziyad had only a political tinge, and was the outcome of the pressure of public thinking. The sermon delivered by Imam Sajjad in Syria and the Qur'anic verses recited by him in the bazaar in reply to a Syrian and whatever else the Ahlul Bayt said produced their result. So much so that the martyrdom of Imam Husayn was mourned first of all in Damascus, the capital of the caliphate, and in the caliph's own house. The Syrian women also came to know the true facts about the tragedy of Karbala. Perhaps the month of Muharram of the year 61 A.H. had not yet come to an end when the news of the martyrdom of Imam Husayn reached various Islamic regions and their inhabitants became aware of most of the events that had taken place. When the storm and thunder of the caliphate subsided the people came to their senses, felt grieved on account of what had happened and reproached themselves for their unpardonable negligence in helping the Imam and supporting Truth. Gradually the same correct view was adopted as had prompted the people of Kufa to invite the Imam before his martyrdom.

Later, they realized their mistake and decided to make amends for it, although the loss of an Imam like Husayn bin Ali, the grandson of the Holy Prophet, was irreparable and wailing and regret could not make amends for it. Muʻawiya had said: "After Ali bin Abi Talib the world has become barren and cannot produce a son like him". Indeed it is so and another Ali cannot be born. Similarly it is impossible to produce an Imam like Husayn, because there must be pure and sacred parents like his to give birth to a son like him. Every loss can be made good sooner or later, but how can the loss of such sublime personalities be compensated?

SERMON OF IMAM SAJJAD IN MADINA

Our discourse with regard to the study of the event of Karbala is now nearing its end, and its last part which cannot be dispensed with, is the sermon which the fourth Imam delivered in the precincts of Madina and in which he informed the people of Madina of what he saw during the course of this sacred rising.

Imam Sajjad praised Allah and thanked Him for the extreme sufferings which he had to bear and then summarized the event of Karbala in a few sentences. In his short and precise speech he said: "Allah is to be praised in all circumstances. He made us bear great hardships. A great breach has taken place in Islam. My father Abu Abdillah (Imam Husayn) and his dear ones and companions have been killed. His women and children were made captives. My father's head was fixed on a spear and shown round the different Islamic cities". It is evident from the speech of the Imam that he did not want to speak only with the object of expressing his sadness and creating a touching atmosphere. He really wanted to put the enemies of Ahlul Bayt to shame and to summarize their oppressions in clear words and bring them to light by means of these brief sentences. He also said: "O people! We were treated as if we were infidels and apostates, although we had not committed any crime or sin and had not in any way betrayed Islam. By Allah, if the Prophet of Allah had ordered them to fight against us they would have done nothing more than they did".

The sermon of the Imam came to an end. The members of the Holy family arrived in their houses. They recorded for ever in the name of Bani Hashim the honour of devotion and self-sacrifice in the path of truth and placed the names of their enemies in the category of tyrants and oppressors. They made patent this honour for themselves and this disgrace for their enemies by means of historical evidence which they placed at the disposal of the unbiased pages of history. It is not now possible for anyone to tamper with history, divest Bani Hashim of their good name and obliterate the digrace and ill fame of others. The discourses and speeches which the Ahlul Bayt delivered during their journeys from Madina to Makkah, from Makkah to Iraq, from Iraq to Syria and from Syria to Madina are recorded in the pages of history. It is, therefore, no longer possible to change the facts of history, to rearrange the positions of the martyrs in the path of Allah. The truthful and self-sacrificing persons cannot now be divested of their honours and good name; and the liars and the oppressors or persons devoid of virtue cannot be shown as manly and sacrificing persons. It is also not possible to do anything so that history may become unthankful and ungrateful and may ignore the services of sincere persons and conceal the evidence in their favour which is available with it, or may commit breach of trust in the matter of documents regarding their virtue, magnanimity and sinlessness. So long as the evidence of history regarding the ancients is available it will testify to the purity, infallibility, faith, piety, religiousness, and godliness of Imam Husayn and his companions and will speak about the oppression and egotism of his enemies. History is the only recourse which should be resorted to for the study of various events, because the lies and fables coined by those given to idle talking and writing cannot deprive history from distinguishing truth from falsehood, and wherever there is any doubt it can be removed in the light of its firm verdicts.

* * * * *

APPENDIX I

ARRIVAL OF JABIR AND ATIYYA IN KARBALA

Shaykh Tusi writes in his book entitled Misbāhul Mutahajjid that 20th of the month of Safar is the day on which Jabir bin Abdullah Ansari a companion of the Holy Prophet came from Madina to Karbala to pay homage to the sacred grave of Imam Husayn and he was the first person who performed homage to the grave of the Imam. Homage of Imam Husayn on that day is recommended and it is this very homage which is called *Ziyāratul Arba'in*. Shaykh Tusi appears to say that Jabir left Madina with the object of paying homage to the sacred grave of Imam Husayn and arrived at Karbala on the 20th day of Safar and not that he reached Karbala after forty days of the martyrdom of the Imam by chance. It is not unlikely that it was so, because after the arrival of Ahlul Bayt in Kufa Ibn Ziyad immediately despatched Abdul Malik bin Abil Hārith Salami from Iraq to the Hijaz so that he might arrive in Madina as early as possible and inform Amr bin Sa'id bin Ās Amavi, the Governor of Madina, about the martyrdom of the Imam and his companions and Abdul Malik proceeded to Madina at once, reached there after a few days, and formally conveyed the news of the martyrdom of the Imam to the governor. In that case it is possible that on hearing about the tragedy of the martyrdom of the Imam and Bani Hashim and the companions of the Imam, Jabir bin Abdullah Ansari, who according to some narration had lost both of his eyes by that time, might have departed from Madina with the intention of paying homage to the graves of Imam Husayn and his devoted friends, who bravely met martyrdom, and might have arrived in Karbala on the 20th of Safar i.e. exactly forty days after the martyrdom of the Imam and the tradition of the *Ziyāratul Arba'in*

209

of the Imam was commenced by him. Jabir did not perform this journey alone and had with him a companion who was younger than him and at the same time very learned and respectable. Owing to ignorance some persons have called this great man the slave of Jabir. In fact he enjoyed a high position which has been misrepresented in many religious circles like many other realities. This great man was Atiyya bin Sād bin Junāda Awfi Kufi who was a distinguished *Tābie'* (i.e. the companion of the companion of the Holy Prophet). Atiyya, though not a companion of the Holy Prophet had seen many of his companions like Abdullah Ibn Abbas and acquired knowledge from them.

Tabari, writes in his book entitled Muntakhab Zaylul Muzayyal that Atiyya bin Sād bin Junāda belonged to the Judaila family of the tribe known as Qays and his patronymic appellation was Abdul Hasan. Thereafter he narrates that Sād bin Junāda i.e. the father of Atiyya came to Imam Ali in Kufa and said: 'O Commander of the Faithful! Allah has given me a son. Kindly propose his name". Ali said: "He is the *atiyya* i.e. gift of Allah". In this sentence Ali also proposed his name and he was named Atiyya.

Tabari continues to say about Atiyya that in 81 A.H. he fought against Hajjaj bin Yusuf Thaqafi, the well-known tyrant Governor of Iraq, in the company of Abdur Rahman bin Muhammad bin Ashath. After Abdur Rahman was killed in 85 A.H. Atiyya ran away to Iran. Hajjaj wrote to Muhammad bin Qasim Thaqafi to summon Atiyya and ask him to curse Ali and, in the event of his refusal to do so, to slash him four hundred times and to shave his head and beard. Muhammad summoned Atiyya and read over Hajjaj's letter to him so that he might choose one of the two alternatives. Atiyya declined to curse Ali and did not do it and had consequently to agree that four hundred lashes might be struck on him and his head and beard might be shaved according to Hajjāj's orders. When Qutayba bin Muslim became the Governor of Khurāsan Atiyya migrated to that place and continued to stay on there till the time when Umar bin Habira became the Governor of Iraq. Atiyya wrote a letter to him seeking permission to return to Iraq. Umar accorded him permission and he went to Kufa and continued to reside there till he died in 111 A.H. Then Tabari writes that Atiyya quoted many traditions and is reliable.

The aforesaid event has also been narrated on the same lines in the sixth volume of Tabaqāt-i Ibn Sād and it has been added that Atiyya's mother was Roman slave-girl.

Besides being one of the narrators of traditions and a Muslim Mujahid Atiyya was a great commentator of the Holy Qur'an and he wrote a commentary on it in five volumes. As reported in Balāghātun Nisa he quoted the speech of lady Fatima Zahra about Fadak from Abdullah Mahz i.e. Abdullah bin Hasan bin Hasan whose father was Hasan Muthanna, son of Imam Hasan and whose mother was Fatima, daughter of Imam Husayn. Atiyya remained a pupil of Ibn Abbas for some time and attended his lectures on exegesis. He himself says: "I had three courses of the exegesis of the Qur'an and seventy courses of the reciting of the Qur'an with Ibn Abbas". It means that Ibn Abbas gave two kinds of instruction, one of which consisted of exegesis of the Qur'an and the other of reciting the Qur'an, and Atiyya attended three courses of the former and seventy of the latter.

HOLY QUR'AN — THE KEY TO SUCCESS

The above narration relating to Atiyya shows how great an importance the companions of the Prophet of Allah and the *Tabi'in* attached to the exegesis and reciting of the Qur'an and how fond they were of acquiring knowledge in this behalf. They knew very well that the glory of the Muslims and their prosperity in this world and in the Hereafter lies under the protection of the Qur'an and it has been revealed so that the Muslims may always recite it and reflect upon its contents. Furthermore, they should learn the meaning of the Qur'an from the Prophet of Allah and should also become acquainted with them themselves and ponder over them. In the following Qur'anic verse the Muslims have been asked to do two things: Firstly they should learn the meanings and the interpretation of the Qur'an from the Holy Prophet, and secondly they themselves should endeavour to understand it and ponder over its contents. The Almighty Allah says: *We have revealed to you the Qur'an that you may explain to the people that which has been revealed for them, so that perhaps they may reflect.* (Surah al-Nahl, 16:44) This verse means that the people are required to perform two things regarding the Holy Qur'an. Firstly they should learn and commit to memory the explanations provided by the Prophet of Allah and should understand by means of his remarks that which needs explanation. It does not, however, mean that an explanation by the Holy Prophet is needed also in respect of those verses which are explicit and clear. Help of explanation by the Holy Prophet is needed in respect of only those verses which are difficult to understand and must be explained in detail, because different persons interpret them differently. The second duty of the Muslims with regard to the Qur'an is that they themselves should also endeavour to profit by it and utilize their intellect to understand it. To say that the Prophet of Allah may recite the Qur'an before the Muslims and explain it to them does not mean that the Muslims should deprive themselves of understanding the Qur'an and should have asked the Prophet of Allah as to what he understood from the verse: *Allah commands (people) to maintain justice, kindness, and proper relation* . . . . . . (Surah al-Nahl, 16:90) The meaning of such verses are so clear that every person even with a smattering of Arabic language can profit from them and be guided by them and none will understand from this verse anything except that Allah has ordered the people to be just, not to be oppressive, to do good and be kind to their relatives. Similarly when verses like these were recited before the Muslims: *Woe be to the deceivers: those who when they take demand it in full, but if they measure to them or weigh for them, give less. Do such men not consider that they will be raised again to an awful Day — the day when people will be brought before the Lord of the worlds?* (Surah al-Mutaffifin, 83:1 — 6) they could not say that they did not understand their meaning and should, therefore, go and request the Prophet of Allah to explain the same to them. The Holy Qur'an contains such clear and explicit verses that the Muslims may read them, ponder over their import and obtain the best code of life. Whenever these verses or their translations are read over to some one he understands that Allah is warning those who weigh or measure less when they sell out something. They give to the people lesser than their right, but take their own right in full from them. Allah says that it appears that these people do not believe in the Day of Judgement, when all human beings will stand before

Him for the accountability of their deeds.

The Holy Qur'an is the Book from which all the Muslims should benefit and seek guidance and should consider it to be the best remedy for their spiritual and moral ailments. Of course, there are some verses which are difficult to understand and even the great scholars are unable to understand their correct meaning. In the case of such verses, therefore, there is no alternative but to resort to the remarks and explanations of the Prophet of Allah and the Holy Imams. However, all the verses of the Qur'an are not like this, for most of its verses are clear and explicit and intelligible to the people.

In many verses of the Qur'an the phrase, 'O people! or the phrase, 'O you who believe! occurs. The meaning of such phrases is that in the Holy Qur'an at some places the entire mankind is addressed, and at some places the believers, the unbelievers, and the hypocrites are addressed. The Heavenly Book is for the entire mankind. Islam too is a religion for the entire mankind. Of course, some persons have embraced it and acknowledge it to be the true religion and others have not embraced it and do not acknowledge it to be true. If some persons do not believe in Allah and have not expressed faith in Him it does not mean that we should say that Allah is the Lord of only the pious and godly people He is the Lord of all the beings which exist or can possibly come into existence and of all the human beings of the world whether believers or unbelievers. The Holy Prophet is also the Messenger of Allah for the entire mankind including those who believe in him as well as those who do not believe in him. The Qur'an is also a Book which has been revealed for the entire mankind and addresses all the human beings including those who consider it a Divine Book as well as those who do not believe in it on account of ignorance or obstinacy. Same is the case with Imam Ali and eleven other Imams who have been the Imams and leaders of the entire mankind and the Proof of Allah during the respective periods of their Imamate. They are the Imams of those who believe in their Imamate as well as of those who, for some reason or other, do not believe in it. Hence, to think that the Qur'an is incomprehensible to the common people and is a sacred Book, which should be kept in our houses only for the sake of felicity and blessings and even if it is read it should be read to earn spiritual reward and that it is not necessary to understand it and act upon it nor to become strong spiritually and morally, is a baseless thinking contrary to the Qur'an and religion. This attitude deprives the Muslims from reflecting upon the verses of the Qur'an so that they may not get an opportunity to become acquainted with it, to understand it, to take lessons from it and consequently to increase their faith by reading and hearing its verses. The Almighty Allah has desired His slaves to ponder over the contents of the Qur'an. He says: *Do they not ponder over the Qur'an or are their hearts still locked?* (Surah Muhammad, 47:24) It is not possible for anyone to recognize Allah and benefit from the teachings of the Qur'an and make it his guide in his life in this world and in the Hereafter without pondering over its contents and understanding it. In the Preface to the Tafsir (exegesis) entitled Majmaul Bayăn the late Aminul Islam quotes a tradition of the Holy Prophet which can help us in understanding this point. That tradition is as follows: The Holy Prophet said: "After reckoning has taken place on the Day of Judgement it will be said to the man of the Qur'an i.e. one who believed in the Qur'an and recited and understood it: "Read the Qur'an and ascend as you read it. Now also read the Qur'an in the same way in which you recited it correctly, slowly, regularly and in good order in the world, and read it as well as pondered over it properly, because your halting-place and residence in Paradise is the same where you arrive at the time of reciting the last verse". This tradition should be understood to mean that in Paradise only that person who has recited the Qur'an in this world and ascends from one spiritual and moral position to another by reading each verse, will recite the Qur'an verse after verse and acquire higher position according to the number of the verses.

In the Hereafter none will acquire a position and ascend to a higher rank unless he has acquired a position here and attains to a moral and spiritual rank. Allah has given the Holy Qur'an to the Muslims so that they may consider it to be a pure and sacred Book, ponder over it and benefit from it.

The Muslims should develop more interest and familiarity with the Holy Qur'an than any other book. They should read it with the intention of acting according to its commands.

What a good thing it will be if every Muslim reads a few verses of the Holy Qur'an with this intention, and podners over them. If he does not know Arabic he should at least study its translation in his own language and acquire blessing from the word of Allah for which no other speech can be substituted. If he reads ten verses to gain spiritual reward he should also read one verse for his spiritual and moral training. In fact the spirit of spiritual reward is that very good impression, which the reading of the Qur'an makes on the soul of man, and if the reading of the Qur'an or performance of any other good deed makes no impression on his soul it will be meaningless to say that any such act carries spiritual reward. You should determine to read a few verses of the Qur'an every day and also to understand their meanings, as far as possible. At present even the educated persons are afraid of Arabic and of understanding the Qur'an. However, one can get rid of this fear very easily. Man is afraid so long as he does not know and does not understand. However, if you get acquainted with the Qur'an and its meanings and develop the habit of benefiting from its teachings and wisdom, you will enjoy reading it. You should, therefore, read the Holy Qur'an and should consider it matchless. Read a few verses of the Qur'an every day, fixing their number according to your own convenience, and try to understand their meanings as far as possible. If you cannot yet follow the Arabic text of these verses read their translation along with them and compare it with the Arabic text. As and when possible talk with the members of your family about the verses which you read. It is not proper for a Muslim to keep aloof from reading and understanding the Qur'an.

The Almighty Allah has revealed the Qur'an so that the Muslims of the world may get acquainted with it, read it and understand it, obey its commands and develop moral virtues and become free from moral vices through their love for this Heavenly Book. The acquisition of spiritual reward from reading the Qur'an does not also mean anything except that it should reform us and purify our soul. If you do good deed and Allah gives you spiritual reward, it means that as a result of that deed your soul is elevated to a higher degree and takes a step forward towards perfection. In other words something is added to your self. So long as a good deed does not add anything to the personality of man from the moral viewpoint it is meaningless to say that it carries spiritual reward. Similarly so long as a bad deed does not reduce something from the personality of man and does not make him inferior as compare with what he is, it will be meaningless to say that he has committed a sin. The deeds which carry spiritual reward are those, which, if performed with good intention, make a good impression on man, increase the purity of his mind, keep good morals alive in his self, and eliminate bad morals from it. As regards sinful deeds they are those, which, if done intentionally, make a bad impression on man, tarnish his soul, aggravate his bad morals, and weaken his good ones, gradually eliminating them totally.

Reading of the Qur'an is a praiseworthy act, provided that it increases goodness in man, reduces his evil deeds, strengthens his good morals or eliminates the bad habits in him.

* * * *

APPENDIX II

DAY OF *ARBA'IN* (40th day of Imam Husayn's Martyrdom — 20th Safar)

It has been recommended that on the occasion of the *Arba'in* of Imam Husayn and his devoted companions visit to the graves of the Holy Imam and the martyrs of the tragedy of Karbala should be paid. The day of *Arba'in* is one of the most crowded days in the sacred city of Karbala. The Muslims and the Shi'ah in particular come to that glorious place from different parts of the world and send greetings to the great and magnanimous persons who performed the feats of highest, bravery, devotion and honour. Of course, the ceremonies of homage can be performed and one's attachment to the sacred mission of the martyrs can be expressed in any words and language. However, it will be much better that whatever has come down to us from the leaders of the religion with regard to the ceremonies of paying the homage should be performed in the same manner in which it has been recommended by the Holy Prophet and the Holy Imams, and the supplications mentioned in the Holy Qur'an itself should be given preference over others. How regrettable it is that, for example, people come from far off places for paying the homage to the sacred grave of the eighth Imam, but during their stay in Mashhad for a few days they do not recite anything except the commonplace homage prepared by the sellers and remain deprived of reading all the homages quoted from the Holy Imams.

MUSLIMS OUGHT TO UNDERSTAND ISLAM

The followers do not recognize Imam Riza except with the title of *Gharibul Ghuraba*. These people may be religious but they do not really understand religion. There are people who believe in Allah, His Prophet and in religion, and make sufficient efforts to perform the religious rites, but they do not understand religion and their efforts are usually based on ignorance and vulgarity. These are the people who at times oppose Allah to seek His proximity, attack religion and the religious persons for the sake of religion and consider the believers to be infidels so that they themselves may not become infidels. Every person, who recognizes Prophet Muhammad to be the Prophet of Allah and admits to be true what he brought from Allah, is a Muslim. However, every Muslim does not understand what is the meaning of being a Muslim, what the purpose of the Holy Prophet's mission was, how supplications and homage should be performed, and which deeds are the means of acquiring proximity to Allah. On the contrary it often happens that notwithstanding the fact that a person or some persons may be Muslims and religious-minded, they may be having ideas opposed to religion, may practise polytheism in the name of monotheism and godliness, and may indulge in hypocrisy in the name of sincerity. Hence, if it is said that such and such person acts against religion or the Qur'an, it does not mean that that person is not religious.

During the course of the history of Islam there have been many persons who have acted against religion while wishing sincerely to seek the proximity and pleasure of Allah. In fact they wanted to defend their religion and even to promote it, but notwithstanding this they took steps against religion. There have been many persons who were interested in the Holy Qur'an and its publication, but they took steps against the Qur'an. There have also been many persons who wrote false narrations and traditions in the books believing that this action of theirs was a step towards the advancement of religion and thus became the source of deviation of many Muslims. There have been still others who wrote things against the contents of the Qur'an and gave them the name of the commentary of the Qur'an.

A large number of myths have become a part of the history of Islam and many vulgar actions have been considered to be a part of the religious ceremonies. It is for the reason, as we have said, that every religious person does not understand religion and the religious persons should more than anything else think about understanding religion so that they may not disgrace religion, and whatever they do in the name of religion should become the means of the acquisition of the pleasure of Allah and His Holy Prophet. The religious ceremonies cannot be left to the personal taste of the individuals, and the homage of the Holy Prophet and the Holy Imams cannot be performed with vulgar methods.

One of the dangerous anti-religious ideas is that whichever action assumes religious bias is good and carries spiritual reward, although it may be opposed to the spirit of the religion, and the Prophet who brought it might be opposed to it and might hate it. Similarly the ceremony on which the sacred name of Imam Husayn is imprinted is considered to be the source of honour in this world and in the Hereafter although it may offend the Imam, and whatever is said from the pulpit of Imam Husayn amounts to worship and entails spiritual reward although it may consist of a lie whether it is in praise or vilification of certain persons.

It was in view of these dangers that some distinguished personalities and scholars of the religion, notwithstanding the fact that they were capable of educating and training others, considered it necessary to present their religious belief before the Imam of the time, lest they should be believing in the name of religion in things opposed to religion, or do things contrary to religion, considering them to be a part of religion. One such great personality was Abdul Azim Hasani who was the great-grandson of Imam Hasan. He was a contemporary of Imam Muhammad Taqi al-Jawād and Imam Ali Naqi al-Hādi and is himself reckoned to be a distinguished member of Ahlul Bayt and a great scholar of Islam. Once he came to Imam Hādi and said: "I wish to mention before you my beliefs so that I may stick to them if you endorse them". After he had narrated his beliefs before the Imam the latter said: "I swear by Allah that the faith which you hold is the same which Allah has chosen for His slaves. You should, therefore, stick to it. May Allah keep you steadfast in truth in this world and in the Hereafter".

It is really very surprising that in spite of his being a very great scholar, Abdul Azim Hasani was not satisfied till he had narrated his beliefs to the Imam of the time, but usually an ordinary person is perfectly satisfied that whatever he knows and does is the same which was brought by the Holy Prophet from Almighty Allah.

Hamrān bin Āayun was one of the distinguished companions of Imam Bāqir and Imam Sādiq. Imam Bāqir said to him: "You are one of our followers in this world and in the Hereafter". He has been reckoned to be one of the reciters of the Qur'an and a scholar of the Qur'an and Arabic grammar. When he narrated his faith and beliefs to Imam Sādiq the Holy Imam said to him: "If anyone opposes you in the matter of the beliefs which you have narrated, he is an unbeliever". Hamrān asked: "Even though he may be an Alawi or a Fātimid?" The Imam replied: "Even though he may be a Muhammadi, an Alawi, or a Fātimid". The Imam meant to say that relationship with the Holy Prophet or Imam Ali or lady Fatima has nothing to do with religion.

Abdullah bin Abi Yāfur narrated his beliefs to Imam Sādiq. Amr bin Hurayth also narrated his beliefs before Imam Sādiq and the Imam said to him: "O Amr! I swear by Allah that my faith as well as of my ancestors has been the same as narrated by you and we have remained steadfast in it. Do not forsake piety in any circumstances and do not utter anything other than a good one. Do not say that you have guided yourself to the right path for it is Allah who has guided you. Hence thank Allah for the blessings which He has bestowed on you".

Khālid Bajali, who was one of the companions of Imam Sādiq, narrated his beliefs in detail before the Holy Imam and the Imam said to him: "What you have said is sufficient. Be quiet, for whatever you have said is true".

Another person named Yusuf who was one of the companions of Imam Sādiq said to him: "Kindly permit me to narrate the beliefs which I hold. In case they are correct you may tell me about it so that I may stick to them and in case any belief of mine is opposed to truth you may guide me to truth". The Imam said to him: "Speak". Yusuf said: "I testify that Allah is One and without a partner. I also testify that Muhammad is Allah's servant and Messenger; Ali has been my Imam; Hasan has been my Imam; Husayn has been my Imam; Ali bin Husayn has been my Imam; Muhammad bin Ali has been my Imam; and now you yourself are my Imam". The Imam said a number of times: "May Allah bless you" and then added: "I swear by Allah that whatever you have stated and expressed is the Divine faith and the faith of Allah's angels and my faith and the faith of my ancestors. It is the faith besides which Allah does not accept any faith".

Hasan bin Ziyād Attār also narrated his beliefs before the sixth Imam and the Imam endorsed them. One of the persons who narrated their beliefs before the Imam of their time was Safwān bin Mehrān Asadi who was a common carrier and who hired out his camels. He says that while narrating his beliefs before Imam Sādiq he said: "I testify that Allah is One and without a partner". He added: "Muhammad is Allah's Prophet and so long as he was present he was the Proof of Allah for the people. After him Imam Ali was the Proof of Allah". The Imam said: "May Allah bless you". Safwān added: "After him Hasan bin Ali was the Proof of Allah for the people". The Imam repeated: "May Allah bless you". Safwān added: "Then it was Ali bin Husayn who was the Proof of Allah for the people". The Imam said again: "May Allah bless you". Then it was Muhammad bin Ali who was the Proof of Allah for the people. The Imam said: "May Allah bless you". And now you are the Proof of Allah for the people. The Imam said: "May Allah bless you".

This magnanimous person who was one of the distinguished companions of Imam Sādiq and Imam Kāzim took Imam Sādiq from Madina to Iraq a number of times and the Imam used to hire his camel. Safwān himself also used to accompany the Imam and by means of the blessings of the companionship of the Imam, he identified the grave of Imam Ali which had not been identified till then, and remained in attendance upon it for twenty years. Safwan is one of the distinguished narrators and has narrated traditions from the Holy Imams. Among them are *Ziyārat Wāritha*, the well-known homage of Āshura of Imam Husayn, Alqama's supplication, and a homage of Imam Ali. In his book entitled **Misbāhul Mutahajjid** Shaykh Tusi has quoted *Ziyārat Wāritha* from Imam Sādiq through Safwān. He (Shaykh Tusi) has also quoted *Ziyārat Āshura* through two media — one from Imam Muhammad Baqir through Alqama bin Muhammad Hazrami, and one from the sixth Imam through Safwān Jammāl.

Safwān said to Sayf bin Umayra: "I was with Imam Sādiq when he performed homage at this place in this manner and recited this supplication (i.e. Alqama supplication)". What is surprising is that the supplication which is known as 'Alqama supplication' and is recited after *Ziyārat Āshura* has been quoted by Safwān from Imam Sādiq and not by Alqama from Imam Bāqir. It should, therefore, have been called 'Safwān's Supplication' and it is not known as to why it has beeen called 'Alqama's supplication'. This very Safwān has also quoted one of the two homages of *Arba'in* of Imam Husayn from the sixth Imam.

The second homage of *Arba'in* is the one, which was recited by Jābir bin Abdullah Ansāri while paying the homage to the grave of Imam and which has been quoted by Atiyya bin Sād bin Junāda from the distinguished companion Jābir. The sentences of the *Ziyārat Arba'in* of Safwān, as translated below are well known. They are the same sentences which, according to Safwān, were uttered by the sixth Imam while performing the homage to Imam Husayn: "I testify that you were a light in your noble fathers and the wombs of your pure mothers. The uncleanliness of ignorance did not contaminate you. The darkness of polytheism, blasphemy and perversion did not put its clothes on you. I testify that you are a pillar of the faith, a support for the Muslims and a refuge for the believers. I testify that you are the righteous, pious, praiseworthy and pure Imam, you guide and are yourself guided. I testify that only the Imams who are your descendants are the paragon of virtue and piety, the signs of guidance, the dependable medium and reliance for the people of the world".

We hinted before that it is possible that a person may be religious and may take much interest in religion and the things related to it, but notwithstanding this he may not understand religion and may believe as a part of religion in things with which religion has nothing to do, and may do things in the name of religion which have no sanction. It is for this reason that according to a tradition quoted by Suyuti in Jāmi'us Saghir the Holy Prophet said: "When Allah wishes to do good to one of his slaves He makes him understand religion. He despises the world and comes to know his shortcomings". Apparently what is meant by the first sentence of the tradition is that when Allah wishes to do good to a person and to make him happy He makes him understand religion so that his faith and deeds may be based on wisdom and knowledge, and he may not add anything to it on account of personal desires, nor subtract anything from it owing to ignorance and lack of insight. According to this sacred tradition understanding religion is the foundation of the happiness and prosperity of a slave of Allah. In fact the reason for the mischiefs and divergences which took place in the history of Islam and the irreparable losses suffered by the Muslims, has been that most of the Muslims did not understand religion. Notwithstandig the fact, therefore, that, according to their own thinking, they served religion, they actually did harm to Islam and the Muslims. Possibly the main reason for this was that during the time of the caliphs the Islamic conquests took place rapidly and every day the inhabitants of a new city or region embraced Islam. In the circumstances it was quite impossible that the persons newly converted to Islam should become aware of its reality and its real teachings, understand this religion and become acquainted with the Qur'an and the commands and morality of Islam through intelligence and knowledge. Making conquests and persuading people to accept the laws of the Islamic Government is one thing and their education and training and acquainting them with the spirit of Islam and the value of its teachings is another. In none of the sacred verses of the Holy Qur'an revealed about the personality of the Holy Prophet it has been said that Muhammad is a Prophet who is a conqueror, and in none of the religious documents conquest has been reckoned to be one of the virtues of the Holy Prophet. The Qur'an describes the Holy Prophet and his duty and message thus: *O Prophet! We have sent you as a witness, a bearer of good tidings, a warner, a summoner to Allah by His permission, and as a shining torch.* (Surah al-Ahzab, 33:45 — 46)

Allah does not say: "We have sent you to conquer lands by Allah's permission and to add them to the Islamic state". On the other hand He says: *We have sent you as a summoner to Allah by His permission.*

We have sent you with the Truth, a bearer of glad tidings and a warner. (Surah al-Baqarah, 2:119)

We have sent you only as a bearer of good tidings and a warner. (Surah al-Furqan, 25:56)

We have not sent you save as a bearer of good tidings and a warner to all mankind. (Surah Saba, 34:28)

223

We have sent you with the Truth, a bearer of glad tidings and a warner. (Surah al-Fatir, 35:24)

We have sent you as a witness and a bearer of good tidings and a warner. (Surah al-Fath, 48:8)

He it is Who has sent among the unlettered ones a messenger of their own, to recite to them His revelations and to make them pure, and to teach them the Book and wisdom. (Surah al-Jumuah, 62:2)

In these verses as well as in others revealed in connection with the duties of the Holy Prophet nothing has been said about conquests. On the other hand in all of them a mention has been made of education and training, encouraging the people to do good and warning them against the troubles and adversities from which the evil-doers suffer.

In 8 A.H. Makkah was conquered and idol-worship came to an end in that city. Thereafter the Muslims gained victory over the tribe of Hawāzān, who had gathered in the valley of Hunayn to attack them. Then the Holy Prophet proceeded to Tā'if to put an end to idol-worship in that city also, and to destroy the temple of Lāt which was reckoned to be the centre of Tā'if. However, after having kept that city under siege for some time, he went to Makkah and then returned to Madina, and the city of Tā'if remained unconquered. However, in 9 A.H. the chiefs of Tā'if and the representatives of the inhabitants of that city themselves came to Madina, met the Holy Prophet and offered to embrace Islam on the following two conditions:

(i) They might be excused from offering prayers.
(ii) The Prophet of Allah might postpone the demolition of the temple of Lāt, even though for a very short period.

If the Holy Prophet's object had been to conquer the city of Tā'if he would have immediately accepted their offer, considered the surrender of those people a windfall and added the city to the Islamic State. He would then have realized *zakāt* and other taxes from the newly converted Muslims of Tā'if, invited their people to take part in the Islamic battles and thus increased the number of the Islamic forces. Embracement of Islam by the people of Tā'if and their surrender on the above-mentioned conditions was undoubtedly in the interest of the Muslims from the viewpoint of organization, conquests and other advantages, but the Holy Prophet was not at all agreeable, and so long as the people of Tā'if insisted on the acceptance of their conditions, he declined to accept their embracement of Islam. The last reply which he gave them was: "As regards breaking the idols with your own hands, I excuse you from undertaking this task, and shall send other persons to do it. As regards prayers *(al-Salāt)* it is a must, for without it religion has no value".

It was usual with the Holy Prophet that whenever he conquered a place he asked its chiefs to pull down their idol-temples with their own hands. The favour which he did to the people of Tā'if was that he excused them from breaking their idols with their own hands, but as regards prayers he told them that the religion of which prayers did not form a part is worthless i.e. even if not only Tā'if but a country is conquered and its inhabitants do not offer prayers that conquest is of no use. In other words it is no good if the people are religious but do not understand religion.

* * * * *

THE END

DR IQBAL ON IMAM HUSAYN

Dr Muhammad Iqbal (1877 — 1938) known to the world as the Poet-Philosopher of the East, devoted his life to awaken the Muslim Ummah and to make it pursue the path of spirituality, knowledge, jihad, sacrifice and martyrdom.

Dr Iqbal had an abiding faith in Ahlul Bayt (the Chosen Descendants of the Holy Prophet). He was intensely moved by the tragic events of Karbala so much so that in many of his couplets he carried a universal message to the mankind for emulating Imam Husayn who sacrificed his life at the altar of Truth. His elegies on the martyrdom of Imam Husayn stand unmatched and are an eye-opener to all those who are giving a mere lip-service to Islam.

In the following couplets Dr Iqbal gives vent to his sentiments and feelings on Imam Husayn:

Jis tarah mujhko shahid-e-Karbala say piyār hay,
Haq ta'āla ko yatimon ki duā say piyār hay.

Dr Iqbal expresses his extreme love for Imam Husayn. Just as Almighty Allah loves to listen to the invocation of the orphans, he also has the same kind of love for the martyr of Karbala.

Roney wālā hoon shahid-e-Karbala kay gham may mayn,
Kyā durrey maqsūd na daingay Sāqi-e-Kauthar mujhey.

Dr Iqbal has a sincere and genuine faith in Imam Husayn. The hero of this episode Imam Husayn, the brave son of the bravest of the brave Ali and grandson of the Holy Prophet, took up a firm stand not to acknowledge Yazid as the Caliph of Islam. It is a fight for the preservation of the principles and tenets of Islam. Imam Husayn arrived in Karbala on the 2nd of Muharram 61 A.H. along with his small children, women, and some comrades numbering 72 only. On the 10th of Muharram he was brutally killed. This was the tragedy over which Iqbal sheds tears. He believes that mourning and wailing over him would lead to his (Iqbal's) salvation. He also believes that *Sāqi-e-Kauthar* Lord of Kauthar (Cistern in Paradise) i.e. Imam Ali loves those, who weep for Imam Husayn. He hopes and prays that since he sheds tears out of grief for Husyan, Imam Ali would give him all the help he needs.

Gharib-o-sāda-o-rangin hay dāstān-e-Haram,
Nihāyat iski Husayn ibtida hay Ismāil.

Dr Iqbal says that the event of the construction of Kāba is very simple and interesting. Prophet Ismāil suffered great pains in its construction. The Holy Prophet purged it from the idols that were in it, and so raised its glory. The first stone was laid by Ismāil indeed. He offered for sacrifice his own life but the sacrifice was not completed as he was replaced by a ram and according to the Holy Qur'an the great sacrifice or *Zibh-e 'Azim* was to come later and completed by one of his descendants, Husayn. So in fact culmination of the spirit of love for Allah was manifest when Imam Husayn sacrificed his life and preserved the dignity of the Holy Kāba.

Haqiqat-e-abadi hay maqām-e-Shabbiri,
Badaltay rahay hain andāze Kufio-Shāmi.

Dr Iqbal here compares two things Shabbiri or Husayniyat, i.e. principles enunciated and adhered to by Imam Husayn, and Yazidiyat, i.e. worldly power and authority. Husayn was the symbol of devotion to and love for Allah, i.e. submission to none except Allah.

The spirit as shown by the rulers of Kufa and Syria, is always changing since it tries to gain strength through fraud, dishonesty, and political expediency and manoeuvring as against this truth never changes. So the place Imam Husayn has achieved, is a reality which shall be hailed and acknowledged for all times to come.

Qāfilāy Hijaz may ek Husayn bhi nahin,
Garche hai tābdār abhi wādi ey Dajlao Furāt.

Dr Iqbal was distressed to note that Iraq was under the yoke of the British. He was disappointed that the Muslims had lost courage and were suffering humiliation. The land of Tigres and Eupharates called some staunch devotee of Islam who could relieve them of their serfdom. Iqbal only wished a man, a follower of Imam Husayn might come up to help the Muslims of Iraq!

Sidq-e-Khalil Bhi hay ishqe sabr-e-Husayn bhi hay ishq,
Mārika-e-wujud maiyn Badr-o-Hunayn bhi hay ishq.

Dr Iqbal says that love of Allah manifests itself in many ways. Prophet Ibrahim had to suffer many difficulties in the cause of Allah. He accepted being thrown into the fire, and the fire was turned into a blooming garden.

It showed his intense love for Allah. Our Holy Prophet conquered the Battles of Badr and Hunayn through his ardent love for Allah. Similarly Imam Husayn showed his patience in the battlefield of Karbala where he, with his family and comrades, not only suffered the pangs of three days' thirst, but willingly sacrificed his life for the cause of Truth and love for Allah. Love for Allah is a quality, a force, an impetus, which creates in us extraordinary patience and forbearance.

Ek faqr hay Shabbiri es faqr mayn hay meri,
Mirās-e-Musalmāni, samāya-i-Shabbiri.

Dr Iqbal says that the life of a dervish is a very noble way of living; but it is different from the life of a mendicant or friar who lives on begging or in seclusion. We should learn from Imam Husayn who while passing the life of a dervish had no other consideration except love of Allah and submission to His will. Our treading the path practised by Imam Husayn will bestow on us the title of Chief among the people. A Muslim has inherited this wealth from Imam Husayn, and we should make the best use of it. Imam Husayn has given us the lesson of self-sacrifice, patience, and forebearance and submission to none except Allah.

Ān Imam-e-āshiqān pooray Batool
Sarvay āzādi ze bustān-e-Rasul.

Now Dr Iqbal opens his praises for the son of lady Fātima. He was the chief of the lovers of Allah, and an evergreen tree from the garden of the Prophet. Imam Husayn who stood against the forces of evil, refused to acknowledge Yazid as the Caliph of Islam, and upholding the dignity of Islamic principles sacrificed his life along with a small band of 72 of his followers, at the battlefield of Karbala.

Allah Allah Bāey Bismillah pidar,
Ma'niye zibh-e-azim āmad pisar.

In a state of supreme bliss Dr Iqbal says, "O' Allah, what an exalted position Imam Husayn possessed, as his illustrious father (Imam Ali) was the first letter of the Qur'an! A tradition says that Imam Ali said, "What is in the Holy Qur'an is in the first chapter (Surah Fātiha); what is in this surah (chapter) is in the first verse (Bismillah); what is in *Bismillah* is in its first letter (Bā) and I am the dot below bā. Doubtless Imam Ali was acknowledged to be the best expounder of the Holy Qur'an. The Holy Prophet had himself declared: "Ali is with Qur'an, and Qur'an is with Ali". Imam Husayn was the son of such an eminent personality. It is Imam Husayn's Martyrdom which is referred to as *Zibhe Azim* the greatest sacrifice in the Holy Qur'an. Imam Husayn was the direct descendant of Prophet Ismāil and had offered himself for sacrifice at Karbala to save Islamic principles from annihilation. The Holy Qur'an says that *Zibhe Azim*, the great sacrifice of Prophet Ismāil was left over for the coming generation. Dr Iqbal alludes to this and says that *Zibhe Azim* in the Holy Qur'an means the sacrifice of Imam Husayn.

Bahray ān shahzādāey Khayrul milal
Dosh-e-Khatmul mursalin ne'mul Jamal.

Dr Iqbal here alludes to an event stated by Tirmizi and others. Once Imam Husayn mounted the shoulders of his grandfather, the Holy Prophet. Somebody said, "What a good carriage it is!" The Prophet said, "And what a good rider it is!" Dr Iqbal mentions this event to show what affectionate feelings the Holy Prophet had towards his grandson.

Surkh roo ishq-e-ghayoor az Khoon-e-oo
Surkhiye in misra az mazmoon-e-oo.

Dr Iqbal says that it is because of Imam Husayn's blood that the modest love has gained honour and dignity. This couplet can well serve a title for the episode of the Tragedy of Karbala which shows how piously and valiantly Imam Husayn defended the tenets of Islam, sacrificed his own life along with his kith and kin, sincere followers, and comrades, and raised the honour of love to its acme.

Darmiyān-e-Ummat ān Keywān janāb,
Hamchu harf-e-Qul Huwallah dar Kitāb.

Dr Iqbal shows here the position of Imam Husayn. He says that among the followers of the Holy Prophet Imam Husayn is like the Divine phrase *Qul huwallah* (Say He is Allah) meaning that Allah is One, in the Holy Qur'an. Since the entire Holy Qur'an turns to this verse — *Qul Huwallaho Ahad* (Say that He is One) similarly the whole Islamic world turns towards Imam Husayn who is the source of our guidance. Dr Iqbal knows the tradition of our Prophet: "Husayn is from me and I am from Husayn" i.e. Husayn is his grandson and that he (the Prophet) would be made known by him, and his mission would be fulfilled by Imam Husayn who sacrificed his life to immortalize Islam and its tenets.

Musa-oFiraun-o-Shabbir or Yazid
In do quwwāt az Hayāt āmad padid.

Ever since the creation of life two opposing forces have been at war with each other — virtue and vice, Right and wrong. Musa (Moses) rose against Firaun (Pharoah) and Shabbir (Imam Husayn) rose against Yazid. These struggles were between the Right and the wrong. Consequently the Right prevailed upon the wrong and it was proved that Right is might.

Zindah haq az quwwat-e-Shabbiri ast
Bātil ākhir dāgh-e-hasrat miri ast.

Dr Iqbal says that Truth or Islam exists today because of the strength shown and the spiritual power exercised by Imam Husayn. In other words Imam Husayn made Islam immortal. The wrong was crushed to annihilation in spite of its apparent success. Yazidism or the principle enunciated by Yazid is looked down upon by all, but Husayn's blood spilled at Karbala still enlivens our hearts and makes us feel that his sacrifice to support the Right against the wrong was unparalleled in the history of mankind.

Choon Khilāfat rishtah az Qur'an gusikht
Hurriyat ra Zahr under Kām rikht

Khāst ān sar Jalwaey Khairul Umam
Choon Sahabe Qiblah Bārān dar qadam

Bar zamin-e-Karbala Bārid o raft
Lalah dar wirānaha Kārid o raft

Tā qayāmat qat'ay istibdād kard
Mauje Khoone oo chaman ijād kard.

Dr Iqbal says that when the Islamic Government severed its relation with the injunctions of the Holy Qur'an the Muslims suffered moral degradation. It marred their freedom. When the rulers indulged in all sorts of vicious habits and satisfied their carnal desires against the clear-cut injunctions of the Holy Qur'an the whole social structure was impaired. Nobody could utter a word against the tyrant ruler and his associates. Then arose that

231

chief of the Muslims (Husayn) like blessed cloud with rain of mercy under his foot. It rained blessings on the sands of Karbala and turned that desert into a garden. It is the place where Imam Husayn with his kith and kin, children and comrades, numbering 72 only, faced a huge army and courted martyrdom after three days starvation and thirst on the 10th of Muharram 61 A.H. Husayn was undoubtedly the saviour of freedom and Karbala has become the symbol of struggle against tyranny. Husayn's role at Karbala was so magnificent that it eradicated for ever the savage idea of cruelty and cold-bloodedness. The wave of his blood has created a garden which is symbolic of his sacrifice for the preservation of freedom and Truth.

Bahre haq dar Khāk-o-khoon ghaltida ast
Pas binā ey lā illah gardida ast.

Dr Iqbal says that Imam Husayn voluntarily gave his life at Karbala for the sake of Allah or Truth. So it goes without saying that Husayn laid the foundation of the cardinal Principle of Islam — *the belief that there is no god except Allah.* Since Islamic principles were being twisted, distorted and exterminated it was Husayn's blood which gave it a new life.

Mudda ā yash saltanat boody agar
Khud na kardy bā chunin sāmmāne safar.

That Imam Husayn's only aim in refusing to accept Yazid as Caliph of Islam was to preserve Islam, can be borne out from the fact that while he left Madina for his journey towards Kufa he had a small band of his relations and followers, including women, and children. Had he the intention of fighting a political battle he would not have gone there with such people as he took with him. Those who accompanied Imam Husayn included his sisters, wives, children (even a six month old child was with him) and some followers, some of whom were more than eighty years of age.

Dushmanān chun rig-e-sahra la tu'ad
Dostān-e- oo bā yazdān ham 'adad.

In the Battle of Karbala the number of the enemy was as countless as the particles of sand, but the number of Imam Husayn's friends was only 72.

Tigh-e-Lā choon az miyan buroon kashid
Az rag-e-arbābe bātil khoon kashid.

Naqsh-e-Illallāh bar Sahra nawisht
Satre-unwān-e-najāt-e mā nawisht.

Ramz-e-Qur'an az Husayn āmokhteem,
Za Ātishe-oo Shoalahā andokhteem.

Imam Husayn took up his sword of 'Lā' or 'No' that is, there is no deity (except Allah) and crushed infidelity. He imprinted the mark of *Illallāh (Tawhid)*, or monotheism in the wilderness of Karbala. It was a title for our salvation. In fact we have learnt the lesson of Tawhid or monotheism from Imam Husayn, who taught us in a practical way the secret of Qur'an by sacrificing his life for the sake of Allah and for completing the mission of his grandfather, the Prophet. We have gathered warmth from the fire of love for Allah that Imam Husayn possessed. Dr Iqbal means that the love for Allah shown and the sacrifice made by Imam Husayn at Karbala should serve as the best lesson for all the people of the world.

Shawkat-e-Shām-o farray Baghdad raft,
Satwat-e-Gharnāta ham az yād raft.

Tār-e-mā az zakhma ash larzān hanooz,
Tazāh az takbir-e-oo Imān hanooz.

Dr Iqbal says that kingly grandeur gained through political battles never survives. The pomp and vanity of the thrones of Syria and Baghdad which were once seats of great kings is no more present. Nobody remembers the splendour of Gharnāta which was the seat of Spanish Kings. But the reverential call of Husayn at Karbala — his call of *Lā Ilāhā Illallāh* is still echoing in our ears and thrilling our hearts.

233

Ay sabā ay payk-e-dūr uftādagān,
Ashk-e-mā bar khāk-e-pāk-e-oo rasān.

Iqbal's intense love for and faith in Imam Husayn is apparent from this couplet. Fondly addressing himself to the breeze, which proverbially carries the message of the lover to the beloved, who is at a remote place. Iqbal asks her to carry his tears to the sacred tomb of Imam Husayn. Dr Iqbal weeps in sad and blessed memory of Imam Husayn and wishes to place his tears over his Imam's grave.

* * * * *

A LIST OF OUR PUBLICATIONS

1. ISLAMIC PRACTICAL LAWS BOOK I & II
2. ARTICLES OF ISLAMIC ACTS
    By Ayatullah al-Uzma al-Khoei
3. THE BELIEFS OF THE SHI'ITE SCHOOL
    By Allamah Muhammad Riza Muzaffar
4. THE SHI'AH ORIGIN AND FAITH
    By Allamah Muhammad Husayn Kāshif al-Ghitā
5. MAN AND UNIVERSE
6. MAN AND HIS DESTINY
7. THE MARTYR
8. WOMAN AND HER RIGHTS
9. MASTER AND MASTERSHIP
    By Allamah Murtaza Mutahhari
10. THE AWAITED SAVIOUR
    *By Allamah Murtaza Mutahhari
    & Ayatullah Muhammad Baqir al-Sadr*
11. ISLAM AND SCHOOLS OF ECONOMICS
12. ISLAMIC POLITICAL SYSTEM
13. A SHORT HISTORY OF ILMUL USUL
14. HE, HIS MESSENGER AND HIS MESSAGE
15. TRENDS OF HISTORY IN QUR'ĀN
    By Ayatullah Muhammad Baqir al-Şadr
16. A PROBE INTO THE HISTORY OF HADITH
    By Allamah Murtaza al-Askari
17. A PROBE INTO THE HISTORY OF 'ĀSHURĀ'
    By Dr Muhammad Ibrahim Āyati
18. ISLAMIC TEACHINGS BOOK-I
19. ISLAMIC TEACHINGS BOOK-II
20. ISLAMIC TEACHINGS BOOK-III
21. ISLAMIC TEACHINGS BOOK-IV
22. ISLAMIC TEACHINGS BOOK-V
23. ISLAMIC TEACHINGS BOOK-VI
24. ISLAMIC TEACHINGS BOOK-VII
25. RATIONALITY OF ISLAM
26. ISLAM – A CODE OF SOCIAL LIFE
27. CHILDRENS' GUIDE TO ISLAM
28. ABUZAR
    By A Panel of Scholars

29. AMMĀR YASIR
    By Sadruddin Sharafuddin
30. BILAL OF AFRICA
    By Husayn Malika Āshtiyāni
31. LESSONS FROM ISLAM
32. STORIES FROM QUR'AN
    By Muhammad Suhufi
33. LESSONS FROM QUR'AN
    By Mohsin Qarā'ti
34. THE MESSAGE
    By Ja'far Subhani
35. PHILOSOPHY OF ISLAM
    By Dr Husayni Behishti & Dr Jawad Bahonar
36. UNIVERSALITY OF ISLAM
    By Allamah Muhammad Husayn Tabātabā'i
37. THE DESPOTIC RULERS
    By Allamah Muhammad Jawad Mughniyah
38. MANNERS AND ETIQUETTES
    By Allamah Majlisi-I
39. A TEXT BOOK OF ETHICS
    By Allamah Muhammad Narāqi
40. AṢ ṢALĀT
41. QUR'AN MADE EASY
    By Raza H. Rizwāni
42. PEAK OF ELOQUENCE (Nahjul Balagha of Imam Ali)
    By Askari Ja'fari
43. THE VOICE OF HUMAN JUSTICE
    By George Jordac
44. TENETS OF ISLAM
    By Shaykh Tusi
45. IT REMOVES MISCONCEPTION
    ABOUT CALIPHS' CALIPHATE
    By M. A. A. Sattar
46. LIGHT WITHIN ME
    By Allamah Murtaza Mutahhari
       Allamah Muhammad Husayn Tabatabai'
       Ayatullah Ruhullah Khomeini
47. THEN I WAS GUIDED
    By Muhammad Samāwi Tijani
48. SUPPLICATION OF KUMAYL
49. THE EVENT OF CLOAK

الخيرية

AL-K